DEDICATION

Dedicated to my mother and father who allowed me the freedom to become who I am; to my wife for loving and accepting me for who I have become; and to our children and their children who will travel their own "roads" through life—long may they ride!

D0036962

CONTENTS

PART III: RETIREMENT'S SIX FUNDAMENTAL BUILDING BLOCKS

"A" to "B"—A Distinction with a Profound Difference ◆ Adapting to Retirement—Overcoming Stress through Positive Action ◆ Different Times, Different Demands, More Stress ◆ Life Is Viewed through Different Prisms ◆ Will You Be Living a Type A or Type B Retirement?—Your Choice ◆ *Going from "A" to "B, and Not the Other Way Round*

BUILDING BLOCK #4:
INTERGENERATIONAL LIFE ENGAGEMENT

12. Why Can't We All Just Get Along: THE IMPORTANCE OF STAYING SOCIALLY CONNECTED 179

Letting Go, Moving Forward ◆ Where Did All Those "Touchstones" Go? ◆ Retirement "Unstructures" Everything ◆ Building Social Assets ◆ New Touchstones to the Rescue ◆ Meeting and Greeting—First Impressions Count ◆ Mature Male/Female Seeking Compatible Others ◆ I Want to Be Alone…Do You, Really? ◆ Is Anybody Listening, Does Anybody Care? ◆ Talk Is Cheap, but I Guess We Already Knew That ◆ New Realities Require New Responses ◆ Don't Let Insecurity Separate You from the World ◆ Did You Ever Notice? ◆ People Reading People ◆ Looking for Friends in All the Wrong Places ◆ Are You Talking to Me? ◆ *The Building Blocks to Better Conversation Checklist*

13. We Are Who We Are Until We Aren't 197

The Games People Play ◆ Prepare to Be Troubled and Enlightened ◆ Behavioral Profile # 1: The Dominator ◆ Behavioral Profile #2: The Critic ◆ Behavioral Profile #3: The Pleaser ◆ Behavioral Profile #4: The Achiever ◆ Behavioral Profile #5: The Manipulator ◆ So Who Gets Along With Whom and Why ◆ Locked In Can Get You Locked Out ◆ The Matrix Is Talking to You, So Listen Up ◆ Reach Out and Really Touch Someone ◆ Can You Sing "Kumbaya"?

PART I
AM I REALLY READY TO RETIRE?

CHAPTER 1

■ ■ ■ ■ ■ ■

Our Real Wonder Years

*Toto, I've got a feeling we're
not in Kansas anymore.*
—FRANK L. BAUM

*Every new beginning comes from
some other beginning's end.*
—SENECA

RETIREMENT: PROLOGUE OR EPILOGUE?

We come from everywhere and anywhere—we share common visions, purposes, and aspirations; we are on the road to the same place, a place called "Retirement." This book is dedicated to the Boomer Generation, all 76 million of us, and to the 10,000 Boomers who will be retiring every day until the year 2029 and are all asking themselves the same question: "Am I really ready to retire?" It is also for the many millions of us who have already retired but are "flirting with failing retirements," who may be asking a different question: "Is that all there is?"

You see, this book is about us, the Boomers, you and me, men and women who were raised by the "Greatest Generation," the children of those who not only saved the world but made planet earth a better (while not perfect) place for us to grow up. And grow up we did, whether we wanted to or not. We took the world we were given, and then, for good or bad, shaped it in our image just as our children are doing today. Then we started retiring to enjoy the fruits of our labors and the retirement trickle soon became a flood. We passed the baton of youth on to the next generation with confidence that our legacy would be recognized, remembered, and reborn in the hearts and minds of our progeny for generations yet to come. We were the:

Bakers, Takers, Commanders-in-Chief;
Dreamers, Schemers, Apparatchiks;
Doers, Darers, Leaders of Fief;
Fathers, Mothers, Providers of Relief;
Builders, Breakers, Persons of Belief;
Inventers, Dissenters, Givers of Grief

STUFF HAPPENS

In the continuum between our youth and old age a lot of "stuff" happened, some good, some bad, some life changing, some life stealing, some painful, some joyful, some memorable. During this time opportunities emerged; hopes and dreams were fulfilled or shattered as we moved through life's ages and stages. Some of us grew stronger in the face of challenges while others weakened; some of us learned from our failures while others were destined to constantly repeat them. But through it all, transitions relentlessly occurred, some silent and barely noticed, others profoundly real and agonized over. Retirement is one of those consequential changes in life, it offers us a unique opportunity to start over, to move beyond the past and to once again live forward.

DOORWAY TO THE REST OF OUR LIVES

Work gave us our status, our sustenance, our structure, our social context; it was how we organized our lives. Even if we did not fully enjoy our work, at least we understood its demands and requirements. Retirement to some is symbolic of our aging selves, of our powerlessness to stop the hands of time; the ending of our life at work. It may be feared or longed for, depending on our perspective. Most of us, however, view retirement as a new beginning where the past is now prologue; it is our opportunity to shape a new life for ourselves without the controls and obligations imposed by work or by others. Retirement presents new opportunities to those who seek them; challenges to those who have yet to understand its full implications; and a threat to those who neither desire nor value anything other than work. Whatever our perspective, our lives should be guided by the singular principle of living in the present while remaining informed by the past and reality-checked by the future, with the assurance that dreams have no boundaries. Dare to keep dreaming, it's our doorway to a new reality—and the rest of our lives.

WHAT THIS BOOK AND RETIREMENT ARE ABOUT

This book is about empowerment and our willingness and ability to shape the rest of our lives in our own image. It's about retirement's three powers that are granted to every retiree: (1) *The Power of Unlimited Possibilities*—our retirements are only limited by our imaginations and our willingness to challenge our minds, bodies, and emotional selves; (2) *The Power of Self-Determination*—we have earned the right to control our lives and our personal destinies, not the other way around; and (3) *The Power to Do Something Simple and New Every Day*—read a book, contemplate the universe, or climb a mountain.

This book is about what retirement is and what it is not. It's about "Retirement's Six Fundamental Building Blocks"; and "Retirement's Ages and Stages." It's about the "soon-to-be retired" who have yet to make one of life's most consequential decisions and the "reluctant retirees" torn between two worlds, fearful of what they will find on the "other side" of work. It's about those flirting with failing retirements and not knowing how to turn them around. It's about coming to terms with our retirements and learning how to psychologically, behaviorally, and financially adjust to our new lives after work. It's about retirement's must-do's and what-not-to-do's. It's about accepting our "aging us." It's about challenging our minds and our bodies and engaging life up close and personal. It's about accepting our new lives with eyes wide open; it's about living forward, not in the past; and about who we will become, not about who we used to be. It's about challenging life and tempting fate; it's about exploration, travel, and adventure; it's about friends and family, about meaning, legacy, reconciliation, forgiveness, and spirituality. It's about optimism, and respect for others and for ourselves. It is about making a commitment to a healthy lifestyle. It's about having a love affair with retirement because some things happen only once. It's about committing to and getting lost in adventure. It's about knowing when we are *really* ready to retire. It's about retiring from work but remaining connected to life. It's about discarding old beliefs and dogmas and letting go of things that don't serve us well. It's about celebrating endings and transitions because they precede new beginnings. It's about enjoying every minute, every mile, every sunrise and sunset *every day,* and about squeezing out all the joy and meaning life has to offer until it's our time to leave this planet.

WHAT RETIREMENT IS NOT ABOUT

Retirement is not about who we were or believed we were in the world of work. It is not about how much money we have or the size and opulence of our houses nor the speed of our cars. It's not about hiding from life behind the protected walls of adult communities or becoming prisoners in our houses with indeterminate, self-imposed sentences. It's not about occupying ourselves with all manner of blinking, winking, tinkling electronic devices, from mind-numbing movies to compulsively playable mindless games, nor is it about having our ear attached to an iPhone, it's not about talking to Siri, our new and ever present mythical "friend," nor is it about constantly pumping music into our earphones, shutting out both people and life. Life is not meant to be lived virtually, rather up close and personal with others. Retirement is not about "finding" ourselves—or losing ourselves in electronic distractions—but about creating a new life for ourselves and those around us.

WELCOME TO "OUR WORLD"

So, welcome to "Our World," where retirement and reality come face to face. We are here, searching for answers, because we have common questions and want to know what retirement will be like. Why duplicate the angst, the bumps and bruises, that others have experienced if we can learn from our collective mistakes and shared victories, then use that knowledge to help us bypass, or at least navigate, the sharp edges and obstacles that are an unavoidable part of retirement's learning curve—in my mind, easier is better. We want to know when we are ready for retirement and when retirement is ready for us. Will we have enough available assets to maintain our working lifestyles into our retirement years? Will we be bored to tears or join the wandering minions in a life without purpose or direction? Or, perhaps worst of all, will we find ourselves isolated, voluntarily or otherwise, in adult communities; or, whatever they call them.

Retirement is one of life's most defining moments. It can be a bittersweet time for some because we all need to come to terms with our aging selves and recognize that life as we know it will dramatically change, hopefully for the better, and that we are on a slippery slope to "old age," whatever that means to us. The decision of whether or when to retire should never be taken lightly. Retirement, if planned properly and lived right, will be the most exciting, most meaningful, happiest, most fulfilling, and best years of your life—plus every other positive adjective you can throw in there. If we retire prematurely, not fully prepared for our new lives, or make missteps or miscalculations in our early retirement years, something so desired can easily turn into a hornets' nest of worries, recriminations, money woes, and fear for our futures. We want to do everything possible to prevent a failed retirement—we worked too long and hard to let the potentially best and happiest time of our lives slip from our grasps.

WITH A LITTLE HELP FROM OUR FRIENDS

So how do we insure that our retirements will live up to our expectations? While I cannot guarantee that any particular retirement will live up to your expectations—because I do not know what they are—I can provide the framework, insights, strategies, personal reflections, and tools needed to build and shape your retirement, consistent with your personal and financial abilities and your visions for life after work. You see, the long march into retirement doesn't begin in our sixties, it begins the day we start our first "real job." As we approach "maturity" and start considering whether or when to retire, there comes a decision point which must be confronted thoughtfully and objectively because this decision cannot be easily reversed—you can't simply say, like Roseanne Roseannadanna, "Never mind." Many have preceded you and can offer wise counsel, perhaps from different perspectives, and that's a good thing; so take advantage of our experiences because life can be made easier with a little help from your friends.

OF COURSE I'M GOING TO RETIRE

Some take the decision to retire for granted: "Of course I am going to retire." Others don't pay much attention to retirement and assume it will just take care of itself, then when the time comes they will "just retire"—ready or not, here I come. Still yet others prepare for it assiduously over many years, constantly thinking about it and planning for it to the point where it becomes an obsession. The rest of us understand that retirement is out there somewhere on the horizon and that it does require serious financial thought and planning; but typically our retirement thinking and planning stops there. Perhaps some will give considerable thought to relocating to someplace with a more amenable climate, or a lower cost of living, or just somewhere different. And finally, we have those who firmly believe they will never retire, such a decision may be motivated by a variety of reasons, valid or not. Retirement, from my perspective, is expected and desired by most, not even considered by few, but neither planned nor prepared for by many.

RETIREMENT: LIFE'S ONLY MULLIGAN

The decision of whether and when to retire is being agonized over by literally millions of Boomers at this very moment. Every one of these potential retirees must ask and honestly answer one of life's most consequential questions, "Am I really ready to retire?" And please keep in mind, retiring from work is the simple part; it's *living* in retirement that can be challenging. So what makes me qualified to help you, my fellow travelers, deal with one of life's most significant pivot points? No, I am not an investment advisor (although I do understand it's not good to gamble all your money in Las Vegas, or in the world's biggest casino, the New York Stock Exchange, or anywhere else the odds are always in the "house's" favor without first seeking wise counsel). Nor am I a life coach—and who are they anyway?—but I do have over 44 years' experience in helping individuals, organizations, nations, and governments transition, change, and adapt to new realities, demands, and circumstances. However, my biggest claim to fame is that I failed—yes, that's right, I *failed*—to freely accept what life offered me, a second chance, a Mulligan, life's one and only do-over, more commonly known as *retirement*. Failure is the "mother" of success, just ask any rich or happy person, keeping in mind they might not be one in the same.

Indeed, in my first try at retirement I faltered, but I did not crumble; and yes, it was those first stumbling attempts that prompted me to find out what this thing called "retirement" is really all about. Admittedly, I wandered aimlessly because I had yet to map a path, indeed I didn't quite know where I was headed, much like Jack Kerouac who wrote in *On the Road,* "There was nowhere to go but everywhere, so just keep rolling under the stars." That was my attitude at first, until I decided to treat retirement as one of life's most precious gifts and perhaps one of its most significant events. It was then that I decided to stop questioning and wandering and start accepting what retirement was offering—not only to me, but to my wife and family as well—and then to apply the same thought and effort to solving the retirement puzzle as I would have given any other task in my previous working life. My new life goal was to accept this gift and then to make my retirement and my wife's the most meaningful, exciting, and best years of our lives because some things happen only once and retirement is one of those life-altering events. *Never look back, and live forward* became my new life mantra. Then I realized the feelings and doubts I had experienced were not unique to me; we are all in this together, every last one of us who is on the road to retirement.

REAL PEOPLE, REAL LIVES

So, how do we know when we are really ready to retire? The answer is: "it depends," weasel words for sure. But it does depend on a whole host of factors including: individual circumstances (both financial and personal); our psychological and emotional readiness to retire and to accept our retirements; our ability to use the time that retirement grants us for positive, life-fulfilling purposes; and our willingness to accept a new life role. Or perhaps we have yet to come to terms with this thing called retirement, and thus feel lonely and adrift in a sea of people, without meaning or purpose. Our previously structured life rhythms have seemingly abandoned us and we find ourselves trying to hide in plain sight from life and from others, asking ourselves, "Is this the way the rest of my life will play itself out?"

The answer is that the path forward is not always an easy one, especially when our expectations for retirement have yet to square with its realities. Please remember that retirement is a *different* way of life, with new challenges and opportunities. You need to adapt and adjust to this new lifestyle, and that takes time, effort, and creativity. But when you learn the rhythms of your new retirement life, its customs, needs, wants, and opportunities, you will embrace retirement like a new lover, never wanting to let go. Success in life or retirement is not measured by how much we have in the bank, but rather by how much richness we have in life. Retirement is not about who we *were*; it is about who we are yet to *become*. Now, as you transition from the working life you knew into the life you have yet to experience, just remember: all of the energy that you once put toward building a career is now free and unattached, ready to be put toward building a sustainable, sustaining retirement. It is fine to honor the past, but not at the cost of your forward momentum. Enjoying life, tempting fate, travel and adventure, friends and family…these are not bound by age or employment. Retirement, at the end of the day, is about inner peace, acceptance of our aging selves, and most of all learning to take control of our futures, and not letting others become our "handlers." Hanging in there until life's last breath—that's what it's all about.

HOW TO USE THIS BOOK

This book seeks to see retirement as a journey, not a destination—a road to travel, with lots of adventure along the way. First, we have to find that place they call retirement and, second, we have to figure out what we are going to do when we get there, what will be waiting for us when we arrive. Think of it as a personal journey of discovery and consider this book your travel guide to retirement.

The book identifies and examines three major retirement themes. First, it explores one of life's most profound "Pivot Points," moving from the world of work into the world of retirement; a transition that is perhaps easy for some and difficult for others. Retirement, while appearing to be a no-brainer, is anything but, and whether it ultimately succeeds or fails depends on understanding five critical concepts: (1) life as we know it will be different, and hopefully "good" different; (2) retirements don't just happen, we have to make them happen; (3) retiring from work is easy, it's *living* in retirement that can sometimes be troubling; (4) the behaviors and dogmas that served us well at work will not necessarily serve our best interests when retired; and (5) when we retire *from* something we have to retire *to* something—we must not view retirement as an opportunity to do nothing, but rather as an opportunity to do *different* things.

The second theme goes on to identify and define "The Retirement Life Cycle," and how each "Stage" and "Age" is different from the other, requiring different responses, behaviors, and mindsets; and, most importantly, full acceptance of our aging selves. It describes how we can build and shape our own retirements, keeping in mind Retirement's Six Fundamental Building Blocks, which are identified, defined, discussed, and analyzed to provide an understanding of how each Building Block contributes to the overall success and cohesiveness of our retirements, and how each Building Block is positioned one on top of the other to form an integrative whole in the form of a virtual pyramid. You will be the architect, builder, and resident of this virtual pyramid. If the design is poorly conceived or realized, the pyramid might collapse around you, and we don't want that to happen, now do we?

The third theme focuses on each of the six Building Blocks individually, describing how every layer connects to the one below and the one above, forming an almost indestructible monolith and creating what I like to call "sustainable retirements." A chapter is devoted to each of those six Building Blocks.

Retirement's Six Fundamental Building Blocks

1: Physical, Psychological, and Emotional Health and Well-Being

2: Financial Security and Sustainability

3: Retirement Transition, Adjustment, and Acceptance

4: Intergenerational Life Engagement

5: The Intellectually Curious and Physically Active Retiree—
Discovery Adventure and Challenge

6: Spirituality, Meaning, Family and Legacy

I ask you all to join me on one of life's most exciting journeys, a trip to this place we call "retirement." And, whether or not I ultimately succeed in my mission is up to you. If I positively impact even one life, then I have succeeded; if I transform one retirement from dull to daring then I have succeeded; if I give new hope to someone struggling with retirement then I have succeeded; and, if I make one new friend then I will have exceeded my greatest expectations. And to speed us safely on our way, I will quote the most famous of Irish blessings,

May the road rise to meet you,
May the wind be always at your back,
May the sun shine warm upon your face,
The rains fall soft upon your fields and,
May God hold you in the Palm of His hand.

CHAPTER 2

■ ■ ■ ■ ■ ■

Reflections from the Other Side of Work

The past is behind, learn from it; the future is ahead, prepare for it; the present is here, live it.
—Thomas S. Monson

The farther backward you can look, the further forward you can see.
—Winston Churchill

EVENTUALLY MOST OF US JUST SAY "ENOUGH!"

Most of us, at some time and for a variety of reasons, will just say "Enough! It's time to retire." Enough of the palace intrigue, the whispering, the union/management drama, the double dealing, the long hours, the time away from family, the "do as I say, not as I do" mentality, the mostly manufactured crises which require all hands on deck and occur with growing frequency, plus the short staffing, and the mental and physical toll that it all takes. Enough of people chewing on us from the bottom and being hit around the head and shoulders from the top—those who say our workplaces are "employee-centered" models of reasoned discourse with customer-first mentalities and better products for a better

America are probably thinking of a different planet. "Retirement, ready or not here I come," we think and believe.

ALL THAT GLITTERS IS NOT GOLD

Not so fast, Cowpoke. Before we pull the plug there is much to consider, particularly the financial issues and the reality of being home with our significant others 24/7 with no place to hide (or more politely put, no way to give each other space). Then there are the feelings of loss, confusion, and even fear about our new life paths; these ride along with self-doubt, but are counterbalanced by our newfound freedom to control and shape the rest of our lives, in our images, along with feelings of relief for coming out the other side of work undamaged and unscathed. Then there is one of the biggest concerns of soon-to-be retirees, the money issue, looming menacingly over many of our heads. Indeed, money is the biggest concern of pre-retirees; although perhaps it shouldn't be because there are other equally profound issues that will also have dramatic impacts on our retirement. Life, however, always gets back to money and to "things." While money doesn't make bad retirements good or good retirements bad, it is an important factor, if not in the quality of our retirements, then in their quantity. Okay, I said it, but don't worry about the "money thing" quite yet because we are only in the second chapter, and we have higher mountains to climb.

Once these pesky financial concerns are put to rest (in our minds if not perhaps in reality), then we can look forward to retirement and getting away from the daily grind, to our new lives and more time with family and friends, to travel and adventure, exploring new interests, refocusing on our existing activities and hobbies, and enjoying a healthy and trouble-free life filled with contentment and wonder. We can also focus on rediscovering the meaning of life and why we were put on this planet. Sounds wonderful, now doesn't it? (If not a tad overly optimistic, which indeed, it is.) Although optimism is an absolute necessity for dealing with life and all its vagaries, we are setting ourselves up for disappointment if we view retirement as a panacea, the solution for all our problems, the redemption for all our misdeeds, the answer to all those emotional, financial, health, and relationship problems that have plagued us these many years. I hate to rain on the parade, but neither retirement nor life is that simple; if it were, you wouldn't need me, or this book, now would you?

WHY IS THAT SPEEDING TRAIN HEADED FOR US?

So where am I going with this? Well with all our retirement thinking, planning, and even some scheming, we sometimes fail to see that speeding train headed right for us. As our working life comes to its inevitable conclusion, we, having survived numerous bosses, restructurings, and competitive challenges, are now newly minted retirees standing on the "other side of work," looking in. We have walked away from decades of problem solving, involvement, activity, and comradeship expecting to easily slide into our new retirement personae. Not so fast—retirement pushes back and pushes back hard. You see, our lives' rhythms will be completely disrupted when the structure that once ordered our world, our thinking, and our actions for so many years is whisked away in a New York minute. We will be out there on our own, looking at our dear significant other across the table asking, "What do you want to do today?" or something equivalent, and the answer will come back, perhaps a bit more emphatically, "Well, what do *you* want to do?" So we wander about undecided, by ourselves or together; we shop, play on our computers, watch daytime television (which can be a "hoot" for the uninitiated), then don't sleep very well because our "wake-sleep" biorhythms have been disrupted as well, and begin to think not so pretty thoughts, and maybe we even start sneaking a look at help-wanted ads to see what's going on out there in the "real world." Some of us may have expected too much too soon from retirement, or we didn't do our retirement homework, which is frequently the case. As the novelty of retirement and our newly found devil may care attitude wears off about what we do, when we do it, and even what day it is, and the realization sets in that those so-called hobbies weren't as fulfilling as expected, we inevitably start thinking *What have I done?* Is it buyer's remorse? Time will tell. You're bored, listless, and hungry for human interaction, maybe you even start thinking about going back to work, "Just part-time, to get out of the house and prove that I am still needed and wanted by someone." *But by whom?* We wonder. Boredom is a breeding ground for discontentment and even more potentially destructive human vices, so work seems the better option.

IT'S NOT JUST YOU FLOATING IN A "MOST PECULIAR WAY"

Life after the initial high-fives, hearty handshakes, funny speeches, and "wish I could go with you" sentiments quickly fades into a very singular affair as we leave our workplaces for the last time. We've been working for over 40 years and now it's over. When the initial enthusiasm of retirement wears off, the memories of our working days get stronger and more nostalgic, doubts about retirement start flooding our minds. We find ourselves transported to a parallel universe, one we had previously glimpsed but with little knowledge or real understanding of what it would truly be like for us. Indeed, it's a "Ground Control to Major Tom" moment. The David Bowie classic "Space Oddity" has a particular relevance to those caught in such major life transitions, *I'm floating in a most peculiar way/And the stars look very different today/Here am I sitting in a tin can far above the world…and, there's nothing I can do.*

When first retired, I, and probably some of you, had a similarly hopeless and helpless feeling—like free-floating in space, not knowing what to do with the rest of my life or how to fully disconnect myself from the world of work I so badly wanted to leave, but perhaps have begun to miss.

THE WANDERER, PERHAPS, IS TRULY LOST

There's something terribly wrong here, we feel. It is commonly said, "All who wander are not lost," but truth be told, some of us are sincerely lost. The isolation and separation from the decades of life at work—what we knew and who we knew—forces some of us, at least, to consider the unthinkable. That is, going back to work, even if it is only part-time, and not necessarily for the money, but to get out of the house and be around people once again. As our angst and loneliness mount we start asking ourselves, "Is that all there is?" It soon becomes obvious that we have to stop whining, complaining, and spinning our wheels and instead figure out why we are not feeling good about retirement, why we have not found a new life rhythm or place in this world after work, and, ultimately, what we can do about it. You see, some of us have contemplated abandoning what we have so long sought—retirement—and kicking a long-cherished dream to the side of the road like so much trash. Remember the sixties cry, "Let's give peace a chance"? Well, that goes for retirement as well.

RETIREMENT IS A PRIVILEGE, NOT A RIGHT

As new recruits into the "army of the retired" we are not yet familiar with the rules and etiquette of retirement or how it needs to be nurtured and fed. Perhaps we expected retirement to just organically evolve, or be delivered to our doorstep like a FedEx® package, only this one would be wrapped and paid for. If so, then both you and I were wrong…really, really wrong. What I finally figured out on the road to the "other side of work" was that retirement isn't a gift or a right, rather it's a privilege, one well worth working for all those many years. But, like any privilege, it becomes a responsibility that should be neither exploited nor squandered but instead encouraged and cultivated. Which, unfortunately, we typically do not know how to do in the early stages of our retirement journeys. Most pay scant attention to planning for retirement other than to make sure there will be enough money; there is little awareness of and concern for dealing with the emotional impact retirement can have on our sense of self-worth, on our feelings of abandonment and the accompanying grief. For many, leaving work is very much like losing a close friend, a loss that takes a big emotional toll.

If this is where you find yourself in the retirement continuum, you have several options: (a) figure out why retirement is not "happening" for you and do something about it; (b) ignore the problem and keep flirting with a failed retirement; or (c) abandon retirement as a bad idea and go back to work. Like most of us, I hate not succeeding at anything, let alone failing at what should be a simple walk in the park. *We need a solution,* we tell ourselves, and so perhaps we seek the advice of friends and family who have seemingly bridged the gap between work and retirement, or we turn to books like this one, or we search the Web to find answers to our many questions. What you will find wandering around the Web, libraries, and bookstores is a lot of financial, trust, investment, and legal advice with scant attention paid to the perhaps more profound nonfinancial issues confronting both the retired and soon-to-be-retired. But after the money matters have been put to rest, many of our concerns are of the "what am I going to do with the rest of *my* life?" variety and the uncertainty of what this new retired life is really all about, and -how we emotionally adjust to such a major life-changing transition after coming off the retirement "high" and settle in to a new life routine that is at first liberating and then confusing, as feelings of aloneness, boredom, and abandonment start banging around our heads.

For some, spirituality and getting closer to God is an answer, and indeed it is the solution for some. But many of us are already convinced that spirituality is important to our aging selves so these insights do not offer any additional wisdom, nothing that would lead us out of our "on the one hand and on the other hand" retirement dilemma.

THE ANSWER PLEASE

So, as I began seeking answers for myself to the "retirement paradox," I unexpectedly discovered that I was not alone. Many of us are experiencing difficulty adjusting to the "freedom" that retirement offers. Indeed, we had become so accustomed and desensitized to living by the "rules"—the structure of work, others, and life—that we either forgot how to, or were afraid of becoming, the "boss of us" after so many years of letting others determine our fates. We were told when to wake up, when we could have vacations, when we could go home at the end of the day and be with our families, when we could eat lunch, and what we must do for the greater part of our waking hours. I used to joke that I spent more time with my colleagues and staff than my family and probably knew more about their private lives than the lives of my wife and kids—but, I reasoned, that's what we did. What was the option? We were climbing the ladder and supporting our families, and wasn't that what we were supposed to do? We rarely ever considered retirement in our early years; we were just too busy chasing life.

RETIREMENTS DON'T HAPPEN, WE MAKE THEM HAPPEN

Well, even as retirement "newbies," it's probably no surprise that successful retirements don't just happen, we have to make them happen, and many have not taken the second part of the calculation into consideration. We naively believed that retirement would somehow magically materialize, arriving fully formed without our care or intervention. Perhaps we made the classic retirement miscalculation that retirement would be "easy," a "no-brainer," provided the financing was in place. Work was hard, so we expected retirement to be simple; we assumed that it would just flow into our being like a friendly spirit, bringing both peace and contentment. Boy, were some of us wrong!

THE MEANING OF RETIREMENT ACCORDING TO...?

As my concerns and doubts about retirement mounted, I sat down at my trusty computer and started jotting down some of my thoughts and beliefs about what retirement meant to me personally and to my life, and perhaps to the lives of others. I hoped to better understand how retirement could be integrated into our lives rather than simply bolted onto our "pre-retirement" selves. Before going full bore into this exercise I first needed to determine if someone else out there had already done the hard work and analysis, and if holistic or integrated retirement models even existed. But all I found were just bits and pieces of retirement advice, some sound, some of limited validity or value, and many pronouncements and dictums about how we should or even "must" live in retirement. But, as anticipated, the only retirement "models" I uncovered were, you guessed it, financial models of the "how to fund your retirement" variety. There was scant literature about the emotional, psychological, and social dimensions of retirement, nothing addressing the separation anxiety, the difficulty transitioning from work to retirement, the acceptance of our aging selves, the innate need for meaning and fulfillment, and how to achieve those. Most glaring of all was the almost total lack of discussion and debate about the necessity of remaining active and continually challenging our bodies and our intellects. And, just as critical but equally ignored, was the human desire and need for companionship, compassion, sharing, and caring with, for, and by others; the critical role "life engagement" plays in the everyday existence of retirees and how we can actually learn to become more socially accepted or adept, and that boredom and loneliness are just as dangerous as the addictive behaviors they can spawn. Now, it doesn't mean that such a model doesn't already exist, only that I was not able to discover anything that satisfied my preliminary concepts and theories of what behaviors and factors contribute to building successful and meaningful retirements.

RETIREMENT'S SIX FUNDAMENTAL BUILDING BLOCKS

So, absent a retirement model that satisfied my expectations, under-standings, and admitted preconceptions of how we can shape life after work, I set out to craft my own integrated and holistic retirement model, one that would have real-world relevance and above all be useful to my millions of fellow travelers as they either contemplate their impending retirements or seek to re-energize existing ones. I quickly settled on the "Pyramid" as my model because it is the strongest geometric shape known, and pyramids have withstood the ravages of man and nature through the ages. So, I commenced building my "Virtual Retirement Pyramid" out of "Retirement's Six Fundamental Building Blocks" and linked it to the more dynamic "Retirement Life Cycle Paradigm," which I call "Retirement's Ages and Stages." Now, we have two retirement models that are inextricably connected and when taken together provide the logic and organization of this book, affording the ability to measure and/or assess our retirements in real time.

MAKING RETIREMENT THE NEW NORMAL

It became clear to me that before we could collectively and successfully move into our new retirement lives, we had to shed the mantle of our former working lives. After all, aren't we all seeking and hoping for joyful, healthful, long lived, exciting, productive, purposeful, and financially worry-free retirements? Regrettably, some of us on our way to retirement fall prey to the "Rookie's Retirement Slump." This happens when the new realities of life after work together with its newfound freedoms conflict with the "old realities" of life at work, its structure, friendship networks, and, yes, its steady income; all things that we clung to for security and comfort regardless of what we said and thought—you see, breaking up is hard to do!

Most of us stragglers, after a year or so of resistance, self-reflection, and recommitment, eventually come around to not only adjusting to retirement, but banishing all thoughts of living any other way. We finally find our "retirement groove," and fulfill our personal quest for retirement purpose, adventure, and meaning. We probably now find ourselves busier, more in tune with life, emotionally and physically healthier, calmer, more accepting of people and events, more self-sufficient and motivated to seek new and different experiences and opportunities for self-improvement than ever before. Likewise, we are more open to others and to this world we share for whatever time is granted us; indeed we are happier, more excited and engaged in life, eager to greet each and every new day. But what made this turnaround possible? Glad you asked. And, the answer is: we now freely accept retirement as our life and desired destiny; we know retirement is the world we want to live in, we choose to be retired and no longer feel uncomfortable with retirement, we have more to contribute to our family and community, and we understand that retirement gives us more opportunities than work ever could or did. You see, at some point we had a retirement epiphany; that is, a hit upside the head that said, "How could you have missed it?" "Missed what?" we likely responded. "The retirement paradox, you dolt," we answered ourselves. *We work so we can retire, but to succeed in retirement requires work.*"

AND THE BEAT GOES ON

So here we are eager, or at least not reluctant, and sincerely committed retirees, doing in retirement not what we *have* to do, but what we *want* to do. Retirement has given us all the opportunity to control our own lives, to pursue interests together and separately, to travel and seek adventure, to reconnect with friends and family and to follow whatever path presents itself and tickles our fancy. Personally, I will always write, I will always test my body, I will always seek enlightenment and knowledge, I will always be there for my wife and family, and I will continue exploring this sometimes scary and sometimes inexplicable world. I want to live the rest of my life in a state of constant wonderment. I have no intention of ever giving up observing and engaging, of thinking and learning, of touching the world in all its glories and diversity, its squalor and anger and cruelty until my last brain cells have died or ceased cooperating. I will always seek opportunities to connect with others, learn the stories of their lives, offer sage advice when asked or quiet comfort when not, and I will live every day like it is my last day, certain that one day I will be right, and when that day comes, I will leave with no regrets because a life well lived is worth dying for. As Sonny and Cher sang, "And the beat goes on."

PART II
THE JOURNEY BEGINS

CHAPTER 3

■ ■ ■ ■ ■ ■

Recapturing Lost Dreams and Missed Opportunities

The optimist sees the donut,
the pessimist sees the hole.
—OSCAR WILDE

What is more mortifying than to feel
you have missed the plum for want
of courage to shake the tree?
—LOGAN SMITH

ON PERSPECTIVE

Age alone grants us neither grace nor wisdom—you have to earn those. What it does give us is perspective, or the ability to look at the present in the context of the past; sometimes this perspective is very personal and introspective, other times analytical and objective, usually starting off, "when I was your age…," and so on and so forth. We all know the drill. The newly found gift of age called "perspective" endows us with the capacity to look at life events not as they were or are, but rather as they should be or could have been—without getting angry or emotionally entangled in mind-draining self-doubt. Just as a fine wine gets more flavorful and full bodied as it ages, it will just as surely turn to vinegar if left too long in the bottle. Likewise perspective can sour as well, if we are unable to reconcile our past selves with our future selves because of doubts, emotional pain, and deep regrets over lost dreams and missed opportunities. The inevitable process of growing older grants us hindsight, or the ability to re-create life events, both joyful and sad, in our mind's eye. We can then stand back without rancor or anger, allowing ourselves to reconcile with those significant life decisions, actions, and pivot points we could have or should have been more thoughtful about or done differently, if not better. We silently complain to ourselves, "If only we had been able to see into the future," or "If we had known then what we know today life would have surely been different," so we think and so we believe. But we must stop punishing ourselves over what could have been or should have been because maturity cannot be rushed. Life cannot be lived through the rearview mirror—we must always look forward, and with renewed commitment, energy, and spirit set out to recapture those lost dreams and missed opportunities. Retirement is our last best chance to heal old wounds, both emotional and physical, and to redirect our attentions to what is most important in our personal lives and for the significant others who surround us. We all should apologize for those misguided choices or inconsiderate behaviors, particularly to our families, if we are to move on in life without carrying the baggage of the past into the present and then on into the future.

CONGRATULATIONS, YOU ARE NOW ON THE ROAD TO RETIREMENT

All of us, whether and when we realize it, are on the road to retirement from the first time we receive a paycheck—congratulations, we are now certified members of the Social Security system—although whether or when we cross the finish line is conjecture. We don't think about retirement very much in our younger years, partly because we have nothing to retire from and partly because we are too busy getting an education, learning a trade, starting a business, raising a family, beginning our first "adult" job, or all of the above. We are young and thoughtful, or young and reckless, or young and oblivious, or some combination of the three. We have little concern even for the concept of what it means to get old, let alone what our lives will be like when we are in our sixties. So even the concept of retirement for a 20-something is just a dim vision somewhere over the far horizon. Interests and thoughts are directed toward more immediate needs, wants, and life priorities, not squandered on even imagining that someday we will be old or ever like our parents. But life has a funny way of catching up to us, and by then it might be too late to make up for lost time.

SOMETIMES LIFE JUST GETS IN THE WAY

In our early years all our energy and efforts are directed toward getting a toehold into life as contributing, functioning adults. Some of us gravitate toward jobs that hold the potential of high rewards, status, and wealth but require significant and expensive preparation and schooling; some are destined for family businesses; yet others just want to get by and end their schooling prematurely, having no interest in learning a trade or profession, and let chance, fate, and serendipity be their guides. Yet others focus like a laser on a preferred career, such as doctor, lawyer, engineer, or small business owner, and then single-mindedly go about connecting all the "life dots" to that end. And some of us choose to live outside the boundaries of life's "coloring book" and follow a different drummer. All of these choices ultimately impact when and how we can fund our retirements. Some of us pursue wealth, some security, some adventure, others opportunity or creativity, and still others just roll the dice. Some retrace their parents' footsteps down the same roads they traveled, while yet others follow the "rule of opposites"—meaning they will do everything in their power not to become their parents, which will eventually happen anyway.

SO MANY PATHS, SO MANY CHOICES, SO LITTLE TIME

We followed many different paths to get on the road to retirement. We came from many parts of the country and from many places around the world; we worked at many different jobs, occupations, and professions. Our occupations defined who we were and where we fit into society, the friends we would have, how well we lived, our station in life, and ultimately, the life we would lead in retirement. We were valued as equals by some and not by others, regardless of what we were paid or how well we performed. We performed these jobs for many years, even though some sapped our strength, eroded our spirits, and dulled our minds, still most of us persevered and reached the other side of work. And while most of us retired gracefully and gratefully, others, like me, followed Dylan Thomas's advice, "Do not go gentle into that good night."

LET YOUR LIFE NARRATIVE BE YOUR GUIDE

And, while history is not necessarily destiny, our life narrative does surround us with comfort and boundaries and pushes us in one direction or another depending on the "story" we and others authored for ourselves. That life narrative, or "story," might or might not put us on the road that will take us through life without fault or failure and ultimately lead to a well-earned retirement. Detours and washouts along the road to retirement can delay or even stop our progress, sometimes forcing us to return to our old lives if we let self-doubt infiltrate our emotional defenses and make us question who we are and where we are going. Before we permit "old negative life scripts" to derail our futures and our retirements we must fortify ourselves against those eventualities and move forward, ever forward, as Winston Churchill said, "If you are going through hell, keep going." And, while we synthesize, analyze, and hypothesize about life and where we want to go and ultimately what road to follow, we are sometimes haunted by past events that unwittingly hide and speak to us from the corners of our minds, urging us to do what we have always done. We must tame that voice and trust ourselves to keep our eyes on the prize and proceed with optimism, vigor, and determination toward this new beginning, this place called "Retirement."

RETIREMENT IS OPTIONAL, OLD AGE AND DEATH ARE NOT

Life offers us untold varieties of destinations. Some are of our choosing, many are not, yet others have been predetermined and programmed within us by our parents, significant others, teachers, institutions, or circumstances. If you don't like the options offered you can always take Frost's "road less traveled," or Hope and Crosby's *Road to Zanzibar*, or follow author Lewis Carroll's sage advice, "If you don't know where you are going, any road will get you there." One way or another, life's many pathways will narrow to just one and then that too will ultimately come to an abrupt end. We all should clearly understand that while retirement is optional, getting older and death are not. So why not enjoy your retirement? You earned it. Think of retirement as the gift that keeps on giving, and it will, as long as you are willing to embrace and nurture it. Treat retirement as your best and last opportunity to conceive, craft, and create your personal life affirming narrative and then make it happen before time and opportunity pass you by.

What we do, where we go, and ultimately how successful we are at navigating life's sometimes calm and other times turbulent waters is guided by several life-affirming traits and attributes: (1) a willingness and capacity to adapt to the new and ever-changing circumstances surrounding us in our daily lives; (2) allowing others into our life space on equal terms as friends, colleagues, and partners; (3) assuming and accepting responsibility for our own actions; (4) forgiving others and ourselves for past transgressions; and (5) understanding and expecting there will be times of joy and celebration as well as disappointment and sorrow, and that we must embrace the joy and overcome the sorrow and loss. Ultimately, how we face or cope with retirement's stages and ages, and its accompanying challenges and changes, whether with equanimity or anger, is within our own control but we must always remember we are the sum of all our memories, habits, behaviors, events, and life scripts and that we were shaped by our parents, relatives, teachers, clergy, friends, the media, and the world surrounding us.

WE ARE ALL BORN EQUALLY HELPLESS AND IMPRESSIONABLE

Life is about decisions. Hindsight can inform the future, but we cannot dwell on the past, rather we must learn from it by not repeating those "life-destroying" decisions that did not serve us well, and by refocusing on the "life-affirming" decisions that stood us in good stead. We must all take responsibility for who we were, who we now are, and who we will ultimately become. It is, after all, our behaviors and life choices that determine, shape, and direct our lives as we move through its various stages and ages. We are more than the sum of our genetic codes. We are also the products of our environments and the significant others who surrounded us and helped create our "personal worlds," in which we live out our lives. We are all born equal at birth, with the same vulnerabilities and impressionableness. We are formed and re-formed by the loved ones who surround us and the societies and cultures in which we live.

IT'S YOUR LIFE SCRIPT, SO WRITE A HAPPY ENDING

In the early years of our lives, our parents, surrogate or otherwise, were the providers of love, sustenance, nurturance, and boundaries. They had the obligation, power, and opportunity, if not always the understanding, to shape and send appropriate life-affirming messages and ensure that constructive behaviors were learned, adopted, exhibited, and repeated. These life-affirming—or in some sad cases "life-destroying"—messages and behaviors were then integrated into our very beings, becoming what we think of as our personalities.

Some of us learned better than others how to counter or cancel the negative, or "life-destroying," messages we all continually receive day in and day out from the media, our computers, our peers, and countless other sources of negative messages and misinterpretations of reality. We internalized what to do and what not to do; what is acceptable and what is not; we understood how to behave and how to respond to disappointments and upsets. We were either encouraged or discouraged by our parents from doing anything even approaching dangerous, risky, or unconventional, or else we were inspired by them to explore and discover, to challenge the status quo and unfairness by others or upon others. We became dependent or independent or somewhere in between. If we fell or failed we were given a hand up, taught how to get up and how not to fail again, or sometimes punished. We learned our behaviors, got our "voice," and became who we see in the mirror from those who surrounded us. We then carried those behaviors forward into our adult lives, either as baggage to ultimately be abandoned when new and more positive life messages were learned or as treasured touchstones to help us find our way in a world that is sometimes scary and always confusing.

WE ARE RESPONSIBLE FOR OUR PERSONAL DESTINIES

We all develop personalities and perspectives, with all their consequent fears, hopes, dreams, and desires, along with a worldview that is either optimistic or pessimistic, life affirming or life destroying, a view that while not immutable, can only be redirected if the will, the desire, the internal drive, and the motivation are strongly present. That is, we can re-form and reshape ourselves, provided we have one of the most critical (if not *the* most critical) of social values and beliefs: the ability to distinguish between what is right and what is wrong, what is acceptable behavior and what is not.

Adulthood and maturity add yet another dimension to our lives, the perception, if not the reality, of "free will" in its broadest context. The corollary to free will is the assumption of responsibility for our own lives, for our successes and our failures, or whether we learn from or ignore the lessons life presents us. Even as adults we continue to be formed and re-formed by forces we fully understand, recognize, and accept but did not initiate; by purposeful actions we take to, perhaps, move us forward in a changing micro or macro environment; or by circumstances and events that blindsided us, even those we should have expected and prepared for but somehow failed to anticipate. Life is never predictable despite our best efforts to make it so. Life can be arbitrary and sometimes capricious, perhaps adding interest and challenges that either move us forward or freeze us in place. It is our optimistic or pessimistic view of life—the "I can's" or "I can't's"—that directly transfers to how we perceive, conceive, and live not only our lives, but ultimately our retirements. Think of retirement as life's second chance at happiness—don't squander this opportunity; there won't be another one like it coming your way any time soon.

As we approach retirement age, whatever that is for us, we begin to mentally tangle with both the prospect and the impending realities of retirement, which for some is a given, not *whether* but *when*. Yet, for others it can be a time of stress, struggle, and anguish as we ponder what to do with the rest of our lives. A few won't even allow themselves to consider retirement as a life option because of personal perspectives regarding the value and worth of work, real or imagined; financial reasons; or, even simply because they never developed hobbies or interests and quite frankly lack imagination, equating retirement with frivolity, decadence, and idleness. And as we all know "the devil makes work for idle hands," or, as Sherlock Holmes tells Watson when asked if he is going to bed, "I never remember feeling tired by work, though idleness exhausts me completely."[1] I am particularly concerned about those who have yet to understand that you retire only from work—not from life—and that in retirement there is joy, adventure, challenge, and intergenerational opportunities to reconnect with friends and family, and to make new friends and try new things and commit to new causes and to put both meaning and perspective back into our lives. Retirement can and will give us those precious opportunities if we give it a chance, as I so fitfully learned.

DON'T FORGET THE PAST, BRING IT FORWARD

Whatever our course in life, whether to retire or to continue working, we must prepare ourselves to move ahead with a renewed optimism for the life yet to come with full realization that the past does not necessarily determine our futures—because only we can do that. While it is comforting to look back to where and who we were, we should not be encumbered or overly attached to life as it was, because it is no longer. Don't forget the past, build on it by bringing the good parts forward and leaving the rough patches behind. Life isn't a Hollywood prequel where we can conveniently reinvent our pasts to make them neatly fit our visions of who we are or who we want to be. Take the past and the present on a journey of discovery because for many of us, or more particularly, those of us who embrace our new lives, retirement is our passport to everywhere. Don't waste mental energy on the "wouldas, couldas, and shouldas" of life. Instead, focus on what you can do, should do, will do, and ultimately must do for yourself and for others as you move on and into your new future.

Because of personal perspectives and perhaps "blinders," most of us view our lives as a series of continuous events when, in reality, our lives are lived in stages with each stage providing us with differing perspectives, experiences, and emotional challenges—some stages pass almost unnoticed, while others are emblazoned in our memories because of life-altering events. Indeed, we can "die with our work boots on," if that is our preference, but we would miss so much that life has yet to offer. Think of retirement as a bequest from our forefathers and mothers because every generation wants the next to have a better, more fruitful, and fulfilling life than they could have ever hoped for; and so we did and so we are.

WORRYING, WONDERING, AND WANDERING

Retirement and getting older, while connected, are certainly not "causative" of each other. Indeed, if lived right, retirement can add years to your life, happy ones at that. So both retirement and growing older are natural progressions with retirement potentially taking us to, as we say, "a better place" and the other just leading us to an inevitable conclusion. I was one of those retirement doubters, or as I like to say, a "Reluctant Retiree," but now consider myself to be sincerely converted and fully committed to retirement, albeit on my terms. It took me about a year of worrying, wondering, and wandering to find my way and to accept retirement as the life I choose to live; as I like to say, "I was lost and now I'm found."

Like some, I hid behind my work and used it as an excuse to avoid and defer life changes, for example being physically active and taking better care of my body. Work was also an excuse for my anger and outbursts, for not being more fully engaged with my growing children, and for not going on the trips and visits to family that my wife wanted to take and that I, perhaps, didn't consider interesting enough or thought too expensive. In retrospect my attitude was selfish and ultimately self-defeating; I didn't even do my share of the household chores. But, once reconciled with my new status as a "retiree," I soon realized there is no better time than life's "third act" to recommit the rest of our lives to self-direction and discovery, to embrace new life experiences and adventure, to make every day a different day, to tend to our intellectual, emotional, and physical well-being, but most of all to recommit ourselves to our spouses, loved ones, and friends, to contemplation, our communities, and our fellow travelers. Life is fragile and retirement should not be taken for granted. If we find ourselves attached to our beds, bored and moping around, then something is wrong, really wrong. Clearly, lots of "somethings" are missing from our lives. Retirement can be the "gift that keeps on giving" for some, but not for others—you choose.

WE DON'T ALL RETIRE—BUT WE ALL STOP WORKING

We don't all retire—but we all eventually stop working. Some of us sadly "die in the saddle," others become incapacitated and are no longer able to work. Many others leave the workforce permanently simply because they cannot find employment or do not possess the necessary skills to procure a job; however, many of us, by far the majority, conclude our work careers by formally retiring.

The decision to retire—that is, to end, sever, or completely disengage ourselves from work and from personal participation in the workforce—appears at first blush to be the fulfillment of a life-long dream, but the reality can be like a nightmare on Elm Street. Retirement can have fearsome repercussions for us, our family, our lifestyles, our health, our emotional and social well-being, and our finances, if it is not thoroughly thought out, fully staged, and planned. Most importantly of all, we must not fail to consider that when we retire *from* something we must concurrently retire *to* something. Otherwise we can find ourselves living in a black hole of boredom and depression.

DOES THIS SOUND LIKE YOU?

Let me introduce myself, my name is: _____. This is my story. I retired four months ago; I just wanted to stay home and decompress for a while after 35 years working for the same company as a middle manager, pretty much doing the same things all those years. My wife is still working. I don't know where to go or what to do. Sometimes I walk around shopping centers just to be near other people; I can't sleep, rarely shave now, and when I call my friends they're either working and don't have time to talk or they aren't home or don't have time to get together. I feel abandoned by everyone. My children rarely visit, only when they need to use my car because they say I have no place to go anyway. My wife gives me a honey-do list every day, but I don't seem to have the energy to accomplish any of those things, and then she gets angry and calls me lazy when she gets home from work. Mostly I just sit in front of the television watching The Maury Povich Show *or* Judge Judy, *even though she scares me. I go online and wander around the shopping sites, buying things I really do not want or need; even worse, I watch infomercials and buy that junk. But I like getting packages at my door because at least someone out there knows I am alive. I am having a hard time hiding all this stuff from my wife—but if she finds out she will kill me.*

This is how retirement is for some people, more than you would believe.

AFTER THE PARTY

After the party and cake, after the speeches of how important we were to the success of the organization or business, after the hardy handshakes and congratulations for a well-earned retirement have stopped, all our colleagues who wished they could retire too have returned to work, and all the presents have been opened. Now the calls have stopped, no one is asking our opinion or coming to us for advice—there are no more meetings, no more lunches with colleagues, no more business trips, no more rushed assignments or crises to face. We are left entirely to our own devices. There were so many things we wanted to do when retired, like work in the garden, make some house repairs, go hiking, or to the gym, or take that trip to an exotic island. But the spouse can't fit such a long trip into his or her work schedule, and your daughter, who lives just a few minutes away, needs you to babysit the grandkids because she is going out of town on a business trip. *No one cares about me anymore,* you moan silently to yourself. *At least at work people cared about me and what I was doing and where I was going. I had people to talk to and things to do, but now I'm just stuck in the house waiting for my wife to get home from work.*

Whatever the reason, we just can't get going—and it feels as if our feet are stuck in mud that is quickly hardening. My friends, retirement can be both a joyous and a scary time. When we stop doing something, particularly something we have been doing for most of our lives—whether it was constructive or destructive, fulfilling, dull, or repetitive—and then sever that connection "cold turkey," without thoughtful planning, we are in for a rude surprise. Because what we did is what we know, and we have not yet gotten to know this thing called retirement. We are suffering from what is called "separation anxiety" where the hype and the reality of retirement just don't meet up; where every day feels like the day before. It's almost as if the movie *Groundhog Day* has become your new life, with you in the starring role doomed to repeat the same day over and over again...until you can "do what?" you ask. Indeed that sense of loss, malaise, and loneliness is a result of getting away from what you thought you wanted to get away from, it's called structure.

It's tomorrow and once again, you drag yourself to the bathroom for morning ablutions, but now you stand in front of the "mirror of life" reminiscing and asking the universal question we all ask at this stage in our lives, "How did all those years pass by so quickly? It was only yesterday that Johnny and Jane were..." Then you wonder whose face that is staring back at you from the mirror and the song "Dream On" starts playing in your head as it so often does these days:

> *The past is gone*
> *It went by like dusk to dawn*
> *Isn't that the way*
> *Everybody's got their dues in life to pay*
> *All the things you do come back to you*
> *Dream on, dream on, dream on...and dream until*
> *   your dreams comes true*

That song, so prescient, was written in 1973 by Steven Tyler, a much recognized and highly talented bad boy of rock 'n' roll. Born in 1948, he is a card carrying member of the Baby Boomer generation. It remains a mystery to me how someone so young could have captured the essence of what "we" feel and see today in our "mirror of life." But regardless of what we see, we give ourselves a mental slap upside the head. Then we wipe away a tear of sadness or a tear of joy, put on our game face, and go out to meet the world yet again—after all, people are depending on us, and life goes on, with or without us.

CHAPTER 4

■ ■ ■ ■ ■ ■

As the World Turns

*Everyone thinks of changing the world, but
no one thinks about changing themselves.*
—LEO TOLSTOY

*You must welcome change as the rule,
but not as your ruler.*
—DENIS WAITLEY

THINGS CHANGE

The world changed around us without our permission or oversight—
shows how thankless that world can be. We were supposed to be freed
from war and from want, we were supposed to live idyllic lives and remain
married "till death do us part," our children were supposed to grow up
and become productive members of society, and work was supposed to
be fulfilling. So we thought and so they said. The reality was, however,
quite different. We faced daily private wars at work and at home, divorce
became commonplace, our children strayed and only some returned,
our country was and is fighting in "pocket wars" around the globe. We
worked harder and harder to achieve the standard of living we expected
for ourselves and for our families and to provide the opportunities that
perhaps were not available to us, but we were hit by successive waves of

recession and economic downturns. Life, we learned, was fickle, full of joy, hardship, victories, disappointments, and sadness.

Did we really believe that when we retired our lives would turn on a dime; that we would suddenly view the world through a different, "happier" lens; that retirement would make everything alright at home and with our families and around the world and our "wall of worries" would disappear? If so I have bad news, retirement comes with baggage too; it's not the walk in the park some have us believe. Indeed, we might just be trading one set of concerns for another—like going from too little time for ourselves to having too much time on our hands; or transitioning from having a steady income to not knowing whether we will have enough to cover our bills because our investments are going up and down like an elevator. Be wary of retirement's siren song and the false expectations we might be building; retirement will not solve all those personal, emotional, and relationship issues in our lives with our partners, our children, or with others.

WORK WAS WHO WE WERE AND WHAT WE DID

Work, for some, was a "power trip," our daily high, for whatever psychological reasons. Work became addictive, our reason for getting up every morning and home was the place we dragged our sorry selves back to, ready to confront whatever real or imagined horribles were awaiting us. So much so that the Food and Drug Administration should probably put a warning label on our retirement papers declaring: *"Retiring can be totally disruptive to your psyche and life rhythms; follow all prescribed retirement treatments and recommendations or retirement will be hazardous to your health—take this warning seriously."* How do we break from that addiction, the thrill of making a big sale, or landing a lucrative contract, or driving a competitor into bankruptcy? That's right—an addiction by any other name is still an "addiction," and many of us were addicted to work; some of us even used it as an excuse to avoid problems at home, like out-of-control children or marital struggles, or even just as a cover for escaping.

How aggressively we pursue retirement and at what age we plan to retire is directly proportional to the pushes and pulls of life; namely, whether we are running away or toward something. Some of us push retirement off, like kicking the can down the road, because we understand our needs, drives, and fears, and also because we get satisfaction from our work, careers, or occupations; it's more than just a paycheck. Some people become consumed with the fantasy of retiring, casting it almost like a Walter Mitty dream where life is always beautiful, without worry or struggle, monetarily or otherwise. Others view retirement as their savior from a dull job, a release from the pressures of constant deadlines, or an escape from a mean-spirited boss who takes great pleasure in publicly humiliating subordinates. Still others are not running away from something, but rather rushing toward something, like time together with loved ones, the desire to help others, or the lure of hobbies and interests and travel, or even just a new vista from a place yet to be decided.

MOST OF US RETIRE FOR THE RIGHT REASONS

Regardless of our reasons, most of us view retirement as the culmination of a life well lived, as the payoff for hard work, financial diligence, being an understanding and successful parent or partner, a reward for generally good citizenship. But in reality, retirement, what we have so diligently pursued all these many years, can be a time of high stress due to the dramatic changes that will literally sweep over us like a rogue wave; the realization that we are getting older and that we are trading a life we know (whether good, bad, or indifferent) for a life we have yet to experience, a life called retirement.

We cannot successfully break our addiction to work—if we actually *have* one—simply by announcing our retirement one day, and walking out (proverbially speaking of course) the next. The fact of the matter is we should have laid the financial foundation for our retirements early in our careers, but we will get to that point later. The decision to retire should not be a reaction to a bad day at work, or used as a threat, because once you utter those words your organization just might accept the offer. The decision to retire must be made thoughtfully and in consultation and coordination with significant others as well as with your employer. There needs to be serious introspection, retrospection, opportunity analysis, and groundwork performed prior to making one of the most important decisions of your life. Indeed, there are multiple decision points on the road to retirement, but the four most pertinent questions we must ask and then answer as we approach the typical retirement age of 62–65 are: (1) Will we retire? (2) If so, when we will retire? (3) Are we "ready" to retire? and, (4) What are we retiring to, or phrased a bit more succinctly, what are we going to do with the rest of our lives?

WHAT ARE WE RETIRING TO?

We move into retirement one step at a time (sometimes easy and some-times hard), but first, we have to decide and define what it is we are leaving, and why we are doing so at this particular time in our lives. Are we retiring from a job, a career, a profession, or a life's work? Then we have to decide and define what it is we are going toward. Is it more time with our spouses and families; improving our personal selves; returning to a passion like music; doing something we could not do or afford when young and raising a family; making new friends; pursuing hobbies old and new; or tackling our personal bucket list? And on and on...But the bottom line remains—there is no such thing as a perfect retirement or for that matter, a perfect anything.

IT'S NOT ALWAYS ABOUT THE MONEY

Most of us believe the core of a successful retirement is money. In reality the most critical success factors are who we become; how we view life, either optimistically or pessimistically; and what we want to do with the rest of our lives. It's about how we wrap our heads around the concept of retirement until we can fully accept and then experience the "reality" of it. Some of us view retirement as being thrown to the side of life's road by an uncaring employer; others see it as a death sentence or as God's waiting room; while still others see it as an opportunity to become whatever we want to be, to go wherever we want to go, an opportunity to pursue lost dreams and missed opportunities. Retirement is truly life's last exit to everywhere.

WHAT DID YOU SAY?

I hear the murmurs of discontent already. Yes, you are correct—life isn't fair. Some of us have more money and things than others, some of us have better health than others, some of us have tighter knit families than others, some of us have experienced loss, hardship, and sadness, and for that I am truly sorry. But, retirement can be life's best and last do-over. We all have to believe in something, so many of us choose to believe that tomorrow will be better than today—no matter the odds or realities we currently face—otherwise we would all pull the covers over our heads and pray not to wake up.

Please accept retirement as a "new day" and as a new opportunity for happiness and fulfillment. We should remember the past, but not dwell on it—and always look and move forward. Retirement can actually enable us to return to those earlier years when our dreams outstripped the hard realities of life. History is not destiny. How we approached life and its challenges in our earlier years, whether constructively or destructively, is not a predictor of how we will ultimately live in retirement; although behaviors, both destructive and constructive, can become fixed and old habits are hard to slip out of, still it can be done. Think about this, if we are always looking back saying woulda, coulda, shoulda, then what will we say when we can? Retirement is our opportunity to say, "Yes, I can."

RETIREMENT ISN'T FOR SISSIES

Throughout life, every one of us has developed, for the right or wrong reasons, habits, behaviors, attitudes, routines, customs, values, principles, and tendencies to do things the same way every day, every time.

But new undertakings require new thinking. Consider retirement as a new beginning, one requiring sincere reflection and thought together with the willingness and strength to change and adapt to a new way of living. Please understand the transition from work to retirement is not a continuum, even though it might initially feel that way. Indeed, retirement requires an entire mind/body reset. Retirement for many is spelled F-R-E-E-D-O-M. But as we know freedom comes with a price, and money alone cannot and will not suffice to make your retirement years full of joy and happiness. When retired we pay a heavy price in loss of status, social connections, purpose, and structure. And unless we have adequately established new friendship networks, new pursuits, and new life interests, our retirements can quickly unravel.

In order to provide a "head start" on the road to our excellent retirement adventure, and to move our thinking from the abstract to the concrete, I am providing some practical suggestions for jump-starting the "work to retirement" reinvention and recalibration process by providing some do's and don'ts of retirement. Remember, your retirement journey is just beginning, so be careful and avoid those potholes.

RETIREMENT'S SHOULD DO'S

FIRST, always explore and challenge your comfort zones—for the first time in your life, events should not dictate your actions, but rather your actions should dictate events.

SECOND, have a bias for action rather than for inaction—break from previous life routines, establish new, much wider life boundaries that your newfound time and freedoms will allow you to pursue.

THIRD, challenge yourself emotionally, intellectually, and physically by seeking activities and adventures that will keep you physically fit, mentally alert, and emotionally balanced.

FOURTH, make it a practice to do something every day, preferably something new. Don't languish in self-doubt or put off until tomorrow what you can do today. Sound familiar? Stay active and engaged, take a walk, read a book, or visit a friend. Demonstrate to yourself and others that you can and are willing to change, grow, and expand your horizons and that you are accessible to new experiences.

FIFTH, seek out new and renew old social involvements and relationships because it is absolutely critical to build new social networks, activities, and interests to replace those heretofore work-structured interactions, and also to provide companionship, meaning, and purpose to your life.

SIXTH, accept people for who they are and what they are—not who you want them to be—and invite new and different people of all backgrounds into your life, be prepared to learn from each other, enjoy the differences and seek diversity in thought, status, and background.

SEVENTH, have a retirement plan, or what I call a "Retirement Narrative," to guide you through retirement's multiple life stages.

EIGHTH, give back to your community, church, nation, or the world, try to make it a better place for those less fortunate by volunteering and sharing your knowledge, wisdom, and skills with others; you will grow and benefit from the experience as well.

NINTH, remain optimistic even in the face of hardship or pain—life throws balls and strikes. Sometimes we hit it out of the park and sometimes we strike out—but every at bat is a new opportunity to hit a winner, no matter how many times we might have let that ball (or opportunity) pass us by.

TENTH, establish a "realistic" retirement budget, one that is balanced between "real" income and "real" expenses. And, I must remind you once again that the number one fear of retirees is running out of money—with good reason, it happens more than you think, so take special care with your finances and have a disciplined approach or your creditors will be your new best friends.

RETIREMENT'S WHAT NOT TO DO'S

Here are some of those pesky human quirks, behaviors, and urges we should seek to avoid or moderate, particularly in polite company, as we move into and through our retirement years.

FIRST, don't even attempt to re-create youth by re-sculpting your face or engaging in dangerous or unhealthy pastimes, if you get my drift. The urge to turn back the clock is almost instinctive as we become uncomfortable with our aging selves. Chasing something we ultimately cannot have, our youth, is mind draining and self-defeating; you earned your "stripes" so wear them proudly.

SECOND, while growing old is inevitable and the preferred alternative, thinking old is not. Fun, playfulness, and, yes, even some silliness should not disappear simply because you are getting older. Your bearing, your behaviors, how you think, your vibrancy and lust for life and how you approach it are not age specific. It's how you view life that matters and just because you are aging or getting older that does not mean you have to act old and think old—there are more topics to talk about than your daily ailments and bowel movements.

THIRD, don't worship false "idols" and/or false symbols of affluence. These behaviors remind me of male peacocks spreading their beautiful feathers, but as pretty and majestic as these birds are, they are still just food for some predator. Some retirees like to spread those feathers to signal importance and status—whether real or imagined. Some of us do this at the expense of our life savings, buying real estate we really cannot afford or expensive cars we really don't know how to drive or need, throwing expensive parties, going first cabin on trips and letting everyone know about it, or buying expensive clothing or jewelry to impress. The only ones that are impressed by these displays are your banker and credit card company.

FOURTH, don't fall prey to stereotypes. We must confront the traditional roles and boxes society wants to put retirees in—the proverbial rocking chair. The world awaits and you are now free to move about the planet seeking new experiences. Seek them out, for they will not seek you. Nothing is out of bounds; you do not need permission from others—you can permit yourself. Follow your own path into retirement. Find others with similar interests and desires and urges to explore. Become an evangelist for an active and adventurous retirement. Don't follow the herd, let the herd follow you.

FIFTH, don't let fear of the unknown, fear of getting hurt, fear of the unfamiliar, fear of what others will think about you, or fear of failing hold you back from fully enjoying the rest of your life. Control that fear and channel those energies into positive life messages, and always remember *The Little Engine That Could*, repeat after me: "I think I can...I think I can."

SIXTH, if you are not prepared to live within your financial means, whatever they are, then you must be prepared to have a failed retirement—there is no doubt about that. You must know, understand, and then accept your financial boundaries and not base your lifestyle on expecting to win the lottery or some other improbable scheme or windfall.

SEVENTH, don't retire without adequate health insurance and don't gamble away your future assuming you and your partner will not get sick until Medicare kicks in, because hospital and doctor bills add up very quickly, and no, they don't forgive those debts. Avoid, if at all possible, the dreaded 3D's—divorce, depression, and disability. Any of these alone can derail a retirement.

EIGHTH, and my final thou shall not, don't wear plaid or drive a golf cart as your primary mode of transportation, there I said it. Don't rush retirement, let it "evolve" not "revolve," or you will make yourself mentally and emotionally dizzy by constantly questioning yourself, rethinking your decisions, and making false stops and starts. If retirement gives us one thing, it is time, time to think and time to do things right. If good information comes in, then good decisions go out. Living in retirement is not a race— you will get to the finish line soon enough. Think of retirement as a slow walk, a mosey allowing you to see, smell, and touch life rather than hurrying past it and missing life's smaller, but potentially just as significant, moments. There is no need to speed by just to check off something on the "been there, done that" card.

THE NOT SO EXCLUSIVE CLUB

Retirement is not an exclusive club—it admits everyone, firemen, teachers, carpenters, truck drivers, doctors, U.S. presidents, business moguls, the poor, the wealthy, the healthy, the sick, and primarily people just like us. Where and how we fit into this club is not predetermined. We could be members who take full advantage of what retirement has to offer, or we could choose to never read any of the memos or attend any of its meetings—metaphorically, of course. Our place in the world of retirement and what we get out of retirement is entirely up to us. So, I suggest that, given the alternative (which is not very pretty), we all take full advantage of what retirement can offer; but keep in mind that to get, we also have to give. In the case of retirement we have to give it a chance to succeed by shedding some old beliefs, behaviors, and "life tapes" that perhaps kept us on the sidelines of life, missing what it can offer. The price of retirement success is our willingness to open our minds, hearts, and souls to new beginnings; to forgive ourselves for our past mistakes and to forgive others for their transgressions; and to ditch the bitterness we carry from work, or failed relationships and marriages, and be prepared and willing to start over and give ourselves a "second bite of the apple." Please don't let this second chance pass you by—there won't be a third.

CHAPTER 5

■ ■ ■ ■ ■ ■

Retirement Is Not a Spectator Sport

Thou shall not be a victim, thou shall not be a perpetrator, but, above all thou shall not be a bystander.

—YEHUDA BAUER

Everyone plays the game of life, but not everyone follows the rules.

—ANONYMOUS

LIFE'S PIVOT POINT

Retirement is one of life's most consequential "Pivot Points" which must be executed precisely and quickly because retirement windows can close unexpectedly. Our futures will happen whether we are ready or not—so we might as well prepare ourselves for the inevitable, and retirement, for most, is certainly an inevitable event. There is no scarier or more emotionally draining task than leaving a life we know for a life we have yet to fully comprehend. Retirement should not be allowed to "just happen" without direction or purpose. We must make retirement occur on our timetable and schedule, if at all possible, and not allow it to be thrust upon us, giving the forces of disorder an opportunity to take control of what can be the most exciting time of our lives. Retirement is a game changer and we must continually follow the bouncing ball. If we divert our attention at a critical moment, or fail to plan properly, or save enough money, or have a purpose in life other than sitting in front of our computers, or begin to follow our significant others around like lost puppies, then we quickly become irrelevant, and life will have its way with us. We must change and evolve as circumstances demand and require, and retirement is one of those circumstances where life should not stand still; or, as Charles Darwin tells us, "It's not the strongest of the species that survive, nor the most intelligent; it is the one that is most adaptable." Is that you?

REALITY BITES

Retirement is a radical departure from the life we knew, a jump into a life we have yet to fully comprehend, oftentimes with little "spin-up." Retirement dreams are one thing, but somehow reality has a way of interfering with our best laid plans. Retirement is more than an alternate reality that we slip into like a comfortable pair of slippers; and it's more than another life phase. In truth, it's another form of life; one in which we need to relearn, reflect, and recast ourselves so we can properly fit into this new life we call retirement. Most of us get to choose our paths through life, so select wisely. For the pessimists among us, life in retirement can be just as mundane, just as mind numbing and frightening and fraught with angst and anger as it was during our working years; but for the more optimistic it can be the "joy ride" that others assure us it is supposed to be. As retirement newbies we are figuratively "babes in the woods." And no one expects an infant to come into our world fully formed, able to feed and care for him- or herself. Yes, we have histories and life experience, and yes, we absolutely need to look back to go forward, but don't expect your retirement to be a reprise of your past life because retirement should and must be new and exciting with a hint of mystery lurking around the corner, or as Jim McKay would intone in the opening of every *Wide World of Sports* live-television extravaganza, "Experience the thrill of victory and the agony of defeat," because from defeat eventually comes victory. We don't want to tame our retirements, we want to play hard, play strong, play big, and experience retirement in all its glory because certainty in all things, while comforting, can quickly become tedious and uninteresting.

SEE AND BE SEEN

Waiting for something to happen, for that pretty girl or handsome boy to ask us to dance, is an exciting prospect that tickles our imaginations and raises our hopes but rarely materializes. Thus still unknown to our "secret partner," we hang our heads in defeat, move silently away, and hide in plain sight, once again invisible to the world and to ourselves. Many of us, by choice or by circumstance, are passive observers of life's tableau—always watching but rarely participating. We desire, and in fact crave, excitement and social contact, the interaction with and the gentle touch of another. But when offered and given the choice to either accept or flee from that wanted, but ultimately feared, serendipitous connection, we panic and turn away for fear of rejection; quickly we avert our eyes and once again turn on our "invisibility cloaks." We approach, but ultimately we avoid—it's not that we lack the necessary social skills, rather it is confidence and boldness that are the missing life ingredients. Life after work wasn't supposed to be like this; it was supposed to be carefree and easy, filled with new friends and exciting activities and interests yet here I sit in the house staring at the computer, living a "virtual life" with no place to go and no one to talk to, at least, not face to face.

Some of us continue to wander this planet after retirement without direction or intention, ever hoping but never having. But hoping for what? For life to come to us, I suspect. And there, at the junction of hope and despair, is where it all goes wrong. Life and retirement don't come to us. We must pursue them like our very existence depends on it, which it does, with all its beauty and blemishes, the good and the bad, the bliss and heartbreak of love, the joy of physicality, and the trauma of injury—it's all there for us to taste and test.

Seize the day, so they say, and it is still true to this day and every day forward. We get out of life what we are prepared to put into it. There are two ways to look at our lives—we can let life control us or we can control our lives, in retirement or otherwise. You can open doors for yourself that others either can't or won't. Bystanders need not apply.

SHAPING OUR PERSONAL RETIREMENT DESTINIES

"Why do I always feel I'm on the outside looking in at life rather than the other way round?" we often ask ourselves—particularly when we've had a bad day. What's out there for us? What should we do differently and where are we going wrong? We do want things to be better—we all think and actually believe that, whatever "better" is. Are we just collectively drifting through our retirements, not knowing where to go or what to do, feeling like a metalized helium-filled balloon buffeted by the fickle winds of fate until "wham," it hits high tension wires and bursts into flame, disappearing in an instant. But unlike the phoenix, many of us will not easily rise from the ashes of depression and doubt.

The truth of the matter is that our "personal realities," and hence our "personal futures" differ and diverge in predictable and unpredictable ways. There will always be alternative futures for us as individuals, as families, as societies, as nations and for our planet as a whole, but the question remains what will those futures be and how they will come about—with or without intervention, by evolution, or by human collusion or worse, collision? Sometimes we tinker too much with our futures and our lives turn sour even with all our good intentions. But from my perspective, it is in our best interests to shape or control our own personal destinies with freedom to select among all those possible future states, rather than be passively subjected to the forces of man and nature. I, personally, choose to control, determine, and shape my own personal destiny as an individual and collectively with my wife and family, because while I can't control society's behaviors, wants, and desires, or the actions of those who say they represent our interests, then at least I can control my own.

RETIREMENT ISN'T ABOUT DREAMING, IT'S ABOUT DOING

We must ask ourselves if the retirement we are currently living or the retirement we are contemplating living is the retirement we *want* to be living—or is there something important missing, either known or unknown. Is this truly the "story" of the rest of our lives; or is there something or someone else out there calling to us? *What's missing?* We wonder. *Why am I so unhappy and unfulfilled?* After all, we have a nice home and a comfortable retirement and money doesn't appear to be a problem, at least, not yet. *What's the answer?* We silently plead. *Is that all there is?*

Retirement is not just another stage of life—it is a rebirth of sorts, a new beginning, requiring us to break away from our old patterned behaviors and abandon the prideful ways we learned from work, as well as our prejudices, and start anew—because in retirement and death we are all equal, it's truly life's second chance.

You see, we can't "will" a retirement to happen or make it fulfilling and exciting just by thinking about it, or even by hoping for it. We have to take personal control of our futures, we have to make it happen, and the sooner we start, the more real and fulfilling our retirements will be. It's good to have dreams of a better place, and retirement is one of those places we all like to dream and think about. But somehow, as is often the case, reality interferes. Retirement is not about dreaming of a make-believe world. It is about doing and living in the here and now and making the best of the hand we are dealt. Retirement is neither myth nor fairy tale, it is real life, up close and personal. We have to believe in ourselves and our ability to make retirement happen and ultimately to flourish, and while the advice of others is valued, we have to make our own way into this new world of retirement because here we report only to ourselves. While our dreams and hopes move us toward retirement, they often present a false picture of reality, they are dreams after all. If we set the bar so high that our dreams can never match our retirement expectations, then disappointment becomes the order of the day. We must narrow the distance between our retirement expectations and life's hard realities, as difficult as it may be. Indeed, most of us will retire, but will we retire to the life we expected or believed we were entitled to?

There are always distractions, lost opportunities, and reasons why our retirements are less than perfect or not as fulfilling and exciting as we had hoped. Don't expect perfection from any part of life because it is unobtainable, rather expect challenges together with joy, times of happiness and sadness, for isn't that the way of life? The secret to a successful life is no secret at all; it is not to let disappointments or setbacks defeat us—victory is so much the sweeter when we can overcome obstacles, be true to ourselves, and still achieve our "personal retirement vision." If we wait for certainty, we might just never retire. We must be prepared to make the best of it, whatever the best of it is, whether in life or retirement.

RETIREMENT: MAKE IT PERSONAL

When are we really ready to retire? Some would say the week after we start our first real job; others might say, *when I have enough money saved I'm out of here*; still others might answer, *never, because I wouldn't know what to do with myself*. Some conjecture they will know when the time is right, when the future happens or the mood strikes them, or when the plant closes or their employer offers an incentive, or even, perhaps when they are politely asked to leave. In fact, there is no real answer to that question because the reasons and rationales differ for each of us, some are valid and others bravado, but in the end it is a very personal decision.

We all have different needs and expectations of and for our retirements. Some of us want peace and quiet, a respite from life; others seek adventure and excitement; yet others want to finish what was started and abandoned when life and family closed in on them, like getting that college degree or learning how to play the piano. There is something special waiting for us all in retirement. But, we have to define those "wants" for ourselves and then go out and find it or do it—it won't come to us. Dreams unfulfilled are dreams denied and you are now the dream maker; this time it won't be life that stops you from achieving those dreams. As Blaine Lee tells us, "Before you attempt to set things right make sure you see them right."

However, in order to retire we must first be willing and ready to leave the safety, structure, social networks, and security of our jobs or professions. It is a leap of faith, oftentimes without a safety net, and requires thoughtfulness and planning as well as confidence in ourselves, our futures, and in our loved ones. Retirement is one thing and fulfillment or meaning another. Many of us are under the mistaken impression that retirement is the absence of work, the tossing off of responsibility and of control by others, when in actuality successful and meaningful retirements require the presence of a new force, a new focus, a new challenge, and a new purpose that we all must define for ourselves.

You see, if we act hastily or without thought, planning, or passion, our retirements will soon fail; conversely, if we are overly cautious, fearful of the future, and unsure of ourselves and what we will be doing in our retirement years, our retirements will lack meaning and purpose. Overconfidence can doom our retirements just as surely as fear and equivocation can. Retirement, for all intents and purposes, is outside our understanding—it is something we read about, hear about from friends and relatives, and see others living. We listen to their stories that make us jealous and desirous without questioning or seeking the realities behind those tales of derring-do. But we ourselves have yet to live in or experience retirement firsthand. What you just might find is that some retirees don't walk the walk, but rather just talk the talk to gloss over their premature or uninformed decision to retire and to convince you (and perhaps themselves) that it is the land of good and plenty. Ultimately, we must chart our own course into retirement, not by the words of others or by the stars, but rather with our hearts, souls, and intellect and also with our spouses, partners, and trusted others.

MAKE OPTIMISM OUR LIFELONG COMPANION

Retirements built on sand will soon wash away, while retirements built on solid foundations will endure the trials and tribulations of life's events. But as in all things there is a fine line between being too fixed and too flexible because retirements that cannot sway and bend with the changing winds of life will ultimately break. If we are too fixed in what we expect from retirement and from others, our retirements will fail; if we are just blowing in the wind, we will never chart a clear retirement path through life. Retirements must be strong enough to withstand the passage of time and the winds of change, yet flexible enough to withstand earthshaking events—they must be both strong and flexible.

As we age and move through the stages and ages of life, we both fear and long for our approaching retirements. Yes, retirement is a new and thrilling prospect, but it remains an unknown quantity until we live inside its walls, for indeed retirements have walls, just as did work. There are always boundaries and constraints in life, some self-imposed and others imposed upon us. Retirement, or just the prospect of it, will be frightening to some and heartily welcomed by others, but we can't let temporal concerns stop us from planning and ultimately experiencing the full joys and sorrows that retirement and life have yet to offer. We will all face storms followed by times of calm, but we will overcome the storms and find sanctuary in the calm, because what we all must confront is the uncertainty of life in all its terrifying glory. Life goes on with or without us.

Optimism is our primary defense against life's many vagaries; it must become our lifelong companion because doom and gloom will defeat us and isolation will destroy our will to live, or as Winston Churchill put it, "Success consists of going from failure to failure without losing enthusiasm"—I love that quote.

Retirement can become our real "wonder years," but our transition from work to retirement can, in the beginning, be one of the most challenging periods of our lives because of uncertainty about the future, loss of structure that work provided, reduced income, disrupted social networks, and overly optimistic expectations of how easy, joyful, and fulfilling our retirements will be. Indeed, retirement is one of life's most transformational events—some will find it unsettling; others welcome it with open arms, perhaps naively unaware of the traps, dangers, and missteps that await us in our complex and scary world. First impressions can be misleading, but time and experience with this new lifestyle will smooth out retirement's rough edges. Above all, never give up, never falter in the faith that retirement can and ultimately will be the best years of your life, and always, always engage the power of possibility—yes, possibility not certainty.

EVERYONE NEEDS A QUEST

Then, a voice booms in my head, *A "Quest"*—say what? I said, *A "Quest."* Repeat that please, I couldn't quite understand what you were saying, and who are you anyway? *I said a Q-u-e-s-t—you gotta have a Quest.* That's not an answer, it's a riddle. *Think what you want, but that's what you need; oh I'm your "Personal Retirement Genie" and I would grant you three wishes if I could—but, you will have to make them happen for yourself, you're not in a movie you know. This is real life and I'm not a real genie, but you can do it on your own, just try, and then try harder and it will happen.*

Everyone needs a Quest—just ask Don Quixote as Dulcinea did. He responded by singing "The Impossible Dream," my favorite song, soundtrack, and musical of all time. Where would we be today if Dr. Jonas Salk, who invented the first anti-polio vaccine, hadn't followed his Quest? I remember being one of the first children to receive the new Salk vaccine when I was in kindergarten; it changed everything. Or what if Columbus hadn't sailed away on a fool's errand, looking for a route to the West Indies and instead becoming the "Wrong Way" Corrigan" of his day when he bumped into what is now known as the Americas? If it wasn't for his mistake we all might be living someplace else, or still stuck in the "Dark Ages." Our personal Quest, whatever that may be, has to be more than finding the dining room on a mega cruise ship—it has to be much, much more. Our Quest has to be meaningful to us and to others, it has to be fulfilling, it has to be life changing, it has to be referenced in songs and poems by our families for generations; well maybe not for generations, but it has to be a Quest for our very being and existence, for our souls, minds, and ultimately our well-being. Our Quest, however we choose to define it, will add meaning and fulfillment to our lives, it will organize our thoughts and behaviors, it will make every day a new day, and it will, above all, provide purpose, direction, and most importantly, keep us growing and healthy emotionally, physically, and socially. It will keep us forever purposeful, it will sustain us through good times and bad and forever banish boredom and loneliness from our lives. Can you say Amen and Amen again?

GET YOUR FREE TICKET TO EVERYWHERE

My fellow travelers, to help you seek, discover, or find your retirement Quest, I am going to give you a free ticket—your last train to everywhere. Your ticket entitles you to roam the planet in search of lost dreams and missed opportunities. There are conditions, however. In order to keep your ticket you must promise never to: (a) start any conversation with "when I was your age"; (b) buy anything advertised on the Home Shopping Network; or (c) wear T-shirts with sexually explicit sayings blazoned across them. Failure to comply will result in your ticket and its accompanying privileges being permanently revoked!

And by now you are likely ready to ask, "What is my Quest?" Pleased you asked: you are reading it now, and there are others yet to come. Let me know what you think. Your comments, input, and wise advice are more than welcomed.

THE RETIREMENT READINESS QUESTIONNAIRE

The decision of when and how to retire should not be left to chance, to the stars, or to emotion—it needs to be carefully considered and strategically analyzed. You are at a crossroads, standing at the precipice of one of life's most important pivot points, awaiting that fateful decision. In other words, your life is at equilibrium, and, that balance needs to be upset, counteracted or altered—the proverbial "hit upside the head"—before you can acknowledge the existence of other "life alternatives," such as retirement. Understand that you need to *want* to retire more than you *want* to keep working. This is a life-altering event with significant social, psychological, physical, and financial implications. In order to take some of the guesswork and emotion out of the retirement equation, I have developed what I call a "Retirement Readiness Questionnaire" to help you to answer one of life's most significant questions: *Am I really ready to retire?*

RESPONDING TO THE INVENTORY

I have aggregated ten of the most commonly stated reasons for wanting to retire, alongside the top ten reasons for not wanting to retire. These reasons (or others like them, depending on your personal situations and preferences) are either pushing you toward retirement or pulling you back into work. As you read each of these 20 statements, rank their applicability to your personal situation. Your answers will in turn be scored on what is called a "semantic differential scale," a metric developed decades ago by Charles E. Osgood.

Remember, no one will know your answers except you, so please be both thoughtful and frank when responding to these statements. There is no right or wrong answer—the only one you would be fooling is you. *I also strongly suggest, if you have a spouse/partner also contemplating retirement, that they should independently respond to the questionnaire.* Use this as an opportunity to discuss your life goals and retirement readiness expectations—or what you want to do with the rest of *your* lives.

> *"Before you attempt to set things right*
> *make sure you see them right."*
>
> —BLAINE LEE

HOW TO SCORE THE QUESTIONNAIRE

There are five possible responses to each statement, separated into two distinct groupings of ten simply labeled **Group A** and **Group B**. These response options are:

- **Strongly Agree** (5 points)

- **Agree** (4 points)

- **No Opinion** (3 points)

- **Disagree** (2 points)

- **Strongly Disagree** (1 point)

Place an "X" in the box that most closely represents your particular circumstance, opinion and retirement expectations.

Sum up each of the columns for both **Group A** and **Group B**. Place the totals at the bottom of the appropriate columns. Now, add the column scores and place the grand totals in the areas labeled **Group A Total** and **Group B Total**. Do that for both sets.

GROUP A

	5 Strongly Agree	4 Agree	3 No Opinion	2 Disagree	1 Strongly Disagree
Work is enjoyable, meaningful and interesting.					
Work structures my day (and the money isn't bad, either).					
These are my prime earning years—the more money I earn, the better my retirement will be.					
I can't retire until I am Medicare eligible, or can afford health insurance.					
My closest friends are my co-workers, and they're still working—so why retire?					
I just don't know what I would do with myself if I retired.					
Work is who I am and what I do—I plan to die with my "work boots" on.					
I'm not emotionally ready to retire—I'm not ready to be "*old*."					
If I retired, I would have a to-do list of household chores; at work I'm the boss of me.					
Being retired is another way of saying I'm unemployed or unemployable.					
TOTALS:					

GROUP A TOTAL: _____

GROUP B

	5 Strongly Agree	4 Agree	3 No Opinion	2 Disagree	1 Strongly Disagree
I'll gladly sacrifice a steady paycheck to free myself from the clock and my bosses.					
Our financial retirement goals have been reached—money won't be an issue.					
My employer is offering a generous retirement incentive.					
Work is stressful, uninteresting, and no one appreciates what I do.					
I want to retire while I'm young and healthy enough to enjoy the rest of my life.					
My co-workers and friends have already retired—I want to join them.					
Retirement is my opportunity to live someplace else.					
Aging parents need assistance and/or children need help with the grandkids.					
There are so many exciting places to see and visit—I need to get that "Bucket List" going.					
Retirement is my time to do whatever I want to do—my life, my way.					
TOTALS:					

GROUP B TOTAL: _____

INTERPRETING YOUR SCORES

The summative scores allow you to compare two alternative retirement scenarios: "Ready to Retire" or "Not Ready to Retire." Note that these scores should not be considered conclusive or set in stone— only *you* should be making this type of life-changing decision.

If the two scores are within 5 points of each other, it is a "Tweedle-dee/Tweedle-dum type situation—in other words, a toss-up. You're at a neutral point in your life with regard to your retirement—not actually sure whether you want to retire or remain working. Some further intro-spection and discussion is required.

If the scores are separated by 6 to 10 points, you are leaning toward one alternative or the other, but something is still holding you back. Take some time to find out what that is. If you have a partner or spouse, now is the time to talk and come up with a jointly agreed-to resolution.

If the scores are separated by 11 or more points, you are strongly inclined toward one or the other category; that is, there is no doubt in your mind as to the path you want to take.

Above all, whatever path you choose, make sure you enjoy the ride!

CHAPTER 6

■ ■ ■ ■ ■ ■

Retirement's Ages and Stages

*Twenty years from now you will be more
disappointed by the things you didn't do,
than by the ones you did do.*

—MARK TWAIN

*There must be a beginning of any great matter,
but continuing unto the end until it be thoroughly
finished yields the true glory.*

—SIR FRANCIS DRAKE

GROWING OLD IS NOT ABOUT AGE,
BUT ABOUT ATTITUDE

Prince or pauper, octogenarian or toddler, saint or sinner, we all face the same biological certainties of life and of death; we will all be getting older and ultimately die. Some of our physical capabilities will deteriorate more quickly than others, while some of our mental capacities may sharpen and others will dull. Don't dwell on what we can no longer do; rather, focus on what we *can*. We might not be able to work as hard, walk as fast, or play as hard as we used to, but we must continue thinking, walking, and playing. Our bodies are machines and those machines need to be cared for and used or they will rust and decay if we stop challenging our physical selves—that easy chair can sometimes be a "siren song" luring us to a life of sedentary indolence that will at first surround us with seeming comfort but ultimately sap our strength and desire for life. The same goes for our "intellectual selves" and our "public selves," they must be kept sharp through frequent use; or, as I like to say, "It's time to get up, get out, and get moving; you will be amazed what you can find out there."

DIGNITY AND PRIDE—OUR MIRROR OF LIFE

Retirement requires us to not only push life's "reset" button, but it also obliges us to confront, negotiate with, and ultimately accept our aging selves as our new life partners, along with our aging life partners, who are also going through a similarly difficult metamorphosis. How others see us, or how we believe they see us, is unimportant because what truly matters is how we see ourselves in the "mirror of life," or as I call it, "our inner aging belief system." Look beyond your physical self and see yourself not as others might see you through their "personal life filters," but as you believe yourself to be. Who knows our physical, mental, and emotional strengths better than us? We must define ourselves for ourselves and not permit others to do that to us or for us; don't let society trivialize your metamorphoses and assume who and what you are simply because you are getting older, nor let it place you in the helpless role or in any way shape you to fit its expectations, because its ideas are typically distorted and wrongheaded. If we buy into those stereotypes and beliefs, we will become those stereotypes and espouse those beliefs, accepting that we are getting old and feeble and taking what is rightfully the province of the young—as if our place on earth is dependent on their beneficence. If we believe we are getting old and feeble then indeed we will feel and act that way; if we worry over every lost or gray hair and new wrinkle we will act old, think old, and then quickly become old— whatever our chronological age. When we feel and act old, others will treat us as such and our "old" behaviors will be constantly reinforced because sometimes we enjoy the perks of being old, like the deference and helpfulness that is often offered to senior citizens and, of course, those ubiquitous senior discounts.

AND YES, WE CAN SEE THROUGH THE FRONT WINDSHIELDS

Now that we are officially "seniors," do others perceive us as slow, sometimes dim-witted, forgetful, and cranky, requiring constant reminding and assistance? Do we play into this scenario because it is comforting that others want to be helpful to their perception of the "older" us? Do we play the "feeble card" or the "forgetful card" to get sympathy and shuffle about, denying our own abilities and emphasizing our disabilities to get attention and recognition that we exist? Do we isolate ourselves in our homes and segregate ourselves in senior centers and in adult communities or do we take to the streets and to the malls and go into the schools, hospitals, daycare centers, and congregate care facilities to visit with the less fortunate elderly who have truly succumbed to life's many illnesses that befall us as we age? Or do we take to the roads, to the beaches, to the mountains, and the theaters to once again remind us what real life is all about and to feel the freedom that retirement gives us as we take full advantage of every remaining moment we have on this planet? And do we assert our independence and inner strength by politely stating that while we appreciate their concern and acknowledge that we might have lost a step or two, we are still quite capable of taking care of ourselves? Sometimes, we use guile and deception to gloss over some of our failings and to prevent children, grandchildren, and family from seeing the "aging us." Other times we welcome their attentions as the inevitable passage of time begins to take its toll, allowing our adult children, who we once cared for and nurtured, to return the love we gave them back to us, allowing them to offer care and concern, friendship, companionship, and memories with the satisfying knowledge that we did a good job raising our children and they are now returning the favor. And yes, we can still see through the front windshields of our vehicles, and pardon us for following the speed limits, stopping at red lights, and for not talking or texting on our cell phones while driving.

BEING YOUNG IS OVERRATED

Personally, I don't want to be younger or even to look younger. Been there, done that. I just want to remain emotionally and physically healthy for as long as I can, and sometimes when I am in my optimistic phase I actually believe that we can "will ourselves back to health" and to hell with all those medical theories and medicines. What I fear most is losing my humanity and my intellect and becoming a hollow shell of protoplasm trapped in a body without conscious thought, unable to tie my laces or even recognize my wife and children. Yes, we earned our right to get old and to remove ourselves from the world of work. We earned the right to no longer deal with the drama, the conceits, the secret alliances, and the bad actors that characterize a typical workplace; but we also miss the friends, the accomplishments, and ultimately, the contributions that make life better for others. As for the commutes, I, personally, never have and never will miss those. We earned the right to age, hopefully gracefully, to retire and take comfort in family, friends, and freedom, and to pursue our personal interests, whatever they may be.

MORTALITY IS FINITE, GOODNESS INFINITE

Retirement should not be about accumulating "things" and spending our remaining years pursuing the excesses that we in the American culture have learned to value. Retirement should not be about dying with the most toys and thus winning; but rather the winner should be the one whose names and deeds are imbedded in the most hearts and minds. Our mortality is finite but the transference of our inherent humanity, goodness, beliefs, histories, and values to others is infinite, and that is how we truly obtain immortality, through others.

Growing older gives us license to shape and share our lives with others in ways we might never have thought of, appreciated, or even considered when younger. In the end, life at any age is what we choose to make of it. My wish for myself and my fellow travelers is that our health will allow us to live stimulating, fulfilling, meaningful, and adventurous lives in our remaining time, however long that may be. And, when our moment comes to pass the torch to the next generation, as it inevitably must, they will carry our collective dreams forward into the future and fulfill those dreams for themselves and for those who follow.

WE CAN'T STOP AGING, BUT WE CAN KEEP LIVING

Don't be misled, there is no stopping the aging process because the clock of life keeps ticking and waits for no person, regardless of how wealthy or important they believe they are. How many times have we attended funerals of friends and relatives, how many visits have we made to hospitals to give succor or to say good bye to loved ones, how many times have we accompanied friends to doctors as the ravages of cancer and dementia attack their brains and bodies? Death is indeed part of life and if we are still able, then we must not deny comfort to those who precede us; we should share memories and kindnesses, tears and laughter. For many of us, this is becoming a more frequent occurrence in our lives.

As we age we become more and more conscious of how we look and more concerned with our self-images. Yes, we have more aches and pains and our hands don't work like they used to and we will turn gray or lose our hair and get liver spots, and ultimately gravity will take its course. But if we worry over every lost or gray hair, new wrinkle, or brown spot, we will feel "ugly" and ashamed of our appearance and consequently either shy away from contact with others or worse yet, attempt to cover up our outer shell with cosmetics, creams, and other hyped chemicals, or even mutilate our faces with plastic surgery. We earned our stripes, so let's display them proudly. While we cannot stop the aging process we can slow it down; but when the good fight is over and our energies depleted, acceptance and resignation become our allies. Don't go screaming into the night but rather go with grace and with the knowledge that we have made this world a better place and that perhaps we too will be going to a better place on our last journey. Above all, we must never permit others to take our humanity, regardless in whose name or under what laws of man they operate. We must be allowed to die with dignity, and when the time is nigh, perhaps, just perhaps, we will be allowed to pass from this world to the next in peace and at a time and place of our choosing—not theirs.

BOTH LIFE AND RETIREMENT ARE LIVED IN CYCLES

Everything has a "life cycle"—plants, people, animals, the moon, the planets, the universe. When compared to nature's power and importance to everything on planet earth, the retirement cycle seems insignificant, almost trivial, but it is not trivial by any means. Indeed, the aging and retirement cycles are inextricably entwined, neither fixed nor fluid but always ever present because we can never ignore our aging selves. The "Retirement Life Cycle" which is calibrated in years, if not decades, is a marker, a guide or a gauge to let us know where we are in time and age, how we are progressing toward our retirement and life goals, and ultimately, where and who we want to be in each of these cycles. And, while not capable of predicting the future, they will help us to shape our futures.

THE FIVE STAGES AND AGES OF RETIREMENT

The "Retirement Life Cycle," as articulated here, is apportioned into five descriptive stages. These stages have fluid boundaries—there are no fixed beginnings and end points, even though age ranges are associated with each individual stage. There are no "hard stops" in life, in human capabilities, or in how we age; we are all different and how we respond to life and the continuous series of events it presents to us affects us all differently. Some of us will live longer than others, some will be healthier than others, and some will be more astute and mentally agile than others. Life has been good to our generation though, and we have been good back; thus we are now the beneficiaries of the fruits of all our labors. Indeed, according to the Social Security Administration, a male reaching age 65 today can expect to live, on average, until age 84; while a woman turning 65 today can expect to live, on average, until age 86. (Gentlemen, we're gaining on them and that's a good thing for us all.) But we do know one thing for certain, that death is inevitable and how we face that inevitability will be our final testament to our families and to future generations. So let's begin our journey through retirement's ages and stages.

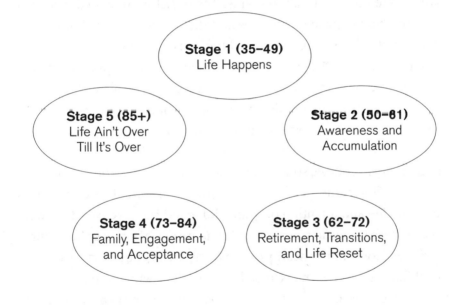

RETIREMENT STAGE 1:
LIFE HAPPENS
(35–49)

We watch the clock of time tick away, at first little concerned with its pace and then more intently monitoring as we move through our thirties, forties, and beyond, and we all wonder—where did time go? We start trying to slow time down and to rekindle our spirits—we go to the gym, get a new hairstyle, or try to cover that growing bald spot, perhaps we even diet away some of those extra pounds or try cosmetic surgery. Youth is fleeting and we cannot play "beat the clock" because in the game of life the "clock" always wins. There isn't even enough time left to sit and contemplate our futures and the passage of time because we have so many competing responsibilities and obligations—work, family, church, aging parents, and perhaps even an unhappy spouse. Oh, and what about college for the kids, how are we going to pay for that, a second mortgage perhaps; or take some money from our savings; or maybe they will have to help by taking out loans? Then what about putting aside some money for retirement? We will have time for that after the children finish college, so we think and so we believe, true or not.

Sadly, illness and death visit our door. Our parents are aging and need the care and attention only an adult child can give. We don't have time so perhaps we arrange for in-home care or we move them into a retirement community nearby or to assisted living; but maybe we forgot one thing, we never even discussed those options with our parents. Then we forget to visit sometimes, saying to ourselves, more as an excuse than a rationalization, "They have people their own age to talk with and be with so they won't miss or even remember they haven't seen us or the grandchildren for two months." We convince ourselves we'll go next weekend. But deep in the back of our minds, we full know that the cycle of life repeats itself and someday soon we will be in the starring role and hear our children saying, "We're busy but we'll see you and Mom next week," but next week never happens. What comes around goes around.

While we don't need to dwell on retirement when we are young and starting out, there does need to be an awareness that someday we will face either a "retirement abyss" or a "retirement bridge." Both retirement and getting older have a way of sneaking up on us; it becomes almost a "Yesterday" moment, as the Beatles so presciently sang.

Our most important tasks in Stage 1 Retirement are to, at the least, recognize that retirement is a future reality and then build toward that reality, perhaps in small steps, but steps nonetheless, primarily of the financial variety, at this stage. Next and more importantly, is to raise our families and attend to our careers, but most of all, to build a strong ethical and moral core, to pass on those values, and to prepare for the future for ourselves, our partners, and for our children.

The Challenges Ahead

The next generation of retirees (unfortunately for them) will face a much different world than we the Boomers are confronting—easier in some ways but more challenging in others. While every generation expects or hopes to be better off than their parents, that might not prove to be our children's reality, but only time will tell. It's as if we Boomers showed up just at the right moment, when everything was growing— families, communities, universities, culture, the arts, you name it, it was flourishing. Our country was thriving, the private sector developed a moral compass, and government was becoming a more pro-active partner (although some would say a too intrusive one). As a result, the public sector was on a hiring binge and we were encouraged to seek government employment to "make the world a better place," and to entice us and keep us in the workforce, we were offered generous health and pension benefits and many of us responded. The private sector, which includes the unions, was also growing in size and complexity, small businesses became big businesses and innovation was the name of the game; we owned the world, so we thought. The unions made sure their members received health and pension benefits comparable to government employees and so they prospered as well. Big Government became "Bigger Government," and then became directly involved in the lives of its citizens at every level—very few of us were left out, and some that were could depend on Social Security or a myriad of "safety net" programs that government threw under us or over us, depending on your perspective.

Today, the outlook is not as sanguine. Governments are shrinking and downsizing pensions, private sector employers are eliminating or dramatically reducing retirement benefits or swapping defined benefit plans for defined contribution ones, which is not necessarily a bad thing. I am not entirely sure that a 25-year-old out of college for four years or so and looking for that first big promotion is going to either care about or ask about "the pension plan"—I know I didn't. They are on the ladder to success and no pension plan would satisfy their needs for financial security anyway; they want to go out and make enough money to satisfy their every need and desire now and "forever," just like we all did. Some of us achieved that goal, but many did not. So, how do we convince our own children to delay gratification and to start saving now, because no one knows what the future holds? Well, it would no doubt fall on deaf ears or get the "I know, I know" routine. No matter how much we rail about saving for the future and trading higher salaries today for better pensions tomorrow, it won't make much of a difference in a career-focused heart and mind—besides, they're probably already in significant debt for the car and the vacations and possibly for the student loans, so to even consider putting money in a bank or investing in the stock market is out of the question. But they will learn, hopefully, before it's too late, when they still have the time and ability to play "catch-up." This, my fellow travelers, is the Retirement Stage 1 story that is being played out all over this country for those between the ages of 35 and 49 years old. If you encounter one of these pre-retirement babes in the woods feel free to offer some "friendly advice" about how the world will appear to them when they are 65 as well as the bridges they must build and rebuild throughout their lives to assure they land comfortably on the other side of work, which is, of course, retirement.

RETIREMENT STAGE 2:
AWARENESS AND ACCUMULATION
(50-61)

Retirement has no set age; it's up to each of us to make that determination based on numerous factors, many already discussed and some yet to be identified. We talked about "catch-up" and it is usually right after we turn 50 that the reality hits us like a kick in the head: yes, we are getting older, and yes, we still have financial obligations like putting our children through college, mortgages, or paying off the debt we managed to build over the preceding years, or even dealing with divorces and aging parents. We cannot stop time and remain forever middle-aged. Remember, Dorian Gray ultimately paid the price for such hubris. We could, once again, think of dozens of excuses and ignore the reality that someday soon we will either want to retire or we will be "pushed" into retirement—and either way we need to be ready for it. A hint of denial creeps stealthily in to our psyches, whispering to us that maybe, just maybe, retirement really isn't for us. We're not the "retiring types" we attempt to convince ourselves. Is it because we truly believe that? Or perhaps it is our age or pride talking, because retirement can be the best years of our lives. Or more likely, it is because we do not believe in our heart of hearts we will have accumulated enough assets to fund our retirements when that time comes; and so we choose to ignore that reality rather than create a new reality by sacrificing today for a better tomorrow. Because it is in Retirement Stage 2 that we should start building our "retirement ark," metaphorically, and loading it with all the necessities we will need to live a comfortable, adventurous, and healthy "life after work." There are no excuses because if we don't come to terms with this next life phase, the only ones who will suffer are us and our loved ones. But facing the future with mutual love and the shared expectation that we will have fulfilling and joy-filled retirements makes sure we don't let ourselves or them down. And, although we probably think to ourselves every time we see a bus loaded with retirees heading here or there or swarming a restaurant rest stop, *I will never get old or be like them*, it's simply not true. Oh, my young friends, it's not a matter of when, but rather of degree. And, as Robbie said in the movie *Poltergeist*, "The storm is getting closer." Keeping the "retirement monster" properly fed requires consistent and concerted efforts now to accumulate personal savings, make wise investments, pay down debts, contribute additional sums to existing retirement accounts, or establish personal retirement vehicles such as an Individual Retirement Account (IRA). Savings in this stage should take priority over spending; easy to say, but recognizably hard to do—*but do it anyway!*

RETIREMENT STAGE 3:
RETIREMENT, TRANSITION, AND LIFE RESET (62–72)

It's time, chronologically at least, to retire…or is it? It's time because we have come to terms with retirement; or not, because we are still fighting the good battle to remain in the workforce, and hopefully for the right reasons (typically financial ones, or ones related to health and the prospect of having health insurance when retired). That is why 62 and 65 are the most common retirement ages, I suspect. First, 62 is the earliest we can collect Social Security. Second, 65 is the earliest we can be enrolled in Medicare, which takes the "no health care" issue out of the retirement equation. While Social Security's full retirement age is on a slow but steady increase to accommodate the demographics of aging and the diminishing Social Security Trust Fund Account, 65 remains one of the most common retirement ages, likely because that was the age first identified in the original Social Security Act, and now 65 has become synonymous with retiring. It's when we reach our sixties that most of us get really serious about asking the "what will we do with the rest of our lives" type questions; but there are as many potential answers as there are options in life after work. Preparation for retirement, while it should start in Retirement Stage 2, is often pushed off because of the reasons previously cited and therefore typically begins in earnest in our early sixties. *Planning be damned,* some of us think, as they take their retirement leap with a parachute named "a hope and a prayer."

Retirement for some is liberating and for others it is akin to being banished to Devil's Island, especially for those who depended on work to provide structure, social interaction, and purpose. Indeed, the more senior we are in an organization, or the more we can control events and not have them control us, the more likely we are to remain in the workplace, while those we supervise likely dream of the day they can retire to get away from people like us. Some in this age group still view work as meaningful and purposeful and good for them, while others, regardless of how much they enjoy the intellectual stimulation of work and the paycheck, have come to the personal conclusion that there is more to life than work and this is "our time" to shape the rest of our lives.

Optimism is crucial to retirement because we are trading a life we fully comprehended and pursued for over 40 years to quickstep into a life called retirement, about which many of us actually have little knowledge. This can be an exciting and frightening prospect at the same time. When the time comes, it takes courage and confidence to walk away from something we have been doing for so long, full knowing it will be the last day we will ever be at that desk, or talk with a colleague or customer that has become like family; plus we will give up the security of that steady paycheck to do something, go somewhere, be someone we have yet to fully define or embrace, the "retired us." Optimism is our bridge from work to retirement, but uninformed optimism can put us on a fool's errand.

Retirement Changes Everything

I know something we all probably know: life at home wasn't always joyful or fulfilling during our working years. It was, perhaps, full of challenges and detours just as life will be in retirement, unless we take affirmative steps to make it work *for* us, not against us, today and every day thereafter. Retirement is a "game changer." Life in retirement requires a complete mental overhaul if we are to move forward and settle in and settle down into the new life patterns and personal dynamics a successful retirement requires. And Retirement Stage 3 gives us just the opportunity to move from the world of work to the world of retirement.

We all, to some degree, have some "hiccups" settling in to retirement, such as letting our successors take control of and credit for what we created. We feel diminished by retirement instead of emboldened and energized by the opportunity to create a new and exciting life after work. We call our friends and former colleagues at work to find out how our "replacement" is doing and get angry when we hear that he/she has gutted some of our most cherished programs, been critical of our "supposed" accomplishments and initiatives, or appears to be purposefully deconstructing much of what we put in place. But of course they are, those replacing us don't want to live in our shadows so they attempt to eliminate that shadow by bringing in new people who will be loyal to them and not to your memory. We need to stay out of this "dog fight" because it's our friends and colleagues who will pay the price, not us. Give solace and encouragement to former colleagues but always let them know that their world has changed as well, and they must cope with and conform to the new regime; we cannot nor will not rush in and save the day—if it actually needs saving at all.

But now let's get back to us. Our lives have changed dramatically as well. We need to decompress and allow our "work addiction" to be replaced by more positive influences, interests, and activities. Yes, some will seriously consider going back to work somewhere, and yes, we will look at the want ads and query our friends about any opportunities that might be right for us, and we might even update our resumes, or at least consider doing so. But I can tell you from personal experience those desires to get back into the snake pit—which we were so anxious to leave—will eventually diminish and then disappear as you come to terms with retirement and actually start enjoying your freedom and your newfound status.

Stage 3 Retirement gives us the opportunity to rethink our lives and to learn new life rhythms and answer the question, *what can or what should we do with the time remaining to us?* Success at finding answers to this question requires the willingness and ability to reimagine our life after work—all options are on the table for us and for our significant others. This retirement stage not only allows, but *requires* us to be bold, to test our boundaries both known and unknown, and to seek adventure and challenge. Please don't let this opportunity pass by—it's a once in a lifetime chance to break from old tired habits and patterns and seek new life pathways. Where do you want to live the rest of your life? What dreams and opportunities do you want to pursue? How much of planet earth have you explored and what more of it do you want to personally touch and smell up close and personal? Question everything but consider all things. Decide who you are and then make yourself who you want to be. Unleash your inner talents and find new passions. You are still young enough and healthy enough to face this world head-on, and pack as much adventure and discovery into this retirement stage as possible. Then go do it! Whatever the "it" is, that is the true test of a life well lived. Welcome to what can, with resourcefulness and initiative, be the most exciting time of your life—enjoy the ride!

RETIREMENT STAGE 4:
FAMILY, ENGAGEMENT, AND ACCEPTANCE (73–84)

Family is central to life at this stage and it is absolutely critical to remain socially engaged and intellectually curious even if we cannot be as physically active as we were in Retirement Stage 3. While science and medicine have done much to relieve us of many health concerns, numerous health challenges still await, some of our own making and others unavoidable and as yet unidentified. We must, and I mean *must*, remain active to whatever degree we can; if we treat our bodies with respect and with activity they will respond in kind. We must not, for any reason, isolate ourselves from others or from life. Continue the relentless pursuit of adventure, even if it must be toned down a notch or two. We must not push beyond our physical limits or capacities. Some of us age more gracefully than others, some of us work at staying healthy more assiduously than others, and for these individuals, age is just a number and has no real meaning to anyone except to those who use it to place us into boxes and build stereotypes about who we are and what we can do. I can tell you I have met many individuals in their 80s who are still practicing their professions, including doctors and lawyers. And I have ridden with 80-somethings in my bicycle club who can far outpace and outride me. Remain active participants in life's changing scenes, and do not become passive bystanders because age itself presents no barrier to curiosity or interest.

Stay connected to family whenever possible—this is your time to share and to pass on your personal histories and your family stories in pictures and words. It is also the time to start distributing those valued, not necessarily expensive, items to loved ones, who can then have a piece of your collective life histories in their possession as a remembrance and to ultimately pass on to the next generation when the time comes. Use this as an opportunity to "show and tell" and you will be amazed at the yarns you can spin, the memories and stories you can conjure up, and the delight they will create.

As we prepare for Retirement Stage 5, consider whether remaining in our "ancestral" homes is still a viable option, particularly if it has become too much of a burden to maintain, move around in, and pay for. Investigate what other living options are available, and how (or if) it could contribute to a better quality of life as we age. If you live in a neighborhood or area that does not provide support to seniors or has a very young demographic and you feel isolated, perhaps relocating to an active retirement community would be in your best interests. Or consider a living arrangement that allows for progressive care with an environment and programs that can support your health, your personal interests, and activities as you age.

This is a time for reflection and contemplation. We have by this stage fully adjusted to and accepted the aging us and the reality that we are getting older and our time on this planet is getting shorter, but that is the rhythm of life just as long summer days ultimately yield to winter's short dark ones. Remain philosophical about growing older rather than worrying about every ache or pain or physical sign that we are aging. Replace the "active" us with the "involved" us as time and tides demand. We need to be comfortable within our own skin regardless of how "well worn" it is, and above all we must be comfortable with who we are and what we have become, but even more so, we must be at peace with our aging selves. Contentment, friendship, and companionship are the order of the day. Honor the past but live in the present. Life is still good.

RETIREMENT STAGE 5:
LIFE AIN'T OVER TILL IT'S OVER
(85+)

Paraphrasing Yogi Berra is one of my joys in life and I thank him for that wonderful line. We are often told that our retirement years will be our "golden" years; and while that may be true for some, it is not true for all, especially not for those who have failed to prepare adequately for our aging selves or our aging partners, those who have not taken adequate care of their physical and mental assets or who suffer from those terrible diseases and deficits that plague the "aging us." As we move into our 80s and 90s, and many of us will, nature takes its course and we become physically frail and mentally less acute. While our gait and balance might be a bit off, our minds will, hopefully, still be mostly intact. Words and thoughts might come slower and are, perhaps, more disjointed but we can still call on most of them when needed.

Above all, we are still on this earth and still have value and worth to society and to our loved ones. Stay active, stay engaged. If you can't walk a mile then walk half that, if you can't walk at all take a ride in a car with the windows down, whether during winter or summer, or mount your trusty motorized wheelchair and take a spin around your neighborhood or around the world. Feel the wind in your face and continue to touch life. My wife recently took her 93-year-old mother, who uses a wheelchair, on the first ocean cruise of her life and she had a hoot. Who says you can't teach old dogs new tricks?

Unfortunately, for those among us who are frail or sick or for those who simply choose to lock themselves behind closed doors, the world starts shrinking around us. We are no longer able to take those long meandering walks through our neighborhoods and visit our favorite shops and restaurants like we used to, or to read the books we loved so much, or even to hear the music and view television without mechanical or electronic assistance. It is hard for us to accept our personal weaknesses and inadequacies and when confronted by family members, we sometimes either deny or attempt to hide our frailties, both mental and physical, if we are even aware of them at all. Our family members grow concerned and encourage or even force us to accept assistance for taking care of our daily needs, oftentimes from strangers. The walls around us keep closing in and the tubes, the adult diapers, the poking and prodding, and the medicines proliferate. We've lived a good life, and perhaps we have been predeceased by a treasured loved one. Our children and their children are grown and doing well, or perhaps not, but we have done our job and done it well as a mother or a father and made our contributions to society.

But some of us will find creative ways to compensate for our deficits and the ravages of age. Many, if not most, of us become more spiritual and philosophical about life. We turn to a higher power for solace and relief and pray it be granted to us and our ailing fellow travelers. If we are no longer optimistic about our futures we become optimistic about the futures of others, our children and grandchildren, and seek in every way to make their passages through life easier, whether materially or through our nonjudgmental love and wise counsel. You see, as we age we become more secure in ourselves and our place in life because we finally accept and understand the "meaning of life," that there will be an ending to life. It's almost as if a cloak of Zen-like calmness is protecting us, bringing peace and tranquility where once lived anger, fear, or doubt. Little things bring us happiness, like the cry of a newborn child, the touch of a hand upon ours, the beauty of a flower; the sunrises and sunsets we once ignored now shine bright in our hearts. Nature has a way of easing our passages and now we are sleeping more than we are awake and we pray to be taken to whatever "resting place" we hope to go—may our prayers be answered. We know that the "final chapter" has to be written whether in a book or a life. Then the cycle is complete and may we all rest in peace when faced with life's endgame.

STAY PURPOSEFUL, MY FRIENDS

Every retirement stage and age presents us with both opportunities and challenges and we must adjust to those "Stages and Ages" because they will not adjust to us. Accept these life cycles as the natural order of things, and at least we know what is ahead of us; for some it is a blessing while for others, perhaps, a scary reality—because sometimes we just don't want to know what's waiting around that next corner; we'll get there soon enough. Regardless of the age or stage always stay engaged with family, friends, and with life. Become senior citizens with a purpose. It's never too late for purpose and passion; regardless of our ages, we still have much to contribute, much to see, and more to learn. You must not hide from your ages; instead be satisfied with what you can still do. But please don't fret over what you can't. Let spirituality be your constant companion and engage in intergenerational mentoring and sharing your singular opportunity to help others—those who will soon follow in your footsteps as you have followed the steps of others.

RETIREMENT AGES AND STAGES WORKSHEET

To help you on your retirement journey, consider the following questions. Hopefully, your answers will shed some light on the future for you and your spouse/partner. Consider your expectations, your fears and hopes for the future. It's better to have a plan than to just let life have its way with you! So, *please*: when responding to these questions, do so thoughtfully and honestly. As our parents always told us when something we weren't going to like was about to happen, "It's for your own good!"

QUESTIONS TO CONSIDER

1. What Retirement Age and Stage are you currently in? Does that "Age and Stage" as described, accurately reflect your current situation? Are you satisfied with your life? Why or why not?

_____

_____

_____

_____

_____

_____

_____

_____

_____

_____

_____

_____

2. Based on what you now know, what would you have done differently in prior "Ages and Stages," if you could do it all over again?

_____

_____

_____

_____

_____

_____

_____

_____

_____

_____

_____

_____

_____

_____

_____

_____

_____

_____

_____

_____

_____

_____

RETIREMENT AGES AND STAGES WORKSHEET

3. What are your "Retirement Life Themes" for the "Ages and Stages" to come? In other words, what do you want your life to look and be like? Are those expectations reasonable and achievable? How are you going to make them happen?

_____

_____

_____

_____

_____

_____

_____

_____

_____

_____

_____

_____

_____

_____

_____

_____

_____

_____

_____

_____

4. If a friend or family member asked your advice about retirement or a particular "Age and Stage," what would you tell them? Would it be a "Don't do what I did" type answer, or a "Let me tell you what we did right and what we did wrong" type of response? Do you have regrets? What are they, and are you willing to let them go and move forward?

_____

_____

_____

_____

_____

_____

_____

_____

_____

_____

_____

_____

_____

_____

_____

_____

_____

_____

PART III
RETIREMENT'S SIX FUNDAMENTAL BUILDING BLOCKS

CHAPTER 7

■ ■ ■ ■ ■ ■

The Retirement Pyramid and Eye

*Manners are the basic building blocks
of civil society.*
—ALEXANDER McCALL SMITH

*If you want to be successful, it's just this simple.
Know what you are doing, love what you are doing,
and believe in what you are doing.*
—WILL ROGERS

BUILDING IT HIGH, MAKING IT STRONG

Successful retirements are built upon strong foundations, just like the Egyptian pyramids, which have survived through the millennia. Pyramids, sacred objects to many and held by some to have mystical powers, are also the oldest surviving architectural structures in the world. Indeed, the four triangles which form the pyramid's structure are the strongest known geometrical shape. Just amazing—no wonder pyramids have become the prototype for building the "modern pyramids" called skyscrapers. Indeed, the Pyramids were the tallest structures known to man, only surpassed thousands of years later by the Eiffel Tower which opened in 1889.

The ancient pyramids' "occupants" were safeguarded by the Eye of Horus, personified as a bird, specifically the right eye and markings of a peregrine falcon, just as our retirements will be safeguarded and enduring if our virtual retirement pyramids are properly conceived, constructed, and maintained. Or, as Yoda would so eloquently declare, "Build it we must."

PLANS ARE "HOPES" WAITING TO HAPPEN

Every complex project, whether it's writing a book, starting a business, building a pyramid, or preparing for a life in retirement, requires a plan; this plan becomes our detailed blueprint for the rest of our lives, and the structure will need to be built as strong as the pyramids if it is to sustain and succor us without worry or want. Our plan must take account of and be sensitive to the retirement stages and ages we must inevitably pass through (or die trying), with every retirement age and stage requiring a different plan "mix."

PLANS ARE NOT INFALLIBLE

Sometimes we get a taste of reality and have our epiphany when we recognize that no amount of money or possessions are as important as our health or the life of a partner or child. Sometimes our priorities get confused and other times they become crystal clear. It is our maturity of mind, not of age, and our willingness and ability to sacrifice immediate wants for more distant goals that separate the future "haves" from the "have-nots." Which side of this equation do you want to be on? That is why we need to think forward. Plans require us to be both sages and prognosticators; to anticipate and predict events before they occur—to control the unknown, if that is even possible. But nothing conceived or made by man is foolproof, as we all know. Plans must adapt to changing conditions, circumstances, and life events, whether expected or not, good or bad. Life happens. We must be prepared to respond with both assurance and flexibility to each obstruction or roadblock. Don't let plans, no matter how well conceived, lock you into unsound rote responses based on old timelines and outdated expectations. Plans need constant adjustment to fit situations as they evolve; that is not failure, it is common sense. Battles are lost by generals who fail to see the realities confronting them simply because they weren't in the plan. We can faithfully execute a plan to the smallest degree and still fail miserably to reach our goal or achieve our desired outcome.

Plans are guides, not "truths." Those you will have to arrive at on your own. We should allow our retirement plans to mature and to adapt—constantly tweaking and updating as conditions warrant and when the plan is no longer relevant, then using new information, intelligence, or insights to guide new thinking and new actions. This is particularly important because as we age our needs, abilities, desires, and our physical, emotional, and intellectual selves likewise transform. Retirement plans and expectations need to be sensitive to the inevitable life changes, challenges, and exigencies that confront us in different forms as we age. But at the end of the day, successful retirement outcomes, at every age and stage, require that our life decisions, hopes, dreams, expectations, and realities be responsive to, consistent with, and integrated into "Retirement's Six Building Blocks."

RETIREMENT'S SIX BUILDING BLOCKS: THE HIERARCHY OF RETIREMENT'S SUSTAINING AND CONTRIBUTING FACTORS

And, just what are Retirement's Six Building Blocks? They are: (1) Physical and Emotional Health and Well-Being; (2) Financial Security and Continuity; (3) Life Transition and Acceptance; (4) Intergenerational Life Engagement; (5) Intellectual and Physical Pursuits, Interests, and Activities; and, (6) Spirituality, Meaning, Family, and Legacy.

First, let me define what is meant by both "sustaining" and "contributing" factors. For example, both money and health are *retirement sustaining conditions*, but money and health alone are not sufficient to cause or guarantee us either "successful" or "fulfilling" retirements, although it would be a heck of a lot easier to achieve those higher order states if we were blessed with unlimited resources and good health. Conversely, we can be rolling in money and have excellent health, and for a host of other mediating circumstances, still struggle with retirement and never come to terms with *retirement's contributing conditions*. Likewise, if we are not in "passable" good health then life at any stage becomes a challenge for survival and a search for normalcy. Just ask any individual with a chronic disease to describe their priorities, dreams, and wishes and you will understand. So without sufficient monies or passable good health our retirements will not have the requisite foundational strength to support the layers above. Health and money are, therefore, fundamental prerequisites for building successful retirements, but money and health alone do not guarantee our retirements will be fulfilling, meaningful, or even a joyful time for those of us actually contemplating or living in retirement.

RETIREMENT'S SIX FUNDAMENTAL BUILDING BLOCKS

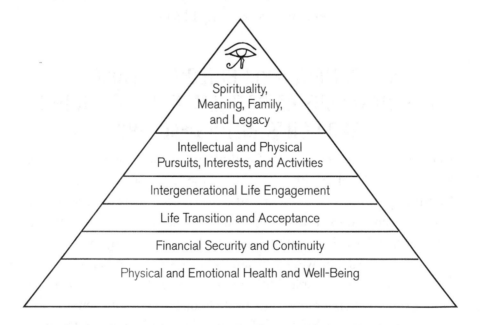

Spirituality,
Meaning, Family,
and Legacy

Intellectual and Physical
Pursuits, Interests, and Activities

Intergenerational Life Engagement

Life Transition and Acceptance

Financial Security and Continuity

Physical and Emotional Health and Well-Being

RETIREMENT SUSTAINING FACTORS: HEALTH AND MONEY; OR IS IT MONEY AND HEALTH?

I was caught in one of those, "on the one hand–other hand" scenarios. I could easily make solid arguments for the primacy of either financial security or robust health, and which should take precedence in life as well as in retirement, as if we had a choice. Both, of course, are pre-conditions for building successful retirements because the lack of either, that is, lacking good health or sufficient assets to fund and maintain our retirements, would be a setback of major proportions, however we define it for ourselves; but, neither on its own guarantees us a joy filled, rewarding, or even an exciting retirement experience.

HOW MUCH IS OUR HEALTH WORTH?

For example, if you or a spouse or partner is suffering from health challenges and life consists of fighting one health battle or one medical condition or chronic illness after another, then retirement becomes just a distant reality that we will have to put off until we can sort all these health issues out, or we live a retirement bounded by pain and suffering, fearful of leaving our homes, our doctors, or our beds. Doctor visits, hospital stays, tests, tests, and more tests; waiting and worrying is not a formula for fulfilling and meaningful retirements. Life is put on hold until there is a positive outcome, or our worst fears are realized and there is a slow and painful (for all parties) walk into the abyss. We have to ask ourselves, *would this outcome be substantially improved if we had wealth beyond our wildest imaginations?* The skeptics among us might say that the well-off have better access to quality health care than the average "Joe and Jane" and maybe in some aspects they do. From my perspective, however, the American health care system, while imperfect, does provide seniors with a high standard of quality care; provided we have an advocate who can fully represent our interests. How do I know? Because, like most of us, I have been through some health challenges as has my spouse, my parents, and other relatives and I advocated and grieved for them all as they approached, entered, and came out the other side of our Medicare and health systems, some with good outcomes and others not. Nature takes its course and may it be merciful.

HEALTH TALKS, MONEY WALKS

Now, let's look at the other side of the coin. You are blessed with good health, but are just getting by on Social Security and other types of government safety net programs, like food stamps or living in public housing. While you worked your entire life neither health insurance nor a pension was ever available. Not the most inviting retirement scenario for sure; but you have not seen the inside of a doctor's office except for routine checkups and have never spent a day in a hospital—you are a very fortunate person. You have few luxuries and don't own a car, but you have a joyful and fulfilling life because you know what is important to you—your church, family, and friends—life for you is good because you don't miss what you never had. Or just conjure up the archetypal noble poor family of all time, *The Waltons*; the made for TV, Depression-era family with a surfeit of love, goodness, and kindness to others and above all to each other—doesn't that just warm your heart. Goodnight, John-boy.

THE MYSTERIOUS CASE(S) OF HOWARD HUGHES AND OTHERS

Then the name Howard Hughes popped into my mind—I had read one of the earlier accounts of his life and been exposed to contemporaneous stories of his interesting comings and goings. Howard Hughes was an aviation pioneer of the highest order, figuratively and literally, who became enamored with the movie business and the starlets they attracted. Hughes, like any red-blooded American millionaire, wanted a piece of the action, again both literally and figuratively, and so made himself into a movie mogul and producer when sound was just beginning to capture the cinema market. Yet most of us remember Howard Hughes for his eccentric lifestyle, his paranoia, and his obsessive-compulsive behaviors. He was one of the early residents of what became the modern miracle in the desert called Las Vegas. Hughes would lock himself up in palatial hotel suites he either owned or rented and essentially lived like an escapee from what used to be known as an insane asylum, but he had one redeeming quality—he was filthy rich and actually continued to operate his aviation and movie empires through his most trusted subordinate, the only one he would let into his inner sanctum. Hughes never let anyone cut his hair, or more famously, trim his nails, and I assume his bathing habits were likewise suspect. Hughes was not only a self-exiled man of immense wealth, he also had access to every variety of narcotic and brain-dulling drug known to man, which he ingested with abandon. When he died in 1976 he was unrecognizable and weighed in at some 90 pounds—and he was one of the wealthiest individuals in the world at that time.

If you need some more examples of how wealth "can't buy you love" or happiness as the Beatles sang, look at celebrities like Michael Jackson, Whitney Houston, Rodney King, or Amy Winehouse, a wonderfully talented songstress who succumbed to alcohol and drugs at a young age. And, if that's not proof enough, a story in the *Detroit News* described the rapid downfall of a young woman who won one million dollars in the Michigan Lottery in 2011, continued to collect welfare from the state, was prosecuted, paid the state back, and within a year was found dead from a suspected drug overdose. Money can buy many things, but some are just not good for you—now are they?[2]

But as they say on those infomercials, wait, there's more! What about Gerald Muswagon, who won 10 million dollars in a lottery and hanged himself after he spent all the money in just a few years; or Victoria Zell, who shared an eleven million dollar Powerball Lottery only to find herself doing time in a Minnesota prison for a drug- and alcohol-induced collision and now all her winnings are gone.[3]

SUDDEN WEALTH CAN KILL

The list goes on and on and statistics demonstrate that at least half of big-lottery-jackpot millionaires self-destruct and end up in poverty within the first five years after winning or they end up somewhere even worse, much worse. It appears that sudden wealth, especially for the unprepared, can kill, perhaps lottery tickets should come with a Surgeon General's warning: Winning Is Dangerous to Health—if you win, run don't walk, to the nearest financial advisor that can pass a "BS Detector Test."

Perhaps this is too much gallows humor, but a sudden influx of anything can kill, especially when it has no antecedent or personal or cultural connection. It's like stuffing severely malnourished children full of high protein prime-cut beef in the belief you are doing them a service when in fact you would be killing them. A severely malnourished child must be brought along slowly so the body is not overwhelmed with the protein it no longer knows how to use and digest. Typically, children in this state are first rehydrated with sterile water infused with some glucose, and then they are given small doses of therapeutic foods, usually containing nutrients and proteins made from low fat milk that are easily tolerated by the body. But interestingly enough, once the children's digestive systems are activated and electrolytes are balanced, enriched peanut butter is the food of choice. Similarly, if you take someone who only knew poverty and want and was addicted to alcohol and drugs then literally millions of dollars are dumped into their "system," this would create not only an internal crisis, but an outward one as well as friends, family, and all manner of bystanders, grifters, and grafters would besiege them with requests for loans and offers to sell them the "good stuff," that, much like high protein beef, would feed their habits but ultimately kill them. In the end, as the proverb states, "A fool and their money are soon parted." Money absent purpose equals problems. So once again, be careful what you wish for, because it just might come true and bite you in the butt, or even worse. And that, my fellow travelers, is why health shall forever be the foundation stone for our virtual retirement pyramids, so let it be written, so let it be done. (My profound thanks to Yul Brynner and the cast of thousands in the movie *The Ten Commandments*.)

CRITICAL "CONTRIBUTING FACTORS" FOR RETIREMENT SUCCESS

I am sure we can all identify numerous retirement contributing factors or those actions, activities, and life events that make our retirements happy, exciting, meaningful, and fulfilling, as well as identify circumstances, behaviors, and actions that are destructive to life and retirement, like drugs and other personal behaviors that make us less than desirable mates or friends. And don't forget, the external forces that complicate, confuse, and otherwise threaten to derail our retirements, like family problems and the dreaded 3 D's—divorce, death, and disability previously identified. I will not go through the list of all possible "horribles" but rather focus on the previously identified "sustaining" and "contributing" factors comprising Retirement's Six Fundamental Building Blocks. This is my way of directing attention onto the types of life events, actions, beliefs, behaviors, activities, connections, and personal relationships necessary for making your retirement the best and most fulfilling years of your life.

BE PREPARED TO SUSPEND DISBELIEF

Indeed, the following chapters are devoted to describing how each of these Six Building Blocks impacts our retirements and the rest of our lives. Knowing about them is one thing, a step in the right direction, but actually integrating them into our lives is another matter. I will be exploring strategies for (1) remaining healthy and describing why some of us ignore our bodies and physical selves by engaging in health-destroying behaviors; (2) financially preparing ourselves for retirement; (3) successfully transitioning to life after work without angst or regret; (4) staying engaged with others and how our "retirement" personalities affect every aspect of our lives; and why some are able to build strong interpersonal bonds while others always appear to be standing outside the circle of inclusion; (5) discovering the "world" that is right outside our doors and how to find the challenge, adventure, and discovery that are absolutely critical to our retirements and to our intellectual, emotional, and physical well-being; and finally (6) achieving meaning, purpose, and inner peace in retirement and in life through spiritual enlightenment and by contribution to family and to others.

CHAPTER 8

■ ■ ■ ■ ■ ■

Taking Care of Our Aging Selves

The first wealth is health.
—RALPH WALDO EMERSON

Those who do not find time for exercise
will have to find time for illness.
—EDWARD SMITH-STANLEY

IT'S NOT ABOUT HOW LONG WE LIVE, BUT HOW WELL WE LIVE

Growing old gives us license to shape and share our lives with others in ways we might never have thought, appreciated, or even imagined when we were raising a family and starting our careers. In the end, life at any age is what we choose to make of it. A good part of this shaping has to do with how we live our lives, or our lifestyles, and how we protect, nurture, and enrich our physical and emotional selves in spite of life's inevitable wear and tear. We can pursue lifestyles that promote physical and mental health, or we can choose to live in ways that seemingly go against our own best interests and those of our significant others and our families. We must all accept personal responsibility for who we are, and for who we are yet to be. While we might accept the inevitable results of our own self-neglect, is it fair to subject our loved ones to the pain and agony of watching us self-destruct or commit slow but inevitable suicide by drink, food, or drugs? When we indulge in these behaviors we are not only hurting ourselves but all those who surround and love us and who see us disintegrating before their very eyes. What I say will not stop anyone from the path of self-destruction—that is something you must do for yourself. Choose life over infirmity whenever that choice is available, because what seems hopeless today can become tolerable tomorrow and ultimately joyful the next. It's really not about the means of our self-execution; it is about how we view the world, either as welcoming, understanding, and accepting, or as hostile and fearsome. Regardless of how far we may have fallen, there will always be someone there to get us back up—but first, we must ask for help or help ourselves—life is transitory and death is forever, end of sermon.

We are living longer and experiencing an improved quality of life as we age due to the availability and ever-improving (thanks to research) new generations of pharmaceuticals, medical, and diagnostic devices, quality of education and training of medical personnel, and innovative surgical procedures. That's the good news; the bad news is that we are now being subjected to diseases and conditions that were either unknown or uncommon just a few decades ago when our life spans were shorter. Some of us are more fortunate than others because of genetics, others because of their ready access to quality medical care, and yet others because they assume personal responsibility for their health. The reality is that our bodies are unique to us, and as a result, we age at different velocities and respond to healing measures with different rates of success. In the same way, the body you had at 45 will be different than the one you will have at 55, 65, or 75, for that matter. Many factors ultimately determine how we age, but disease is not always in the equation. We can accelerate or retard our aging or die from many causes that are not disease related, some self-inflicted like addictions, some injuries from falls or accidents or environmental factors, or sometimes our bodies just wear out—the "machine" simply breaks down over time, but life should not be about how we die, rather how we live.

WE ARE ALL DIFFERENT

While there are many similarities in how we age, as a group, across comparably aged individuals both male and female, the actual pace of change, the actual sites of change, and the actual impacts of these changes are specific to every individual. Our genes play an important role in how we age; but not necessarily in how we cope with aging. Most of us ultimately come to terms with our aging selves, some with a sense of inevitability or resignation, others with reluctance fighting all the way, and still others with a "bring it on" approach promising themselves they will never give in to age—never, never. But in the end, our health, and how well we care for it and how well it cares for us, ultimately determines our quality of life into our sixties, seventies, eighties, and beyond. In order for us to appropriately respond to our aging selves it is important to fully understand how our bodies and our emotional and mental capacities will change as we move through the Five Stages and Ages of Retirement." Here are some of the physical transformations we can expect to encounter, to some degree or another, as we age grace-fully—or not.

WHAT WE WILL SEE IN THE MIRROR

One of the most visible signs of our aging selves is written in our skin and tells the story of our lives. Our skin becomes drier, more fragile, and thinner as we age, hence the lines or wrinkles and the brown spots, which are made worse by smoking and by exposing our skin to repeated bombardment by the sun, either out of vanity or because we work and play outside. We also lose the skin's underlying fat layer which makes our skin appear as if it is hanging, especially around the jowls and the neck. Because the skin is thinner, we start seeing the underlying blood vessels in our cheeks and noses and all over our bodies. Our skin becomes less efficient at moving sweat away from our bodies, and wounds heal slower. Our hair turns white because of the reduced production of melanin, and we lose hair in places we don't want and get hair in places we never even imagined that hair could or would grow. We bruise more easily because our blood vessels are more fragile and less protected by our skin.

Our posture becomes more stooped and we even get shorter, and our joints, particularly our knees, start aching and no longer work as efficiently; we find it harder to walk and to bend because our much-used joints are degenerating. Our muscles, if not used, atrophy at higher rates and bones start losing density and weaken. This is especially a serious concern for menopausal and post-menopausal women, who become more vulnerable to bone damage and breaks.

Our eyesight starts to fail and we are more susceptible to eye diseases such as cataracts, glaucoma, and macular degeneration. It is harder for us to see at night or in dimly lit spaces—if you haven't noticed. Our senses of taste and smell are diminished because the taste buds on our tongues are less sensitive and fewer in number, and our nose sensors become less efficient as well—more chilies please. Our hearing is less acute with some 33 percent of us between 65 and 74 having hearing problems—what did you say? We are suffering more upset stomachs and finding ourselves out of sorts; well, that too is just another aging side effect. As we grow older our metabolisms slow, in fact, up to 5 percent per decade—and now you know why you are packing on the extra pounds. Our stomachs empty more slowly which increases our risk of reflux disease, and because our large intestines (our bowels) work more slowly, we feel constipated—not pretty but at least now you know.

Some forgetfulness is to be expected—don't panic, it is not necessarily an early sign of Alzheimer's, a devastating cognitive disease that first takes our humanity and then our lives and currently affects some 5 million primarily elderly victims. Our brains continually manufacture new brain cells to replace those that die well into our sixties allowing us "old dogs" to learn new tricks. This mild forgetfulness we sometimes experience happens because our brain synapses work a bit more slowly as we age—nothing to worry about.[4]

NOW FOR THE BIG STUFF

Please remember, aging is not a disease, it is a process that moves slowly in some and more rapidly in others. But because we are living longer, on average and for many different reasons, we become exposed to more of life's potent slings and arrows. Some of us manage to avoid being hit while others become their targets.

The most prevalent disorder confronting seniors over 65 is cardiovascular and heart disease, which includes hypertension, vascular disease, congestive heart failure, and high blood pressure. Heart disease is the number one killer of our contemporaries accounting for 20 percent of all deaths among men and women between the ages of 65 and 74. The hit parade on this list of "killers" and "disablers" also includes stroke, followed by cancer, pneumonia, and the flu, with the "C" word being the most feared. In fact cancer is actually over 100 different diseases in which abnormal cells grow out of control with some 1.5 million new cases being reported every year—of course, not all of these are in the elderly.

Other common afflictions on the list of our worst fears include dementia, diabetes, lung disease, breathing problems, and Parkinson's disease, which is a chronic neurological disorder that is particularly devastating, and I know because my father suffered from it. We also are prey to sleep disorders including insomnia, apnea, and movement disorders like restless leg syndrome and arthritis which target the spine, neck, back, shoulders, hands, wrists, knees, ankles, and feet, and which can be extremely painful and immobilizing. And we should not leave out accidents and falls which oftentimes lead to particularly bad outcomes for seniors and are frequently caused by loss of balance and stability, which often have organic origins. This rounds out our rogue's gallery of diseases and other conditions that can attack our bodies and our minds, but there are many more varieties, both new and old, waiting in the wings to reappear at any time, like tuberculosis, and even smallpox and polio.

FOOD CAN KILL

There is one disease, affliction, personal responsibility issue, or whatever we want to call it that has yet to be discussed but nonetheless is a condition that almost one-third of us literally carry around every day of our lives. I am talking about obesity, a silent, or perhaps a not so silent, co-conspirator in many of the diseases and conditions that attack us. Indeed, according to the Congressional Research Service Report titled "Obesity Among Older Americans," the number of obese older adults has increased dramatically in recent decades, having more than doubled to 30 percent of the elderly population since the 1970s.[5] The document attributes this increase to a confluence of factors including the lowered cost of food, more sedentary types of employment, and the decline in the amount of time seniors spend in physical activities. It also points out that we are eating some 300 calories more per day when compared to the base year of 1985, and we are eating less nutritious food, also known as "junk food," that coincides with a general shift toward eating out rather than at home. In 1975, 25 percent of food spending went toward meals in restaurants, but in 2004, that number jumped to 44 percent of our food budget spent in restaurants and primarily in fast food establishments. Even more alarming is the spike in obesity among the Baby Boom Generation with 40 percent of women and 38 percent of males in their 50s and 60s considered obese. Trust me; this is not a contest Boomers want to win. If the trend line continues it is projected that half of the elderly population will be obese by 2030. Remember, obesity increases mortality risk and contributes to other serious chronic conditions, including cardiovascular disease, stroke, diabetes, a growing list of cancers, and, according to recent research, even to Alzheimer's disease, and directly hastens functional decline after age 65.

Obesity is a primary instigator of type 2 diabetes; the prevalence of diabetes increased by 49 percent between 1990 and 2000, reaching nearly epidemic proportions, and in 2010 both diabetes type 1 and type 2 were estimated to affect nearly 30 percent, or some 10.9 million people aged 65 and over.[6] Think about that for a second: almost one out of every three people over the age of 65 has diabetes, a serious disease that is silently, or not so silently, attacking their bodies and threatening their well-being. Fortunately it is a disease that is easily controlled and/or avoided by carefully monitoring what we put into our mouths.

Both obesity and diabetes type 2 are considered "lifestyle diseases" and for good reason because, by accepting personal responsibility for our own health, we can self-eradicate one of the most common ailments afflicting aging adults. According to Holy St. Lifer, as written in the "AARP Health Report," we can dramatically reduce our risk of becoming diabetic by following five effective strategies. Ms. St. Lifer suggests the following:

- Eat breakfast every day and opt for healthy choices whenever possible; this will lower your risk of diabetes by 34 percent.

- Eat more natural foods such as fruits and vegetables, and avoid sugars, sodas, and foods sweetened with corn syrup called "fast carbohydrates" (more about that later) whenever possible, and this will reduce your risk of diabetes by 21 percent.

- Stop smoking! Smokers have a 40 percent higher likelihood of contracting diabetes than nonsmokers.

- Sleep more than six hours per night. Those night birds among us who sleep less than six hours have a 60 percent greater risk of contracting diabetes.

- Get physical and increase your aerobic activity.[7]

OBESITY DOESN'T HAVE TO BE US

There is no nice or easy way to say this, so here is what happens when we opt to satisfy ourselves with food rather than more healthful alternatives. Obesity will shorten our lives, affect our personal relationships, restrict our willingness and ability to move around the planet, make it difficult for us to play and interact with our grandchildren, create psychological distress, challenge our willingness and ability to even leave our homes much less experience the outside world, and above all, make us more vulnerable to numerous diseases and conditions that will cause us pain and immobility and bring our family heartbreak as they watch us spiral into despair and physical collapse. I know this is not a pretty picture, but unfortunately it is an accurate one. Obesity is not the only self-afflicted abuse we heap upon our bodies. Smoking and other addictive behaviors, such as alcohol and recreational drugs as well as prescribed medications, can have serious debilitating consequences for our aging selves.

The bottom line is that we all need to maintain a healthy weight, but don't get too caught up in the BMI, or Body Mass Index Scale, because in my mind it tells us very little about our bodies. Rather, rely more on measures of body fat percentage, which is more accurate and more informative and helpful as we seek to lose weight, or better yet, to reduce body fat and replace it with muscle—which, by the way, weighs more than body fat. So, in reality you can look slimmer and trimmer and be physically healthier and still gain weight because you have substituted muscle for fat, and the BMI is woefully inaccurate in those types of situations. Many home bathroom scales now have body fat calculators.

LIVE IN REAL TIME, NOT VIRTUALLY

It is often difficult to separate physical from emotional disorders; each can be causative of the other. However, for the purposes of this discussion I am treating them independently. We never have to feel alone if we consider "virtual relationships" as proper substitutes for reaching out and touching someone in real time. More and more of us (and yes, seniors as well) have become accustomed to and dependent upon smaller and smaller electronic devices, never having to leave the comfort of our chairs and able to satisfy all our needs and wants with a few keystrokes. Instant gratification has become the norm—I want it now! How many of us start hyperventilating if we leave home without our smart phones, and how many of us have witnessed very young children expertly manipulating computers and electronic devices? We are raising a generation of children that might never know the joys of the outdoors, of climbing trees and of testing their bodies, or of exploration or the excitement of discovering a new bug or bird. We stare into our computers looking for minute-by-minute updates of what our friends or grandchildren are doing, but we are living through our electronic devices, disconnected from the touch and feel of others. And even more disturbing we have accepted our "virtual realities" as the real thing. Are we all becoming social media junkies, a nation of voyeurs living through others, watching rather than doing? Please, get outside, smell the roses and the freshness of life; if we challenge our bodies, our minds will follow—and our bodies and brains will thank us every day for the rest of our longer-lived lives.

Some seniors are fully engaged in this "brave new world" of technology, while others have no clue and have to communicate the old way, face to face and, perhaps, even by writing an email, if not a letter. Life is about balance and if we find the proper balance for the role and function of technology in our lives it can enrich us rather than overwhelm and overtake us. Taken in that context, can social media and technology actually work for seniors? Yes, in some cases it can, especially for seniors with limited mobility. Today, almost anything can be delivered to our doorsteps. Just log on to Amazon.com or eBay, or any major store's virtual site, hit a few keystrokes, and the richness of the world (and yes, I am being sarcastic) can be ours within days. Indeed, my wife has taught her 93-year-old mother, who lives a plane ride away, how to use Skype, and now they enjoy weekly "I can see you" conversations that have allowed them the perception of personal interaction, if not the reality. Unfortunately, we all—young and old—have fallen prey to the lure and easy fixes of fast foods, to indolence, and to the assumption that there is a pill or a cure for everything, and that substituting electrons for human interaction is the new reality—well it might be for you, but not for me. Please think about that and act accordingly, and if you are looking for an answer, keep on reading.

IT'S NEVER TOO LATE TO BEGIN AGAIN

Many of us need lifestyle makeovers. The first step is to seek and then get involved in physically active pursuits by ramping up our physical profiles. Take stairs instead of escalators or elevators, walk, walk, and do more walking. Go skiing, go bicycling, go hiking, but most of all, keep moving. Get involved with clubs that are organized around physical pursuits like bicycle clubs, environmentally focused clubs, kayak and watersports clubs, mountain clubs, hiking clubs; there is every variety of club to match every level of competence from rank beginner to world class expert in any type of physical endeavor. Organize vacations around physical activities, not indolence, and stay away from those "all-inclusives" where you can eat and drink yourself silly. My new office is a snow-covered mountain, with nary a desk in sight, and I get to interact with and teach skiing, a sport I love, to people of all ages, backgrounds, and skill levels. Now my mantra is, "Every day I walk off the mountain is a good day"—oh, and the same goes for my clients—I haven't lost one yet. You too can seek part-time jobs that challenge your bodies as well as your minds or volunteer opportunities that will keep you actively engaged. Please, for yourself and your family, do something, do anything, just keep moving.

There is another approach to keeping our weight under our control. This is my personal secret for maintaining a healthy weight. First, do not obsess about the number on your scale; obsess about your girth or waist size, if you must obsess about something. Then, identify a pair of pants you might already have in your closet or basement, or purchase one with a waist size considered ideal for you. These pants will replace every fad diet known to mankind, because you are not measuring or counting calories, rather you are focusing on what is truly important, your body, because it doesn't lie. If you stop fitting into your benchmark pant size, it's time to do one of two things, which are (a) eat less or (b) exercise more. Scales can sometimes be deceiving; you can fool your scale, but you can't fool your pants.

Another approach, this time using our scales, is not to set an ideal body weight and try to hit it with pinpoint accuracy, rather set a self-determined acceptable weight range. Note, I said "range." I don't have a number that I obsessively worry about because weight changes throughout the day, month, and season; so we shouldn't get bent out of shape if we gain a pound or two. Instead, establish a comfortable weight range and endeavor to stay within that range. In establishing that range, look back and ask yourself what was your ideal comfortable weight and then set that at the bottom of the range and set the upside weight number typically three to five pounds above your ideal weight. And, if you exceed the upper limit, the basic principle remains the same: eat less and/ or ramp up your activity levels. Another way to keep our weight within an ideal range is to balance food intake with activity levels so as you get more active in the summer, then perhaps your body requires more calories; or if you are an active cold weather person, winter pursuits like cross country skiing, or downhill skiing, or snowshoeing burn gobs of calories; and therefore, you need more fuel, also known as food. Start thinking about food as "fuel" for your body and keep in mind we neither want to overfill nor underfill our machine with calories. Eventually we learn how many calories our bodies need or will tolerate before losing or gaining weight. *Keep moving, life is gaining on us.*

THE ELDERLY AND DEPRESSION

Our journey through all the "possible horribles" that can afflict us as we move into and through our retirement years isn't over yet—to be forewarned is to be forearmed. As we age, our "emotional selves" could quite possibly be more troubling to us than our physical selves because we know more about our bodies than our minds and emotions.

Interestingly, depression is more common in the elderly than any other age group, affecting approximately 20 percent of seniors living in the extant community and 40 percent living in care homes, according to the Mental Health Foundation; those are huge numbers. So what's the explanation—is depression in the elderly organic, psychological, situational, or all of the above? Let's examine some of the factors that would make our emotionally challenged brothers and sisters more prone to mental health issues than the population at large.

This is probably not rocket science but when we age we have many more encounters with life, both positive and negative, than younger cohorts, and life takes its toll not only on our bodies but on our psyche as well. The chances are very high that seniors with coping problems in their younger years would still have those coping problems as they age—unless there has been a successful intervention. The National Institute of Mental Health reports that over 26 percent of all adults in the United States may have a mental health disorder, or one out of four adults and 6 percent have what is termed serious mental health issues.[8] Depression, whether moderate or severe, is both internally and externally manifested. In other words, while you can't see and touch the sufferer's mental anguish you can view its outward displays and behaviors. Depressive symptoms include overwhelming sadness, loss of interest and pleasure in nearly every type of life activity, confusion and forgetfulness, constant fatigue and low energy, irritability and anger, feelings of hopelessness, acting out, sleeping too little or sleeping too much, agitation, loss of concentration, anxiousness, disconnection from others, and eating too much or too little. These symptoms can mask physical ailments or physical ailments can mask depressive disorders because along with the psychological damage comes physical manifestations such as persistent aches and pains, headaches, stomach disorders and digestive problems that never seem to go away, even if treated.

So what causes or triggers depressive behaviors? Indeed, we all become depressed at some time or another but most of us can shrug it off and re-engage using our own inner resources, strengths, and coping mechanisms, tested and strengthened by the many challenges we all confront in every stage and age of our life cycles. Some of us, however, haven't fully developed our coping mechanisms and we become prey to the psychic slings and arrows life throws at us. Others are overwhelmed by life events, such as the loss of loved ones, divorce, health challenges, accidents, or living through horrific events, either manmade or natural disasters. Finally, some believe there are biological and organic precursors that trigger depressive behaviors, and here once more, we move into the ongoing nature versus nurture discussion. Depression to the sufferer can be more devastating than physical disabilities, so don't think it's just an act or expect that it will go away of its own accord because it won't.

Why the Elderly Are More Vulnerable to Depression

So, now let's get back to the subject at hand—depression among the elderly. Keeping the above in mind would we be surprised to learn that the elderly are more prone to depression than the general population? Not in my thinking, at least. Consider what we face as we age: (a) health challenges, some temporary with quick recoveries, some chronic, many debilitating and long lasting; (b) changes in our brains resulting in different forms of dementia; (c) outliving loved ones and profound feelings of loneliness and loss; (d) changing sleeping habits; (e) leaving behind our family homes and neighborhoods, often under duress, with all the connectedness and memories being shattered; (f) finding ourselves dependent on others for our every need and being a burden to our families; (g) loss of personal mobility and driving privileges and the feeling of being trapped; (h) turning to negative or addictive behaviors for comfort, escape, and solace; and (i) loss of freedom and the ability to control our own destinies.

Is it any wonder we would suffer from depression? The miracle is that it does not eventually engulf every last one of us as we age.

Available Treatments for Depressive Disorders in Seniors

How do we treat mental health disorders in the elderly? The good news is that we have an arsenal of mood-altering drugs and the bad news is we have an arsenal of mood-altering drugs. It is a quick and easy solution, particularly for those among us who exhibit unpleasant behavioral symptoms like acting out, or violent reactions to being touched and handled by others. These medications oftentimes have more benefits for the caretaker or family members than they do for the depressed elder. While I am not a big fan of psychotherapy or counseling for the depressed elderly, a case can be made for group therapy, or counseling sessions that give the depressed elderly an opportunity to see they are not alone in their affliction and perhaps to establish bonds that could ultimately have a positive effect on their well-being. In my thinking the best defense is a good offense; that is, to identify the signs of depression early in the cycle when success of intervention is highest. Also, adult children and family need to take an active role in forestalling depression by being proactive, particularly when a life-changing event is imminent, like the death of a spouse, a move to a new home or into institutional care, diagnosis of a serious health challenge, and the like. It is absolutely critical that families do everything in their power to keep their aging parents engaged in their lives and around the grandchildren whenever possible and help them to preserve their independence, if not in the family home, then in an apartment or home where our parents can age-out without having to move yet again. The same dicta apply to friends whenever possible. Make every effort to keep parents and/or elderly friends active and involved in community and family. Social engagement is a, if not *the*, most critical ingredient at this stage of life—do not forget that.[9]

BOREDOM AND LONELINESS CAN KILL— SO CAN DRUGS

Boredom, loneliness, and loss can kill us literally and figuratively, they will suck out our souls and damage our psyches, turning our gaze inward to a world only we have knowledge of and access to. The physical shell, while still recognizable to some, will have a hollow core. When this happens we look for ways to numb our pains, both psychic and physical, and absent constructive alternatives, outlets, or healing therapies we replace heretofore life-enhancing behaviors with life-destroying behaviors when life turns sour and when it seems there is little or no hope for redemption or renewal.

Boomers especially are no strangers to seeking unhealthy substitutes when feeling unhappy, stressed, or unfulfilled; many grew up in the drug infused sixties when illicit drugs of all stripes and kinds were readily available—remember the battle cry: sex, drugs, and rock 'n' roll. So it would not be a giant leap to conclude that aging Boomers, when in a fragile or emotional state, return to what many Boomers considered to be the "best times of their lives," and once again seek solace, maybe not in sex or rock 'n' roll but certainly in drugs. According to Dr. Gayathri Dowling, of the National Institute on Drug Abuse, as reported in a *Herald and News* article, "The Hooked Generation," he states, "We can't ignore that older adults are using harder substances, and that we are seeing increases in emergency room visits where people present with drug abuse." But when we think about these addictions we tend to think about younger people." According to the National Institutes of Health (NIH) 2010 survey on abuse of prescription or illegal drugs in people ages 50 to 59, 2.4 million people admitted to abusing either or both prescription or illegal drugs. The NIH became so alarmed they issued a consumer alert on prescription and illicit drug abuse on its website directed to seniors.[10] Common age-related chronic conditions like diabetes and coronary disease are worsened by substance abuse with some 315 Floridians ages 55 to 64 dying from drug abuse or poisonings in 2010. Furthermore, statistics show that individuals in their 50s are far more likely than previous generations to be involved with dual addictions to alcohol and prescription or illicit drugs, the article goes on to report.[11] This is not a very pretty picture, and I strongly suspect it will get worse.

WHO ME, I JUST HAVE A SOCIAL DRINK OR TWO, MAYBE MORE

The "drug" of choice among seniors is alcohol, because it is so easily obtainable, legal, and socially acceptable. Substance abuse, whether drugs or alcohol, can be a long-standing behavior carried over from our younger years as we aged and entered retirement communities and even congregate care facilities. Conversely, substance abuse that begins later in life is usually triggered by a life event, such as death or separation from a partner, health challenges, the stress of leaving our working life and entering retirement, or simply boredom and loneliness. I would definitely add nicotine addiction to this short-list, because smoking is an addiction with devastating effects, not only on the individual who partakes, but on anyone in proximate contact with a committed smoker, because secondhand smoke can be just as harmful, unfortunately, to anyone and everyone, particularly to children and individuals with compromised health.

Also, the abuse of prescription medications can be just as addictive and injurious if they are not used according to recommended protocols. Overmedication can be purposeful or not and seniors suffering from various forms of dementia are at particular risk, unless their medication schedules are carefully monitored. Furthermore, seniors with multiple prescriptions and complex schedules must be particularly cautious about managing their medications. It is fairly easy for seniors to obtain drugs because they quickly learn how to present different ailments in order to obtain some of the more potent pain relief and mind-altering drugs of choice; thus medical personnel must remain particularly vigilant and sensitive to the symptoms of elderly substance abuse.

AN OUNCE OF PREVENTION IS WORTH A POUND OF CURE

Some of the more common warning signs of drug and alcohol abuse in the elderly (and those not so old) include: decreased coordination and balance, unsteady walking; falling and unexplained bruises; memory loss; unexplained chronic pains; chronic diarrhea; changes in sleeping habits; lack of interest in previously enjoyed activities; frequent sadness, irritability, and depression; dramatic weight loss; and cutting oneself off from friends and relatives. As you can see, many of the indicators for substance abuse mimic other mental health conditions, particularly depression.

While prevention is easier than treatment, little has been done to recognize the threat that elderly substance abuse presents to this community. The formula for prevention for those who do not have a prior history of substance abuse is to: (a) pay attention to the signs of substance abuse in those around us and intervene before it becomes a full-blown addiction; (b) avoid the problem entirely by helping our parents or loved ones manage their complicated medication schedules; (c) keep our elderly family members, whether in a congregate care facility or in their homes, physically and mentally active and engaged, remember boredom and loneliness kill; (d) go to doctor appointments with a family member suspected of abusing prescription medications and alert them to your concerns. If the worst is suspected and a family member is in full-blown addiction, seek professional help and perhaps either outpatient or inpatient treatment at a specialized facility, preferably one that focuses on elderly substance abuse.

OPTIMISM—IT KEEPS SHOWING UP SO IT MUST BE IMPORTANT

Optimism is a key ingredient in a happy and fulfilling life—but optimism must be followed by positive action, and unfounded or unrealistic optimism will surely lead to disappointments. We cannot be passive bystanders to life or life will have its way with us. We need to accept responsibility for ourselves and for our loved ones and be prepared to shape our personal futures physically, intellectually, and emotionally by differentiating between life-affirming decisions, actions, and behaviors and life-destroying decisions, actions, and behaviors and to avoid the latter and to accept and actively pursue the former. Life in retirement, no matter how dedicated we are to the superman credo of "Truth, Justice, and the American Way," will not be without trials, heartbreak, and disappointment (it's still life, after all), but we must constantly redirect our energies toward opportunities and away from unreachable dreams, no matter how real or close they appear in the rearview mirror of life. Always dream forward and move forward.

CHAPTER 9

■ ■ ■ ■ ■ ■

Your Retirement, Your Money, and You

*Show me the money... I want you to say
it with me, with meaning, brother.*
—FROM THE MOVIE *JERRY MAGUIRE*

*You can be young without money,
but you can't be old without it.*
—TENNESSEE WILLIAMS, FROM
CAT ON A HOT TIN ROOF

DO I HAVE ENOUGH MONEY TO RETIRE? IT DEPENDS

I can think of no better opening for a discussion about money than these two quotes, one from the movie *Jerry Maguire*, which enshrined "show me the money" into the lexicon of the English language, and the other from the famous—or some would say infamous—poet, playwright, and author Tennessee Williams. Let's assume (for my amusement and yours) that we are thinking about retiring and schedule a visit with our financial advisor and/or pension fund counselor, and when we arrive for the appointment he or she asks, "How can I help you today?" And our response is, "I would like to know if I have enough money to retire," and she or he responds, "That depends ..." "But on what?" we respond. Going in circles and getting nowhere fast, so it seems. But, we have broken the ice and potentially made a life-changing decision, or at least, we are considering one, if the "money gods" are smiling upon us today. And the advisor/counselor is correct—it does depend on a whole host of factors.

"Do I have enough money to retire?" is the most frequently asked and most often discussed issue, worry, or concern of every pre- or post-retiree. Perhaps the emphasis on money is misplaced in the pantheon of things to ultimately really worry about, but nonetheless it typically is the most discussed subject related to our upcoming retirements. But, you have come to the right place, not for a definitive answer from me because "it depends"; but, rather, a definitive answer from you. I will provide the tools so you can answer the "it depends" questions for yourself—particularly "how much money from pensions, savings, investments, and/ or Social Security is needed to have financial security in your retirement years and beyond?"

I don't want to be disingenuous about the importance of money because in reality it is really just a piece of paper or numbers in your savings, investment, or retirement account. It does not exist outside of what is called "exchange theory." That is, people are willing to accept money in exchange for something else—like a good or service. In reality, our financial system is at its core, an act of faith. In other words, if we desire a good, for example a new vehicle, more than our money, then we exchange these pieces of paper as represented today by an electronic transfer, a check, or a credit card for the new shiny car we had our eyes on for weeks. If we do not have sufficient ready dollars to purchase a product we just "have to have," we either borrow it from a bank or similar financial institution, reputable or otherwise, or just put it on our credit cards. Which, by the way, contradicts one of my favorite adages, "If you can't pay cash for it—then you don't need it, whatever it is."

WANTS ARE INFINITE—INCOME IS FINITE

Our income is finite and our desires, wants, and "got-to-haves" infinite. We all need to exercise some self-limiting spending behaviors and ramp up our saving instincts if we are to accumulate sufficient assets for a financially secure retirement. Unfortunately, we have come to judge the value of people by the amount of money they amass; the type of luxuries they surround themselves with; the size, opulence, and number of homes they flit between; or the brand of their vehicles—without knowing how much debt or other people's money they had to borrow to surround themselves with such symbols of affluence. We tend to place people into social hierarchies based on outward appearances, such as displays of power and wealth, as opposed to their inherent worth and goodness as human beings, their value systems, their willingness to give back to society, to help and act respectfully toward others, whatever their social standing. Unfortunately, many of these same people not only build psychological separations between themselves and others, they also build real fences around their homes and communities.

If we value the size of our bank accounts over everything else, including spending time with our families, seeking new experiences, improving ourselves as individuals, or maintaining our health, this will set us up for a "money chase" to fuel a retirement lifestyle that is perhaps not financially sustainable. Sometimes we do this to find the joy and satisfaction from life in retirement that might have been denied us in our "go-go" working years. "Show me the money" is what most people think retirement is all about—the more money we have, the happier we will be, so we believe. In reality it's about who we are and what we consider to be fulfilling and meaningful. Don't be a follower, or wear plaid pants for that matter, be a leader, not of others, but lead yourself into a new and exciting life by cutting out of the "retirement herd" and by pursuing discovery, meaning, and adventure in addition to financial security.

WHEN IS ENOUGH, ENOUGH?

Indeed, I am certain we all want or hope to have accumulated a sufficient basket of financial resources from all sources to allow us a retirement lifestyle equal to or better than that of our working years. But when is enough, enough? We keep receiving mixed messages on this subject. We have often been told by the media and financial gurus that it costs less to live retired than it does when working—once again, it depends. So why worry if our retirement income is less than our working income? Well then, how much less retirement income will you have? And do you really believe that somehow your needs and wants will diminish all that much when you stop working? Prepare to be surprised—very surprised.

Money alone does not guarantee our retirements will be either joyful or meaningful. We must step into our new lives slowly at first, settle in and take measure of this thing we call retirement. As we gain comfort with our newfound freedom, we need to allow new experiences to first creep and then rush into our lives and become the "retirement gold standard" we all should strive to achieve. Retirement allows us to re-imagine our lives in its broadest context, allowing for continuous wonderment and renewal without the fear of criticism or judgment by others. It's your turn to call the shots.

NO ONE HAS A MONOPOLY ON HAPPINESS

Retirement is truly the one time in our lives when we can actually control our personal destinies as well as write its rules and life engagement protocols. There are many paths to retirement happiness, as there are many paths to retirement discovery, as there are many paths to retirement self-renewal—and none of these charges a toll. Retirement allows us to dream forward and to renew our commitments to life, family, and friends, and while money or financial security is one way to ease our travels down these paths (which are rarely easy and rarely paved for our convenience or easy access), no one regardless of their wealth—great or small—has a monopoly on happiness, discovery, and self-renewal. Yes, many challenges will confront us all as we walk the retirement walk and talk the retirement talk but challenges should not be viewed as obstacles, rather they should be treated as opportunities for growth and learning, teaching us not to fear the unknown but to embrace it. Get there any which way you can because with struggle comes accomplishment, and the victory, once realized, is so much sweeter. Life without challenge and purpose will dull your mind, spirit, and body. But, neither should anyone be denied a modest but joyful retirement because of financial challenges that some will surely face as we get older; many not of our making. So, I repeat the question, how much money is enough to live a meaningful and purposeful life in retirement without fear of want for your basic needs of food, shelter, and access to health care? Only you can put a number to that, so once again—it depends, but this time it depends on you.

WHAT THE EXPERTS AND THE NOT SO EXPERT TELL US ABOUT MONEY AND RETIREMENT

There are four rules of thumb commonly used by financial advisors for determining how much money we "need" to live comfortably; or to maintain an equivalent pre-work lifestyle into and through our retirement years without running out of money. They are: (1) fixed percentage of pre-retirement income approach; (2) pre-retirement income multiplier; (3) retrospective budget, or the look back, spend forward approach; and (4) retirement's Holy Grail, the financially self-perpetuating retirement.

1. The Fixed Percentage, or "Magic Number," Approach

The fixed percentage, or "magic number," of pre-retirement income required to maintain a consistent retirement lifestyle, appears to be moving ever higher. If these formulas are new to you, get ready for dis-appointment, or at least some healthy skepticism. In the 1980s the com-mon wisdom and prevailing recommendation for soon-to-be retirees to live well in retirement was to have access to a "household" replacement income, from all sources, of 70 percent of our pre-retirement incomes. Soon after we were told that 80 percent was a more realistic number, then 90 percent, and now some "experts," or financial advisors, are sug-gesting we need 100 percent of our household pre-retirement incomes to fully fund our retirements and maintain our working lifestyles. This calculation doesn't quite square with the Employee Benefit Research Institute which estimates that our household expenditures drop by a third between the ages of 65 and 85—although I have my doubts about that as well, given my personal experiences, but then again I might be the outlier here.

I suspect some of us are getting a bit twitchy by now—don't go into panic mode quite yet, and no 100 percent is not a misprint, but neither is it the final word on the subject because it all depends, but on what? So, what income are we talking about—is it our household's combined income in the years prior to retirement, or is it an average of our household income over the past 20 years, or is it our median household income, or is it our gross income, or is it our net income, or is it all of these or none of them? And, why should income be the retire-ment driver at all? For example, what if you had a household income of $100,000 your last working year but that was wildly insufficient to fuel your current standard of living, let alone your future standard of living in retirement because you borrowed significant amounts to maintain your apparently unsustainable lifestyle.

2. Pre-Retirement Income Multiplier Approach

Other financial retirement formulas don't necessarily focus on final household income as the benchmark, net or gross, but rather on the retiree's best judgment of how much annual household income is required to provide a fully funded retirement that supports a targeted retirement lifestyle, regardless of final actual household income, which might be higher or lower. Advocates of this approach use "multipliers" to get to the "retirement number." Most financial advisors adopting this methodology recommend "multipliers" ranging from 20 to 25 times your estimated annual income requirements, and that includes all wage earners; the exact multiplier depends on the financial advisor or expert you are discussing this with at that particular moment. So, if you estimate your annual household income requirement to be $100,000 per year in retirement, and that is without factoring inflation into the equation, and multiply that by 25, you would have to save $2.5 million to continue your pre-retirement lifestyle into and through your retirement years. "That's a mighty powerful number to fully fund our retirement," Hoss Cartwright, the Ponderosa's "Big Boy," might have responded, if asked while the family sat around the dinner table he so much enjoyed.

3. The Retrospective Budget: Look Back, Spend Forward

Yet another method for determining how much money is required to have a financially fulfilling and relatively "worry free" retirement is what I call the "retrospective budget." Here we have gone to the other side of the equation by focusing on the expense side; or what it "actually" costs us to live the lifestyle we are attempting to emulate in retirement as opposed to guessing how much money we need to fuel our retire- ments, as in the Multiplier Approach. Think of your household as a small business enterprise with you and your spouse/partner as the chief operating and chief financial officers, charged with joint responsibility for managing and paying for all household activities, functions, and operations; and for the financial integrity of the enterprise as well. As in any business, or in our case household, a certain amount of revenue is required to maintain ongoing operations like vehicles, cable or satellite, utilities, food, maintenance, capital goods, infrastructure, personal items like clothes, recreation, entertainment, and vacations; in other words, everything needed to maintain a "happy household" and happy household members. As in most businesses we need to save for a "rainy" day when things might not be so advantageous, and therefore like a business we strive to build cash reserves for unanticipated expenditures and emergencies like replacing the old fuel guzzling heater or the house's roof or other pressing needs like paying for your daughter's or son's wedding, or college tuition, or helping your parents out because they need to move to an assisted living residence, or some uncovered health challenges. Without these cash reserves, you could find yourself overwhelmed with debt regardless of your good intentions. As quick as a flash your "in-go" and "out-go" are completely out of whack.

So when "it" hits the fan, what is the first item we cut back on—that's right—savings, or even more concerning we withdraw from our savings and 401(k) accounts, or increase our pension payouts, or borrow money, or perhaps even consider declaring bankruptcy. Unless quick and decisive action is taken, you will quickly fall into an unrecoverable downward financial spiral; or, even worse, you will be forced to go back to work. Please, please don't let this scenario describe you someday. So how can you avoid it? No, I can't manufacture or send you money, but I can give you a powerful tool, which requires your financial sleuthing abilities, to determine whether you will have sufficient income to fund the retirement of your dreams, or at least one without need or want when it's your time to end your working life and retire.

4. The Financial Holy Grail: The Self-Perpetuating Retirement

The Self-Perpetuating Retirement model is actually a combination of the best bits and pieces of the other three financial models; we sometimes call this "cherry-picking." Budgets are forward looking documents, and as such they are best estimates, or sometimes "best guesses," of how the future and our plans will converge, and with diligence and focus, ultimately yield the expected outcome. This is a fancy way of saying that budgets are really just best guesses, or estimates, of future conditions that might or might not materialize. Governments have overruns because of unanticipated events; but when this happens a government, in its infinite wisdom, just writes these losses or bad investments off without a thought or concern and dips right back into the "pool" that seems filled with endless funds. How do they do it? By printing money, of course, because in the United States only the federal government can print money, alas we cannot. So, budgets can be wildly inaccurate, sometimes we "low balled" because we were working with inaccurate or incomplete information, or we even did it purposely to make things appear better than they are. Perhaps we were overly optimistic about the growth of our funds, or how much income we expected to receive, or how much we needed to spend to maintain our pre-retirement standard of living, causing us to make expenditures appear to match income; or maybe we were fooling ourselves and overestimating income so it would appear to match expenditures, any or all of these actions can cause substantial inaccuracies in our calculations causing us to play catch-up or to fall back. The truth of the matter is that some, if not many, of us know, in the back of our minds, that our financial expectations are unrealistic and we convince ourselves that we will adjust things up or down as conditions warrant—so we think and so we hope.

Just what is a "self-perpetuating retirement" and why is it important? It's the cornerstone of successful retirements and the remedy for every retiree's greatest fear; that is, running out of money before running out of life. Scientists, inventors, and tinkerers have long sought to build perpetual motion machines of all types, which would run forever without an external energy source. While many have tried, all have failed—except, of course, the tricksters and con artists who occasionally dazzle us with "Rube Goldberg" type machines for fun and profit—because even the concept of perpetual motion violates every principle we know about the natural world. In fact, Newton's first law is "a body in motion or at rest will tend to stay in motion or at rest, unless acted on by an outside force"—something we all learned in high school science class. But, if we put the object in motion, then, according to Newton, it should stay in motion forever. Right? Wrong. The second part of the law states "unless acted on by an outside force," which on earth is gravity and friction, and they are always present on our planet.

JUST STEP INTO MY TENT

Ladies and gentlemen and children of all ages, welcome to the greatest show on earth and step into my tent—for just the price of a ticket I can show you how to suspend the laws of man and nature. I will demonstrate my perpetual motion money machine; and no, the U.S. Mint is not inside my tent, young man, and this perpetual motion money machine is now available to everyone for three easy payments of $1.25 million dollars; but wait, if you act now, I will make one payment for you, so for just $2.5 million dollars you can guarantee that you will never run out of money, and that your children and their children will enjoy the fruits of your labor in perpetuity! So who will be the first to purchase my perpetual motion money machine? Does that sound too good to be true? Well, it is both "good" and "true." Provided you only withdraw what is replaced by safe investments usually pegged at around 4 percent per annum, or what you can "safely" earn without risk of losing principal and you keep total expenditures at or below $100,000 per year, or maybe even less depending on your available savings, investments, and, of course, your retirement lifestyle.

A self-perpetuating, or a "financially sustainable retirement," is not a static "hold on to your money and live off the land in a shack" approach to money management, but rather it is a dynamic process which allows individuals, who are prepared to live within their available financial "envelope," to achieve their personal goals and lifestyles without significantly depleting their financial assets.

PRINTING MONEY: WHAT A NOVEL IDEA

Remember my "perpetual motion money machine" allegory? So what if you came into my tent and ponied up $2.5 million to buy my money-spewing perpetual motion machine; would that have been a good retirement investment decision or a bad retirement investment decision? Now, let's assume you need approximately $100,000 per annum to cover your real annual expenses and to fully fund your retirement—how long would your money last? And the answer is…into perpetuity or more simply, forever. Assuming, of course, you earn at least 4 percent in interest or dividends from investments and 401(k) accounts, supplemented by fixed pensions or other retirement vehicles that taken together would yield $100,000 of income per annum. And, if your annual disbursements are $100,000 per year or less, your principal will remain intact; in other words, it would survive you and anyone else covered under the $100,000 umbrella. The 4 percent number is itself another general rule of thumb and assumes (always dangerous when dealing with investments and money) that if you annually spend 4 percent of your principal, the remaining principal will earn on average 4 percent per year or more, effectively cancelling out the impact of any withdrawals. There is a big "if" in assuming your assets will in fact earn 4 percent, especially in the artificially created "low-interest" environment we find ourselves in today.

WHY SOME DARE TO RETIRE AND OTHERS FEAR TO RETIRE

Some of us put off retirement by ignoring its many possibilities because we are locked in to the rhythms of working life—the structure of work and the structured relationships that work provides—and perhaps fear the loneliness or intimacy, depending on individual circumstances, that retirement presents; but, most of all we dread leaving a life we know for a life yet to be experienced. The more optimistic among us often embrace the concept of retirement and want to retire, but become reluctant retirees due to "separation anxiety." This anxiety isn't necessarily about a separation from colleagues, but from the security of regular paychecks; even though we very well might have sufficient savings and pensions to maintain our current standards of living into retirement. Unfortunately, even the thought of outliving our incomes causes some potential retirees to behave like misers, afraid to spend a penny for fear they will live in rags when retired, if they ever do. So they end up working until the "music stops." Yet others are addicted to their high salaried jobs and the status and perks these jobs bestow upon them. Some of us measure our worth based on the amount of money we earn, or put too high a value on dollars and not enough on living a fulfilling life free from the obligations of work. Some are just not willing to trade income and status for the freedom to control the rest of their lives. Absent financial necessity, the decision to retire pits the value of money against the value of time. But, the value of time decreases as more time becomes available to us. The question to ask ourselves is, "What is more important to me?" Is it my income, or the time and the freedom to allocate my time any way I choose? Put another way, are you willing to trade income for "time"? If the answer comes back that time is more valued than income, then you are ready to retire; if it is the opposite, that income has a higher value than additional personal time, then remaining in the world of work is your future... at least for now.

Yet to some, the calculus is not that simple; they can't retire because they have not saved enough to fund even a modest retirement and continually kick the "retirement can" down the road, hoping someday they can stop kicking and start living their retirement dreams. Yet others might never experience the freedom of retirement as a result of late starts, working in low wage jobs or for employers that do not offer retirement plans or pensions, or because of family obligations. Finally, some are worried their lifestyles will be diminished or compromised as will their places in the community; they believe it is essential to live as they always have or even more grandly in their retirement years, and so they opt to keep accumulating for that day, which will probably never come. However some of us choose not to view retirement solely as a financial transaction, but as the life-changing event it really is, or even as something to be eagerly anticipated, savored, and tasted at its height of readiness, because that is what retirement is all about. Retirement offers us the joy of discovery and exploration, a chance to reconnect to the world and our families on our terms; and that is what a financially secure retirement offers us, the confidence to not want to know what is around the next corner, to desire uncertainty, to find the road to a place called "Retirement" and see where it takes us—enjoying the ride all the way down the road.

FINANCIALLY SUSTAINABLE RETIREMENTS MUST DO'S AND SHOULD DO'S

- Lifestyle and income must be compatible; that is, our income must be self-renewing in financial times, both good and bad—it cannot be a "fair weather friend." In other words, the cash flow must either come from defined benefit plans and pensions like Social Security and many other government-style pensions or annuities, or from non-volatile investment streams. What we receive or what is distributed to us monthly or annually must be balanced with our expenditures and we can't allow "lifestyle creep"—that is, letting our wants and desires overwhelm good judgment with the consequent implosion of our heretofore carefully planned financial strategies.

- We must not finance a self-perpetuating retirement on credit cards, on the installment plan, or through borrowing, and we must never raid our "rainy day" fund if it isn't truly raining—debt is the last thing we want to "grow" or leave to our children.

- If at all possible, do not carry a mortgage into retirement. Paying off our mortgages before retirement was almost a given in previous generations, but now an increasing number of households are carrying their mortgage debt into retirement. According to the Federal Reserve's Survey of Consumer Finances, almost 1 in every 3, or 29 percent, of retired households had housing debt in 2010, up from 16.7 percent in 1989, and more alarmingly, the number of households headed by people 75 and over with a mortgage went from 5.8 percent in 1989 to over 20 percent in 2010. The "go-go" fast-money era apparently enticed retirees to trade up to bigger homes or to take equity lines of credit—a big mistake because now many soon-to-be retirees will be heading into retirement with substantial mortgage obligations at a time when we are faced with decreasing retirement incomes.[12] If we want truly sustainable retirements, we must keep both our structured, or fixed, known costs down, and our wants and desires under control. Establish an annual budget that will keep assets safe from our whims and fancies; yes, that vacation to Tahiti looks like a good deal, but can you spend $8,000 for a two week binge vacation without jeopardizing the "sustainability" thing? You might be like the Little Dutch Boy who saved the town by putting his finger in the dike, except in your case, the hole will get bigger and bigger and the water, in the form of money, will rush through and take you with it—or as bankers like to say put you "underwater," pun absolutely intended. Rather, seek travel, hobbies, activities, and interests that don't have high entry and maintenance costs and there are many of these; please don't tell me you can't find one.

- Not saving enough is a sustainability nonstarter, as is believing the "world is your friend," or that good times will roll once again, or if we spend it, it will come. These are all recipes for bankruptcy and heart-break—we might as well go to Las Vegas, bet it all at the blackjack table, and get it over quickly. The net result is that we may become a burden on our children. Or we may have to liquidate assets or go back to work—neither option is very appealing now is it?

- Absence of adequate health care coverage and/or insurance could cause more financial damage than the illness itself. This is the number one reason for bankruptcy, all our savings could be completely wiped out if we are uninsured or under-insured and face a serious health issue. This is particularly worrisome for those retiring prior to Medicare eligibility.

- Stay the course if we want sustainable retirements, and don't retire before we have accumulated enough assets to "play" the sustainability game. While many of us dream of retiring early, probably starting in the womb, some of us are not financially ready to fund those additional years, let alone to have sustainable retirements, since our later years are our highest earning ones—for most of us. Additionally, those added years could be used to "top off" our pension if we have one, give us more time to save, and receive a higher payout from Social Security.

- Be aware of the impact of inflation, especially on fixed income retirements—it's being kept artificially low now, but down the road who knows how high it will go?

- Prepare an estate plan and trusts that can protect your assets so that your survivors, including spouse/partner and/or children, don't have to turn over hefty chunks of "your" hard-earned money to the government, or even better don't have to fight over "leavings."

ARE YOU REALLY READY TO FINANCE YOUR RETIREMENT?

Okay, we have visited most of the possible financial catastrophes that can befall us if we play fast and loose with our retirement finances, as well as many of the possible advantages that truly financially self-perpetuating retirements offer. The optimal time to perform an in-depth financial retirement readiness review is when retirement is in sight and mind, and not after submitting our retirement papers and writing that not so friendly "I'm out of here" letter. If the retirement endgame is looming, this is your best and last opportunity to objectively analyze and then determine whether or not you have sufficient income to sustain pre-retirement lifestyles into and through your retirement years—however long that may be. The results from this up-close-and-personal financial review will be the ultimate test of financial viability, and whether or not you can join the "sustainability club" and live out your retirement without the fear of outliving your money. Unfortunately, retirement's Holy Grail is sought by many but ultimately reached by few. Accomplishing this rare feat requires us to hit the books—the financial books, that is, because this could very likely be the most important financial decision of your life, and a simple miscalculation could literally leave you adrift in a sea of debt, disillusionment, and despair—and that is not what retirement is supposed to be about.

THE FINANCIAL READINESS AUDIT

The audit approach, while not conceptually difficult, requires attention to detail, time, patience, and simple math skills. It takes the guesswork out of the "how much money you need to retire" question and avoids being blinded by "fortune cookie optimism" and overestimating your financial assets and capacities. The best way to achieve an accurate assessment is not to guess forward, as budgets do, but rather to look backward. While we can interpret the past, it is difficult to alter it unless we are attempting to fool ourselves—which is not in our best interests at this critical time in our lives. You can accomplish this by comparing your financial "bottom line(s)" pre- and post-retirement. For example, if you weren't "income positive" in the year immediately preceding retirement what makes you think you will be "income positive" in your initial retirement year?

The Financial Readiness Audit is a "look back" and a "look forward" financial assessment. First, you will be asked to analyze your current financial status; in other words, the pre-retirement costs of running your household. During this stage, you'll also be determining if that was in financial balance with the "available income" from all sources.

Then, you will be tasked with estimating both the expenses and income required to finance your first year, post-retirement. Will that be in financial balance? This is one of the most critical data points in the entire retirement decision process, because it will let you know if you are *really financially ready to retire*. While you can fudge the data or put your rose-colored glasses on, the only ones you will be fooling are you and your family.

The financial review should be conducted at least 6 months prior to making your final retirement decision. I purposely put the focus on "expenses" rather than "income," and on balancing actual annual expenses with income, not the other way around. The reasoning behind this shift is actually quite simple: expenses are easier to control than income. In other words, we can determine what we buy, when we buy it, and how much we spend for it, but we can't control (for the most part) how much we will receive from our various investments, pensions, and 401(k) accounts—although pensions do tend to remain constant, sometimes too constant, with many not being pegged to inflation. So get out your spreadsheets, your calculator, and a pencil, and place it all on the table.

At the end of this process you will have the answer to one of retirement's most asked questions: "Will I be able to maintain my current lifestyle going into and throughout my retirement years?"

Whether you accept the reality it presents is completely up to you.

THE FINANCIAL READINESS AUDIT

PART I:
COMPLETING THE PRE-RETIREMENT FINANCIAL READINESS REVIEW

First, gather all financial documents for the most recent "completed" tax period for you and your partner/spouse and any other household member who contributes or expends money on behalf of the household for any purpose. This will include all local, state, and federal tax documents and accompanying attachments; all credit card and debit card statements from all sources, particularly the annual summaries; all bank account statements, annual pension statements, 401(k) statements, IRA statements, investment statements, and checkbook registers; tax receipts and statements, and any other financial documents that contain information regarding expenditures, payments, and income from all sources.

STEP 1:
Identify, List, Record and Total Gross Income from All Sources

Wages, bonuses, gratuities, business income; dividends/interest; tax refunds; Social Security Income, disability income, child support and/or alimony income, and other related income for all household members. Total and record all income from all sources for all household members.

STEP 2:
Collect, Review, and Record Annual Expenditures by Category

Household Expenses: mortgage/rent; home insurance, utilities including electric, gas, fuel oil, or any other heating source; water, sewer, trash; telecommunications, cable/satellite, Internet, mobile phones, other subscription services; lawn/garden; maintenance, repairs and supplies, appliances, furniture, cleaning services; and any other household expenses you might have, then enter annual totals in the appropriate box.

Transportation Expenses: vehicle payments, loans; auto insurance; fuel; repairs, maintenance and equipment; registration/license fees and taxes; commuting expenses, other-related public transportation, then enter annual totals in the appropriate box.

Consumables/Daily Living: groceries, paper goods, cleaning supplies, personal care items; clothing; dining out; veterinary and pet care; alcohol/wine; cigarettes/tobacco; other related, then enter annual totals in the appropriate box.

Health Expenses: health insurance; doctors/dentists/specialists; medicines, all out-of-pocket health-related expenses, over-the-counter supplies, equipment and prescriptions; health clubs; life insurance; other related; then enter annual totals in the appropriate box.

Vacation and Leisure Activities: vacations and vacation travel (aggregated costs); entertainment, movies, theater, and concerts; sports, hobby equipment and supplies; sports-related equipment; memberships and dues; special events; celebrations; parties; weddings; other related, and then enter annual totals in the appropriate box.

Taxes/Contributions/Loans: term payments; savings, investments; retirement plan contributions; gifts; charitable contributions; stocks, bonds, mutual funds, other related, and enter then annual totals in the appropriate box.

STEP 3:
Do the Math (Total All Expenditure Categories as Described)

First, calculate the totals for each category. Then, sum up all the category totals to obtain your "Total Annual Expenditures," and record it in the appropriate box.

THE FINANCIAL READINESS AUDIT

THE FINANCIAL READINESS AUDIT

PART II:
COMPLETING (ESTIMATED) FIRST-YEAR POST-RETIREMENT FINANCIAL READINESS REVIEW

Pick a hypothetical retirement date. Estimate and identify all available retirement income streams, or replacement income, for the anticipated 12-month period from all household sources. Please do not include one-time income boosts that often follow retirements, such as being paid for unused vacation and/or sick time.

STEP 1:
Estimate, Identify, Record, and Total All Retirement Income from All Sources

Call your retirement account administrators or use online tools to calculate what your income flow will be once retired—you will have to provide a real or theoretical retirement date and identify all available retirement assets, such as savings, pensions, 401(k) accounts, IRAs, investments, and any other hidden stashes. Total and record the gross income amounts in the appropriate boxes and sum the totals.

STEP 2:
Estimate, Collect, Review, and Record Annual Household Expenses by Category for the Selected 12-Month Period

Work off of your prior year expense pattern. Some expenses (like commuting) might very well go down, while others, such as leisure and vacation, might indeed go up. Various retirement experts have estimated that post-retirement cost-of-living could be reduced by 20 to 30 percent, while others estimate no appreciable cost difference. In other words, depending on who is pontificating at the moment, you need anywhere from 70 percent of pre-retirement income, all the way up to 100 percent, to maintain your post-work retirement lifestyle. In reality, these numbers cannot be generalized, since it depends entirely on personal circumstances; and life-after-work expectations.

STEP 3:
Do the Math (Total All Estimated Post-Retirement Expenditure Categories as Described)

First, calculate the totals for each category. Then, sum up all the category totals to obtain your "Total Annual Expenditures," and record it in the appropriate box.

ANALYSIS AND CONCLUSIONS

Subtract actual Annual Expenses from Annual Income for the identified Pre-Retirement Year and do the same for the Estimated Retirement Year." If income exceeds expenses in both these years, pick an actual retirement date. If you find yourself a bit underwater for the projected retirement year, some serious thinking is required—the last thing you want to do is carry significant debt into your retirement years.

So, what are your options? First, you can bring your expenditures in line with your income, and then follow the above rules and requirements. Second, you can keep working (if that is an option) and start packing away the savings and building your retirement assets, getting yourself closer to full Social Security and Medicare (if you're not there yet). These actions just might relieve you of some financial obligations and put you back into income-positive territory. Third, you can retire and supplement your retirement income by working part-time. Fourth, you can shed financial obligations like a second home or third car—any expensive toys and activities you were able to fund previously by accumulating debt. Please don't be cavalier with your definitions of one-time or non-repeating income or expenses. Then, you can revisit the Pre-Retirement Financial Sustainability Audit, and this time, you just might get a passing grade!

GROSS ANNUAL INCOME (ALL SOURCES)

	Pre-Retirement	Post-Retirement
Salaries/Wages/Gratuities/Business Income		
Social Security/Disability		
Investments/Dividends/Interest/Tax Refunds		
Alimony/Child Support/Gifts		
All Other Income		
TOTAL ANNUAL INCOME		

ANNUAL EXPENSES (ALL SOURCES)

	Pre-Retirement	Post-Retirement
HOUSEHOLD EXPENSES:		
Mortgage/Rent/Insurance		
Utilities/Cable/Internet/Telecommunications		
Water/Sewer/Trash/Landscaping		
Repairs/Maintenance/Supplies/Appliances/Furniture		
All Other Related		
TRANSPORTATION EXPENSES:		
Auto Loans/Insurance/Fees/Taxes		
Fuel/Repair/Maintenance/Equipment		
Commuting Expenses/Public Transportation		
All Other Related		
CONSUMABLES/DAILY LIVING:		
Groceries/Paper Goods/Cleaning Supplies		
Clothing/Personal Care/Tobacco/Alcohol		
Dining Out/Veterinary And Pet Care		
All Other Related		

	Pre-Retirement	Post-Retirement
HEALTH EXPENSES:		
Health Insurance/Medicare		
Out-Of-Pocket Medical/Dental Expenses		
Prescriptions/Over-The-Counter Drugs/Supplies		
All Other Related		
VACATION AND LEISURE ACTIVITIES:		
Travel/Vacations		
Entertainment/Hobbies		
Recreation/Sports/Memberships/Dues		
All Other Related		
TAXES, CONTRIBUTIONS, LOANS:		
Federal/State/Local/Taxes/Special Assessments		
Social Security/Investments/Savings/Retirement Contributions		
Loans/Credit Card Payments		
Alimony/Child Support/Gifts/Charitable Contributions		
All Other Related		
TOTAL ANNUAL EXPENSES:		

TOTALS

	Pre-Retirement	Post-Retirement
Total Annual Income		
Total Annual Expenses		
Total Annual Surplus/Deficit		

THE FINANCIAL READINESS AUDIT

CHAPTER 10

■ ■ ■ ■ ■ ■

For Every Exit There's an Entrance

If you haven't the strength to impose your own terms
on life, you must accept the terms it offers you.
—T. S. Eliot

To accomplish great things we must not only act,
but also dream, not only plan, but also believe.
—Anatole France

THE CYCLE OF LIFE

Our life journey begins the instant we draw our very first breath outside
the comfort of the womb when we are literally thrust into this world.
From that moment our lives become a series of passages and transitions
because neither time, nor the earth, nor age stands still. Some of these
life transitions are easy and almost imperceptible, some are more known
to others than us, some are obviously consequential, while yet others are
hard fought and sometimes the outcomes are in doubt. We metamor-
phose from mewling, diaper-laden infants to upright take-charge tod-
dlers; from innocent children to brooding, hormone-fueled teenagers;

from teenager to responsible (or not) adults; from single life to perhaps a marriage or partnership; and from partner to parent and familyhood. Life is on track, so we think. We work, we struggle, we succeed, we divorce, we fail, but yet we endure and overcome. Our progeny, if we have any, leave the nest and repeat the cycle when their time comes, and the beat still goes on.

MEET AND GREET OUR AGING SELVES

But another, perhaps more subtle and challenging transition also awaits us; it is almost imperceptible at first, moving in slow motion in the beginning, but then it appears to speed up as we continue to view ourselves in the mirror of life—we are aging. We all respond differently to our aging selves. Some of us accept aging as the natural order of things and are comfortable with our aging selves, as our bodies and minds slowly but inevitably do what they were programmed to do. Others try to mask those wrinkles or ignore the aches and pains. Still others fight their aging selves or go to war with their bodies, going to extremes such as plastic surgery to give the appearance—if not the reality—of youth or engaging in extreme sports and dangerous pastimes and activities to prove they are just as capable and "heroic" at 70 as they were at 25.

But age has a way of catching up to us regardless of how hard we try to outrun it. We resist the temptation that retirement offers because in our heart of hearts we fervently believe, rightly or not, that retirement is surrender and should be pushed off with every fiber of our being— because we never, never want to admit, to ourselves at least, that life as we know it could possibly come to an end. Life is a rat race but at least it's our rat race, and this, after all, is what separates us from the Sun City, Land of the Living Dead retirees, or so we reason. But the world starts closing in on us, eventually we tire of the pressures, the deadlines, the meetings, the "same old, same old" that work now offers after forty or so years of the daily grind. And then a new life picture slowly emerges and this one is in living color with the words "Liberation Day" constantly scrolling through our minds. Is this our brave new world, our happy place where we are in charge of us? A world in which we can decide what to do and when to do it? But what turned us into retirement believers; when did that last straw finally topple the pile? Or is this merely a conversion of convenience, an escape *from* something rather than *to* something. Is it truly real and heartfelt? The tipping point from work to retirement usually comes with the profound realization that retirement is not an ending, but a new beginning, and that the world of retirement is not to be feared but welcomed; the sanctity of our futures will not be diminished by retirement but rather preserved and enhanced. It is at that very moment our journey begins, when we fully realize retirement is the natural order of things, part of life's evolution, then our transition into retirement begins, while we well know it will be neither easy nor without challenges or setbacks; but understand, above all, that it will be a compelling trip. You see, most of us succumb to retirement's siren song, some more forcefully and affirmatively than others, while some, like myself, are more timid and questioning, but at some point we "learn to stop worrying and love retirement," my thanks to *Dr. Strangelove*.

OUR BRIDGE TO ANYWHERE

While many transitions occur throughout our lives, the retirement transition occurs only once, and thankfully so—the road ahead is our final destination, it's a dead end of sorts, so make the journey matter to you and to your significant others. As we move from one life stage to another we must build bridges from where we have been to where we are going, and in order to build these bridges and make them strong enough to carry us across we should or even must:

- Understand what we are leaving and what we are going toward because retirement is not about who you were but about who you are about to become.
- Accept that life in retirement will be different than life at work, and accept the reality that this transition from work to retirement will not be flawless nor easy, but that there will be stumbles and setbacks and that our desired end is worth some struggle and angst.

- Learn from our mistakes and the mistakes of others—talk with those who have preceded us, don't reinvent the known or suffer the slings and arrows of the journey on your own if someone else has a map. Remember, easier is better.
- Have a vision of where you want to go and who you want to be when you get there. For if you don't know where you are going, then how will you find it?
- Plan, plan, plan.
- Accept the old saw that life and retirement are not about the destination, but about the journey.
- Be comfortable with and actively seek the unfamiliar and the unknown…walk new ground.
- Continually explore the three powers: the power of possibility, the power of self-determination, and the power to do something simple or new every day.
- Build on the past, take what works and discard what hinders—it's a new life, a new day; make your retirement personal, one size does not fit all.

WE'RE NOT IN KANSAS ANYMORE: BEWARE THE VELVET PRISON

There is a second, and potentially even more emotionally charged transition, that is oftentimes considered and debated concurrently with our retirement decisions. We think, "in for a dime in for a dollar." If we are going to retire anyway, we no longer have to live near our work, so why not move to a warmer climate where we can be outdoors the entire year, or where our friends have moved, or to that state with lower taxes where our retirement income will go further, or where houses and communities are specifically designed for "us" seniors.

There is something alluring about moving from our ancestral homes to places that are warm and welcoming, populated by people who act and look just like us, where every day looks like the day before, where every house looks like every other house, where the men wear plaid and drive golf carts instead of Mustangs and motorcycles, and the women wear tennis skirts without ever having been on a tennis court, let alone played a single set. The image, if not the reality, of these active adult communities is almost irresistible, and for some they might just be perfect.

MOVING HOME AND HEARTH

The moral of this little story is to think long and hard about where you want to live after retirement. Indeed, there are many considerations to take into account. My wife and I have been discussing them, just as many of you might have. We are not immune to the higher cost of living prevalent in some states compared to others. It is tempting to contemplate putting more money in our pockets by moving to a state or community with a significantly lower tax burden, or to one of those that actually welcomes retirees by not taxing our pensions and offering significant property tax relief to seniors. It is likewise appealing to contemplate living in a climate that would allow us to pursue our outdoor interests almost the whole year round, and when you consider that the cost of living in some of these "warm wonderlands" is significantly less than in some other areas, it is a very compelling proposition to consider. But, then again, we realize we would be leaving our memories, friends, and perhaps our families behind, we would be leaving the known for the unknown, we would be leaving our familiar places of worship, the activities we so enjoy, the clubs and the causes we are members of or support, but most of all we would be leaving our comfort zones. While I am not a fan when it comes to active adult communities (or whatever they call themselves), I do understand their appeal and the benefits they offer. But—and there is always a "but"—we must fully consider the emotional side of the equation. Our roots where we live have grown long and deep, much like the proverbial oak, and it will be emotionally challenging, no it will be a wrenching experience, for any one of us who ultimately accepts the siren song of starting over in a new location. But at least it will be our choice for our reasons, whatever they may be.

SOMETIMES YOU JUST HAVE TO BREAK FROM THE PAST

There is no doubt that leaving our homes is in many of our futures, one way or the other, and I would rather do it voluntarily and on my own terms. The simple truth is that many of us live in homes that do not readily accommodate our aging selves and the ravages of aging that some of us fall prey to. While our houses may have been ideal for raising children, located in safe neighborhoods with good schools, an array of recreational opportunities, excellent medical facilities, and close to shopping and mountains and lakes or cities chock-full of cultural opportunities, they might no longer meet our needs as we age. Our homes and communities, for the fortunate among us, offer us everything but the ability to "age out" successfully, when the time comes.

My biggest personal concern, and perhaps yours as well, is finding a home where we can live out the rest of our lives without moving yet again. As hard as it may be, I know that at some time or another, I will have to clean out my "man basement." Sound familiar, boys? No, it is not a "man cave," rather it is a storage facility for all my tools, shelves loaded with spare parts for every occasion, storage for long unneeded papers, records, and mementos, old clothes we promised ourselves we would once again fit into, our kids' old toys which are now being happily used by their kids when they visit, our "toys" and paraphernalia—you get the point. Moving to a new location would require us to utter the dreaded word "downsize." You see, we have emotional attachments to our homes and the "things" of our life. Moving means leaving all those memories behind, requiring us to choose between what is kept and what is discarded, to leave our friends and what is familiar, but most of all to leave our children and grandchildren, or perhaps move closer to them. But yet it must be done at some point; so I promised to clean out the basement, and no, I didn't have my fingers crossed, but I didn't set a date either, now did I?

Leaving anything behind is extremely hard, whether it is our youth or our memories, which indeed remain in our hearts and minds wherever we are. This emotional break with the past, while necessary, is very soul consuming. It is our acknowledgement that life as we knew it will be no more, but that life ahead will be different in so many ways, and even more, it will be getting us closer to our dreams, our newfound freedoms as well as our biggest fears of leaving our loved ones and families, not only geographically but literally. Above all, be cognizant of Dorothy's mantra after she got what she wished for, "There's no place like home. There's no place like home"; but, then again, home is where our heart and hearth are and our heart and hearth are wherever we live.

RETIREMENT IS LIFE WITHOUT TRAINING WHEELS

When all is said and done, retirement is about engagement—engagement with life, engagement with family, engagement with others, engagement with destiny and adventure. We typically live every day like the day before because routines are comforting, they help organize our lives, as do the roles we have been assigned, learned, or replicated from childhood. Roles and routines are coping mechanisms to help protect us from change and possible failure; but in reality they might also protect us from happiness and discovery and from ourselves. Or, perhaps our jobs or careers have beaten us down to a shell of our former selves, and our inner voices are constantly wishing and hoping for something, anything, to give us hope and to raise us up from the "pit of despair" and provide a new start and a new perspective on life. *Retirement is the answer*, we quickly think and believe; we can start life over. *Yes, you can*, the inner voice responds, *but this time you are doing it without training wheels*. Imagine hitting the brakes when a deer crosses paths with your car, speedometer pegged at 75 mph—the forces on your body will thrust you into the windshield and steering wheel (just ask Newton), and the only things that keep you from becoming one with the vehicle are your seatbelt and the airbag, which you profoundly hope will deploy. It does, thankfully, so you are battered and bruised and shaken but you walk away physically unscathed at least; however, the memory of that three second event will last a lifetime. That is what retirement will be like if we are not prepared; that is, wearing our seatbelts and having airbags that will absorb some of the shock of the "life collision" called retirement. You leave work for the last time with a spring in your step and joy in your heart. Something you are intimately familiar with and have been doing for your entire adult life for better or worse, for richer or poorer, in sickness or in health is now over—for weren't some of us really married to our work and doesn't retirement feel like a divorce on some level? But we believe—or hope—that retirement will be the answer to our prayers, to our dreams, to our profound unhappiness. This may seem overly dramatic, but retirements are neither cures for what emotionally ails us nor escape capsules. Unhappy people will have unhappy retirements, and pessimists need not apply; other, more profound life changes must occur prior to the retirement announcement, if we are to have successful retirements because, repeat after me, *retirements don't just happen, we have to make them happen.*

RETIREMENT DOESN'T CHANGE LIVES, WE CHANGE OUR LIVES

We can't will a retirement to happen by thinking about it, hoping for it, dreaming about it, or expecting to win enough money to fund it at the blackjack tables in Las Vegas. We have to do something about it to make it happen, and the sooner we start, the more possible it becomes. While our dreams move us toward retirement by envisioning what it can be, we must above all remain realistic, otherwise we just might find disappointment rather than the "promised land" we had so hoped for. Contrary to popular opinion, retirement will not change your life—you have to change your life. Anyone can retire, but can you retire to the life you expected to have or believed you were entitled to? There are always distractions, lost opportunities, and reasons why our retirements are less than perfect or not as fulfilling as hoped and dreamed. Don't expect perfection and then you won't be disappointed. Do expect challenges and joys—times of happiness and sadness, for isn't that the way of life? The trick to life is not to let disappointment or setbacks defeat us—the victory is so much the sweeter when we can overcome obstacles and still reach our personal "promised land," whatever that is for us. If we wait for certainty, or more money, or more things, or for the children to stop being so needy or to graduate from college, or for that perfect moment, whenever that is, we might just never retire.

Many of us literally plunged into the retirement "dream" unprepared and unacquainted with retirement's new and untested life forces, its customs and its challenges. In life there is almost always a corollary downside and retirement is no exception. These downsides usually result from emotional un-readiness; inadequate preparation and planning; over-promising and under-delivering on our personal goals, such as not losing the extra weight, or not taking care of our health or staying intellectually and socially engaged as we had promised ourselves and our partners; under budgeting and overspending; being out of sync with our partners or significant others because retirements not built on mutual respect and common understandings will falter. These are just some of the slings and arrows that can quickly doom our retirements. Avoiding the downsides, no matter how small or insignificant you believe them to be, is truly the difference between successful and failed retirements. It's better to find the downsides before they find you and, as they say in the Old West, "head 'em off at the pass."

Our life and work experiences may or may not serve us well in retirement; some will carry over and some work lessons will have to be relearned, renewed, and refreshed. Life in retirement is different from life at work, make no mistake about that. Crossing over from work to retirement demands a "life reset," a total transformation, but first we must let go of our former selves and our former lives at work. We must recast ourselves, reshape our lives and our very existences. We need to reconsider those old dogmas, perspectives, and beliefs about what was important in our lives at work, and learn to live anew, to understand, finally, that joy, acceptance, serendipity, optimism, passion, and purpose are truly the fruits of the "retirement tree." We must all turn our energy and focus toward a new quest—a quest for purpose, for passion, for introspection, and for retrospection, and most of all, for compassion for our families and fellow travelers because it's *our* time; or, as Denis Waitley tells us, "Expect the best, plan for the worst, and prepare to be surprised."

RETIREMENT: WHEN IT'S OUR TIME

And then we realize, the life journey begun such a short time ago—marriage, our first real job, our first child, our first promotion—is now swiftly approaching its final destination. The best is yet to come, we confidently assure ourselves. I will get that promotion or raise; after all, I am the last one standing, the most experienced and knowledgeable one left. You look around and all you see are 20- and 30-somethings; you are indeed the last one standing—but it's not over yet, or is it? "I am not ready to retire," you think; but, it's not entirely up to you. You can read the writing on the wall and take the initiative and cut the best retirement deal possible, or you can hold out as long as possible and suffer the subtle and not so subtle hints that retirement is in "your" best interest, enduring the humiliation of being assigned to a much younger manager with significantly fewer years of seniority, or being given all those mind-numbing tasks usually done by clerks and secretaries. It's your choice, but I know the one I would take, how about you? Yet you still equivocate, saying to yourself that they "need me," or I need more money in my retirement account before I can retire. Are you lying to yourself or are you just concocting excuses to avoid making the decision to retire; or is it that you are afraid of retiring because you won't know what to do with yourself? You continue to equivocate, If only they understood that I'm afraid, but frankly "they" don't care. You see, they could hire two younger, better-educated, more tech savvy employees with your salary. Finally, a retirement incentive is announced, perhaps aimed just at you, and you have had enough of the humiliation, and besides the extra money will allow you to live a comfortable retirement, and so you accept the offer and the opportunity. You are now retired, but to what?

You have choices about how to approach life after work, you can: (1) do what the "experts," pundits, advertisers, and world of commerce and its hordes of hucksters trying to make money off the backs of our nation's retirees tell us to do, and accept their recommendations on how to behave, what to buy, and where to go; or (2) create and shape your own retirements based on your desires, needs, wants, physical and financial abilities, hopes, and dreams—not the dreams of others as filtered through movies and the media; or (3) remain passive and let life and its events push you first one way and then another, much like the rise and fall of the oceans at land's end.

You see, our time has come—no, not to just retire, but to retire with passion and purpose, for those of us already retired to awaken from our "retirement stupors"; we were lured from our dreams much like Lorelei lured sailors onto the rocks and shoals with her plaintive songs, ending their dreams forever. We need to ignore those false promises of wealth and a life of ease—move outside of our comfort zones and go where we have never been before. It's time to stop dreaming of what we want to do or should do in retirement and start living and doing it. *But why should I do this?* you might ask. I would answer because time is passing and without purpose there is no meaning and without meaning there is no joy and without joy all that remains is sadness.

I invite all my "brothers and sisters," all those retired or soon to be retired, to join me on this life journey of exploration and discovery to test our physical limits, to challenge our intellects, and to confront belief systems and dogmas that have grown old and tired and to answer the question that has plagued probably most of my fellow travelers for some time, *"What are we going to do with the rest of our lives?"*

CHAPTER 11

■ ■ ■ ■ ■ ■

What's Your Retirement Personality?

All changes, even the most longed for, have
their melancholy; for what we leave behind is
part of ourselves; we must die to one life before
we can enter another.

—ANATOLE FRANCE

The greatest weapon against stress is our ability
to choose one thought over another.

—WILLIAM JAMES

NOT EVERYONE BELIEVES RETIREMENT IS A GOOD THING

Why is this even here? You might ask. We all want to retire—don't we? Well, not necessarily, because not all of us actually look upon retirement as being a good thing. There is always an adjustment period with some of us taking longer than others; and still yet others will never reconcile with retirement. Some of us don't really know what to do with all that newfound time or how to positively and creatively fill the void that the absence of work leaves in our lives. This adjustment period is not unusual; but some of us just never adjust, or adjust in negative ways with anger and a constant sense of loss and mourning for our previous lives, perhaps like losing a dear friend. So, how we individually deal with both the prospect and the actuality of retirement encompasses a wide range of emotional responses going from hope to dread, expectancy to hesitancy. So is retirement a dear friend or a despised foe?

If we remain mired in old work habits, beliefs, and behaviors, needing the certainty of structure and knowing what we will be doing this day and every other day; and are financially, or emotionally, dependent on the security of a paycheck, then retirement will be a constant struggle, at least, in the beginning. That is, absent a personal epiphany or the willingness to let go of our previous working life. In these situations there is little chance that such retirements will succeed with every day becoming a search for meaning and identity; or at a more basic level, the self-worth that the world of work previously provided. Life is full of self-fulfilling prophesies, so don't even think about bringing old baggage on this journey to the "other side of work."

Our initial feelings about retirement are often dictated by the "how" rather than the "why" of retirement. Some of us were downsized or forced to retire, others enticed to retire, yet others retired happily. If we perceive retirement as a punishment or as a statement about our personal value, as a "dead end" with no place to go, or as a life failure because we weren't smart enough, needed enough, or wanted enough to be asked to remain in the workplace, then it will take a very long time to come to terms with our new life, if we ever do. If, on the other hand, we lusted after retirement or jumped at the opportunity to take the retirement incentive because it allowed us to retire sooner rather than later, then retirement is more than welcomed—it is, indeed, considered a gift.

YOU GET OUT OF RETIREMENT WHAT YOU ARE PREPARED TO PUT IN

How you approach your retirement, how you respond to your retirement, how you behave in retirement, how you handle retirement, and ultimately how you live in retirement is really up to you. We all need to cultivate retirement friendly personalities well before we leave the workplace—it's like performing our own "personality transplant," would that be possible. These new "personalities" or more appropriately "life behaviors" must be consistent with our new lives and those of our spouses or partners who are joining us on this journey. Don't misjudge others; I have seen some of the most dedicated, hard-driving managers and employees, the ones you thought would have to be carried out feet first, not only accept retirement but actually transform themselves almost overnight and quite easily adjust to their new lives. Some treated retirement as their new "occupation" and took all the things that made them successful at work and applied them to making their retirements successful as well.

Conversely, I have seen individuals who should have retired decades ago—and in fact maybe they even did, but this retirement was "on the job,"—fall completely to pieces when their time came to leave the workplace. Their lives were probably as dreary and unrewarding at home as some of us find work because of marital problems, a house full of adult children and grandchildren living on the parental dole, or a myriad of other family dysfunctions that needed to be avoided; thus work was actually an escape from those negative life forces. For some of us, retirement, rather than being a joyous time, creates a basket full of anxiety because the last place someone forced into retirement wants to be is home. Work, at least, gave them some structure, a place to go every day and escape from unhappy circumstances, and it provided much needed socialization and comradeship. One really never knows what goes on behind a colleague's doors at home, no matter how much we banter about it, because we all tend to hide our inner fears and life secrets so we won't be placed in the class of people we often refer to as "losers."

Don't despair, we will be exploring several concepts and approaches to coping, adjusting, and responding to retirement and describing what types of "personalities" readily accept and adapt to change, to retirement, and to life; and what types tend to resist change and new circumstances. Indeed some of our "behaviors" that served us well at work might not serve us well in retirement. So, we either have to discard or modify some of those nonconforming "behaviors" once retired, or seek other options for "spilling-off" and channeling those behaviors in more positive ways—like a part-time job or volunteering. Indeed, it is the human dimension that ultimately determines whether our retirements will succeed or fail. And, this is right up there with financial mismanagement and our constant need to keep up with the "working Joneses" as a primary cause of self-destructing retirements.

LIFE AS WE KNEW IT, AND LIFE AS IT WILL BECOME

Whatever the reason(s) prompting you to retire, be assured your life will change—dramatically so. Even those looking forward to this time with every neuron in their bodies will go through the equivalent of withdrawal as we pass through one of life's most pivotal transitions.

The "act" of retiring, while important in and of itself, pales in comparison to the challenges and stresses retirees will confront when actually "living" in retirement, because sometimes our dreams and expectations have realities of their own. Life clearly will be different in retirement with most retirees optimistic that these differences will be positive while the pessimistic others will see tragedy looming behind every shadow. We can either worry ourselves sick about what we don't have, real or imagined (like enough money), or fret that our health will suddenly fall prey to every disease known to science, or that we will be bored to distraction. All these and many other concerns are indeed legitimate; but for most retirees, especially those who are, at least, welcoming and prepared for their retirements, a failed retirement is a low-probability outcome.

RETIREMENT CHANGES EVERYTHING

Any major life change, whether good, bad, or indifferent, causes stress, and retirement is not an exception because it requires a complete rethinking of how we want to live the rest of our lives and all the details that ride along with that decision. When we were working, much of our thinking was done for us. Work ordered our day; we knew when we had to wake up, where we had to go, what we were going to do that day, who we would report to, and when we would be getting back home. Our daily interactions, for the most part, were ordered as well by the organization chart so we knew whom we reported to, whom we could talk to, and what we were responsible for. In return, we were paid a salary or wage that put food on the proverbial table and kept a roof over our heads; for many of us health and dental insurance might have been provided along with a pension program of some type that offered some hope that we would have the means to finance our retirements.

OF COURSE, WE'LL GET TOGETHER
FOR LUNCH EVERY WEEK

Often we developed significant friendships at work. We ate with certain colleagues at the same time, in the same place every day, and probably knew more about their private lives, their children, and their fears than their spouses or partners did—we mourned together and celebrated together as the tragedies and the joys ebbed and flowed; we were always there for each other. We debated or even heatedly defended our political beliefs, our social beliefs, and who would win the Super Bowl or the World Series. This was our "work family," but it was more than that—they were our support, our shoulders to cry on, and a neutral port in a time of family war, a place to get solace not accusations, our work family was our safety net. And retirement, what many of us so longed to attain, regardless of our protestations that we will get together every week or we will stay in touch, rips all that away.

Many of us actually liked our jobs, what we did and its challenges, the people we met, the status and the perks, the social relationships that surrounded us—but retirement changes everything—it's like being born again but this time into a parallel universe, one we never even knew existed. So you asked why retiring would be a stressful event: now you know.

STARTING OVER

Life gives us few "Mulligans," or do-overs, but retirement surely is one of them. This is our chance, perhaps our last chance, as adults, to actually shape the rest of our lives by ourselves *for* ourselves; or perhaps just to let the fates guide us, which is not recommended by any means. At any rate, whether you take advantage of this opportunity or not it is entirely up to you.

Think of retirement as a trip of discovery, not one to distant lands, but rather a voyage to self-determine who you are and who you want to become. You are entering a new world, a new social order, one you neither created nor fully understand. "Where will I fit, and will I be accepted?" you silently ask yourself. In order to answer those questions we must first define how we see ourselves in the mirror of life, and this is not an easy task because many of us try to project a self-invented image of who we believe we are and how we want others to view us. In other words, we define ourselves and others define us as well; sometimes those definitions match and other times they deviate wildly. For example, we might see ourselves as patient and understanding while others, like perhaps our friends and colleagues, might view us as a screaming harridan; or, we see ourselves as compassionate and understanding while others think of us as a self-centered SOB, who would walk over anyone who got in the way. Now stay with me on this—it gets a little circular, almost like a dog chasing its tail. Our images create us, and we in turn create our images; but in the end, our false images crumble when confronted with the reality of how we behave toward others and how they respond to us, and not who we *want* to be or think we are. So whether we are accepted by others or not is ultimately based on imperfect perceptions of ourselves and the imperfect perceptions of us by others. Perhaps, in this case, a double negative equals a positive. Retirement gives us the opportunity to redefine ourselves, who we are and who we want to become—that is the gift that retirement gives us all. Unencumbered by the routines of life at work we can leave our baggage, old conceptions, and timeworn definitions of our "work selves" at retirement's threshold and redefine who we are and who we want to become. It's our life, it's our Mulligan—so use it or lose it.

A NEW PERHAPS BITTERSWEET REALITY AWAITS

Some of us never enjoyed our work, perhaps we worked solely out of financial necessity or we found the work and the work environment akin to Dante's *Inferno*. But, we may have found solace in our fellow sufferers and in the hope or knowledge that we would one day escape, and perhaps retirement is our escape—but an escape to what? Some of us will have regrets or misgivings about retiring, particularly if the decision was not fully under our control; let's say, our partner wanted us to retire, or the company or organization made it known that it was time to leave, or perhaps a retirement incentive made you jump too quickly. There is no inconsistency between retiring and having regrets about retiring; or even between being simultaneously happy and sad.

But, in the end—and please, please remember this—retirement is not about what you are leaving, but rather what you are *going to*. Don't look back because you can't go back—it won't be the same—instead remember the good times and bring them forward because that is where your future is.

OUR RETIREMENT PERSONALITIES— NATURE OR NURTURE

How we adapt or what we accept or reject, including our values, our beliefs, and our behaviors, is a function of two major life forces which to this day are being challenged, refuted, once again sustained, and refuted yet again—that is, nature versus nurture. In other words, it has been postulated that who we become—happy person or sad person, genius or jester, giver or taker, optimist or pessimist, and on and on—happens at the crossroads of nature and nurture. In other words the "naturists" among us believe how we respond to life is to a great extent hardwired into us at birth and passed on through our DNA from generation to generation, and that destiny and DNA are one in the same. Others, however, believe that "nurture" has the more profound influence on who and what we become, for as John Locke, the famous philosopher, opined over three hundred years ago, "we are all born with the same blank slate." This debate will never be resolved here, so let's just agree, for the sake of this discussion, that both nature and nurture are equally as important until proven otherwise.

Two ancient parables will demonstrate the nature versus nurture debate that has been ongoing for millennia.

The Scorpion and the Frog (Anonymous)

A scorpion and a frog meet on the bank of a stream and the scorpion asks the frog to carry him across to the other side on his back. The frog asks, "How do I know you won't sting me?" The scorpion says, "Because if I do, we will sink and I will die, too." The frog is satisfied, and they set out, but in midstream, the frog feels the scorpion's sting and with his last breath asks, "Why?" and the scorpion replies, "I could not help myself, it's my nature."

The Two Dogs (Aesop)

A man had two Dogs: a Hound, trained to assist him in his sports, and a Housedog, taught to watch the house. When he returned home after a good day's sport, he always gave the Housedog a large share of his spoils. The Hound, feeling much aggrieved at this, reproached his companion, saying, "It is very hard to have all this labor, while you, who do not assist in the chase, luxuriate on the fruits of my exertions." The Housedog replied, "Don't blame me, my friend, but find fault with the master, who has not taught me to labor, but to depend for subsistence on the labor of others."

You see, you can't stop a hunting dog from hunting, or a herding dog from herding or a cat from eating little mammals and birds, or a wolf from killing weaker animals for food, because that is in their nature and that is how they survive. But you can breed, over time, hunting instincts out of dogs and end up with lapdogs and house dogs and pretty dogs and dogs of all mixes and varieties that have no other function than to entertain us, be our ever-present companions, and reassure us of unrequited love, obedience, and loyalty.

NATURE JOINS NURTURE: SCIENCE WEIGHS IN

So where are we going with this? Well, let's rewind to the 1950s when two cardiologists Meyer Friedman and Ray Rosenman, published an eight-year study of healthy men between the ages of 35 and 59 that focused on personality type as a potential risk factor in heart attacks. The question they were attempting to answer was whether individuals who were otherwise equally healthy but had different personality "stress" profiles would have higher or lower probabilities of experiencing a heart attack. The two cardiologists, following commonly accepted research method-ologies, divided the subjects, according to their personality types based on psychometric testing, into one of two groupings: Type A Personalities and type B Personalities. Based on their findings, the study concluded that individuals with type A Personalities were two times more likely to suffer a heart attack than those with type B Personalities. This was a groundbreaking study in that it was the first to identify psychosocial and behavioral factors as major contributory or risk factors to coronary heart disease (CHD), when it had previously been believed that lifestyle and genetics were the primary predictors of CHD. This study did raise much controversy in the medical and psychological communities, and its validity is still being argued today, but personality types, or certain psychosocial factors and behaviors, became suspected risk factors in many other diseases as well. It also directed much research toward understanding why individuals with type A personalities were more prone to heart attacks than type B's, but also to understand the mechanisms that turn stress, depression, and other psychological conditions into physical illnesses and the converse; that is, whether physical illnesses can increase the likelihood of psychosocial-based illnesses. One of the primary mechanisms allowing psychosocial disorders to morph into physical- or disease-based illnesses has been linked to depressed immune systems making those with mental or stress disorders more vulnerable to a host of physical- or disease-based illnesses.

GETTING FROM "A" TO "B"—A DISTINCTION WITH A PROFOUND DIFFERENCE

"So what are type A and type B Personalities?" I am pleased you asked and while reviewing the characteristics of each, please consider where you fit into this new "world order" that divides us into two primary personality groupings.

Type A Personality

These individuals are the "poster child" for a coronary incident and they are characterized by their intense drive, focus, ambition, competitiveness, rigidity, and "my way or the highway" approach to life. Punctuality is almost a religion for them and they always try to play "beat the clock." Type A's are sometimes truthful to a fault, often on the verge of being impolite; and, they don't enjoy casual conversations, perceiving them as time wasters. On the other hand they are the first to volunteer for a new job or task even though they are already overloaded because only they know how to do it properly; they are self-confident perfectionists who often miss the big picture because they are focused on individual tasks. They are loners who don't like working on teams and are impatient at meetings, eschewing "small talk." Type A's are characteristically mentally agile and alert, but they don't know how to or when to relax, and always want to be treated with deference because they are very status conscious and have a high opinion of themselves—even if others don't share their view. Type A's don't like to hear excuses, regardless of their validity, are constantly pushing themselves, and are often labeled as "workaholics." They tend to develop addictive habits such as smoking, eating quickly, and salting foods before they taste them; they are impatient with others and quick to anger and are often aggressive drivers, quick to react verbally and sometimes physically to real or perceived slights on the road or in person. Type A's enjoy helping others, although in some cases only to show their superiority and greater knowledge, but they will turn their energy and aggressiveness as quickly to an organization "fund drive" for needy children as they will to any other task and can be proactive, stopping little issues from becoming big ones.

Type B Personality

These individuals are "team players" who enjoy working with others and don't always need to be the boss; in fact, they usually encourage others to take the lead. Type B's err on the side of trust and optimism, as opposed to suspicion and pessimism; they are social beings always willing to hear someone else's "sad" story, whether personal or work related, and give sage advice; they understand that sometimes schedules slip because not everything is under their control. They are patient with people, encourage and indeed make it very clear that all individuals treat each other with respect and dignity, they tend toward creativity not always looking for the easiest solution but for the best solution even if it takes longer to achieve. They do not shy away from competition and want to win—but not at *any* cost. Type B's can be reflective about life and fully understand that bad things happen to good people and that good things happen to bad people; they can be tardy to events or meetings because they lingered too long with a friend or colleague who had a problem. They get the "big picture," encourage communication between people both horizontally and vertically, and are not sticklers for formality and rank. They don't always look to assert their authority but let others lead—provided they are on the right track; they are interested in the development of others and not necessarily in promoting themselves; they are more than willing to share the glory. They are quick to praise, have high standards for performance and competence, but would prefer to spend time working with someone rather than rejecting them outright; they are always polite to everyone regardless of where they are, either in life or on an organization chart. They are slow to anger, although when they do get angry, they express themselves forcefully; they are patient but focused on outcomes and will intervene when teams get off track.

Again, while research is divided on the validity of the original conclusions, it does appear, even to the layman, that individuals with pent-up hostility and aggression, which can be triggered by even minor events, who are impatient to a fault with themselves and with others, and who indulge in addictive behaviors viewing life as a constant battle between themselves and the world "writ large" would be victimized by all sorts of stress-related diseases, including coronary heart and artery diseases as well as a host of others. Statistics have borne out this sad reality for them and for their loved ones.

ADAPTING TO RETIREMENT—OVERCOMING STRESS THROUGH POSITIVE ACTION

"So how does stress play out in retirement and in how we adapt to retirement?" Glad you asked; let's examine the interplay between retirement and stress. Retirement, which most consider a good and welcomed outcome, can become a major stressor—not necessarily because it is good or bad, but because it presages a major life change requiring a complete re-thinking of how we want to live the rest of our lives and all those issues and decisions that confront us when in the throes of such a major life shift, which triggers stress and stress-related disorders. Our minds and bodies respond to stressful situations and to caustic or stress-loaded environments, not necessarily in positive ways. Stress and stress-related conditions and diseases, especially among the elderly, have become one of the most prevalent causes of health problems in our country.

DIFFERENT TIMES, DIFFERENT DEMANDS, MORE STRESS

Today we live in a different world. One that is always on the brink of war, constantly flirting with economic collapse; our families are riven by divorce and separation, our children are having children, our neighborhoods are no longer compact but spread over wide swaths of what was once farmland, now known as suburbia, and we have abandoned the poor and the elderly to the slums that are no longer socially or even physically secure, our institutions—particularly government at all its levels, our schools, and our heretofore sacrosanct religious institutions—are no longer seen as social integrators but rather as "dividers" or at best as providers of money without requiring personal responsibility or expectations. We see great wealth and great poverty in real time, living cheek by jowl, and our politics are now politics of difference rather than common agenda. Where do we go, who do we turn to when stress takes over our lives—oh yes, we can watch others less fortunate than we are display all their worries, foibles, and anti-social behaviors in living color on television every day of the week, and we feel secure in the knowledge that we are not them—at least not yet. We say we live in "stressful times" when in fact we are in times of plenty, but have yet to figure out how to distribute mental well-being as efficiently as financial largesse to those not able to cope with or live successfully in the world we find ourselves in today.

Oftentimes, we are our own worst enemies, manufacturing our own stressors by placing impossible demands on ourselves, our children, our loved ones, and our institutions; then when they fail us we become angry, disappointed at being abandoned by those we believed would be there for us in our time of need. Our institutions, likewise, are stressed by the constant wants and needs of those they were supposed to serve because they too have a mission and a purpose they no longer are able to fulfill due to ever increasing wants, needs, and demands for assistance, lack of political will to make personal responsibility a benchmark for assistance, or limited responsiveness to our modern way of life. Everyone feels let down, both the givers and the receivers. In other words, when there is an imbalance between our internally generated expectations, or what we wanted to happen, and actual outcomes, what did happen, internal stressors are generated and activated; you know, that angry feeling and the ache in the pit of our stomachs. Pessimism places us on the road to self-destruction, while optimism is our lifeline to reality.

LIFE IS VIEWED THROUGH DIFFERENT PRISMS

Stress, or the inability to square life with reality, can manifest itself in many different ways and forms and often starts out with a sense of inexplicable unease with the world and with ourselves. It can transform into many different emotional disorders including anxiousness and nervousness, which can grow into panic attacks and a general discomfort and fear of life, which can lead to depression, impulsive behavior, destructive relationships, uncontrolled anger that can cause harm to others and ourselves, and shutting ourselves off from the world and not being concerned with how others feel, becoming completely self-centered and caring only about our needs and feelings and not the needs and feelings of others.

We all see the world through different prisms, some of us are able to absorb or shake off or better cope with highly stressful situations than others. Understanding we are confronting a stressful situation, interaction, or environment is the first step to not only reducing its impact on our mental and physical health, but ultimately adapting to the stress and finding positive mechanisms to cope with it, to accept and adapt, and reconcile with the stress rather than fighting it through internal and external conflict, whether at work or in the family or in your neighborhood. Successful coping is the fastest way to reduce the damaging impact stress can have on our minds and bodies. Stress and stress-related conditions have been implicated directly or indirectly in coronary artery disease, strokes, migraine headaches, lowered immunities, neurological disorders, fatigue, lethargy, gastrointestinal disorders, and also to addictive behaviors like overeating, obesity, alcoholism, drug abuse, accidents, diabetes, tobacco use, and a general lack of caring about yourself, your appearance, and ultimately your hygiene. Stress, depression, and its precursors can destroy us and those around us if we allow the stress to control us rather than controlling our stress. And, if retirement is the stress trigger you have to confront it, control it, solve it, and ultimately defeat it by finding constructive ways of adapting to your new life—one that is purportedly the "last time for life's best time."

Now that we know a bit more about the impact stress has on our lives, others who surround us, and ultimately on ourselves, let's go back to our two personality types once more, type A and type B, and hypothesize how each might adapt to, and either accept or do battle with, their new life in retirement.

WILL YOU BE LIVING A TYPE A OR TYPE B RETIREMENT?—YOUR CHOICE

Personality Type A's and Retirement

I would suggest that a type A person, male or female, would see retirement as a malaise or an illness, something the weak would succumb to; something that needs to be cured or sweated out of them— "why would you even want to retire when there is so much to do at work" might be the response to a colleague announcing their intention to retire. Type A's see "no life after work," with retirement being akin to walking the earth like the "living dead." As a result, Type A's are the ones who vow to never retire because a life without work (a.k.a. purpose) is not a life worth living—they are the ones who want to die with their "boots on." And quite frankly, because of who they are and what they are, A's don't do well in retirement unless, of course, they get the big wake-up call from above; that is, they see the light or they see and feel that first heart attack and then not only seek medical help and advice but also perhaps psychological counseling—but that is not always the case. Retirees have no organization chart, and type A's want to know precisely where they fit in, who they can manage or control, and that their word is the word of authority. That kind of approach is off-putting to fellow retirees who also had successful careers but now have a new focus and life mission; that is, to make retirement the best, most exciting years of their lives. Type A's need tasks and objectives and deadlines to keep themselves occupied; they never learned how to use time for relaxation, for discovery, or for socializing—you see, that impatience and pent-up hostility just doesn't go away. At work, others "had" to communicate with you or report to you, but in retirement we are all freed from the tyranny of the organization chart, and some of us learn to love it, while type A's attempt to re-create that hierarchy and status in retirement. Bottom line is they want to be the dominant person in every situation and discussion or to turn every recreational activity into a competition rather than an opportunity to get moving and to network with friends. Type A's are constantly replaying their working lives in their minds, bemoaning what they are missing and wishing there were more people like themselves that they could befriend—and I am sure there are but they have "moved on with life" and learned to love retirement and all it offers. It's as if type A's suffer from a form of PTSD, or Post Traumatic Stress Disorder, and must be brought down gradually from where they were in the world of work to where they are today—not an easy task, but doable if the will to change is there.

Talk to the Animals

In the animal kingdom there are different mechanisms that determine who leads and who follows—oftentimes violent and sometimes olfactory. But in the human kingdom, we express position and dominance through other mechanisms, like the way we dress, how we behave, by displays of wealth and power like big homes, expensive vehicles or telling others about our yachts and trips to far off lands and displaying our peacock feathers, or by letting others know who we know and by doling out little favors to the less fortunate retirees among us; or, by inviting them to cocktail parties to let others know we are king and queen of the roost or even by displaying superior knowledge of anything, but mostly of how to make money and protect assets. We all try to find our place in this new retirement "social order" that informally takes shape among the newly retired; and type A's, if you let them, will do everything they can to organize those "lazy retirees" into high-functioning groups with schedules and objectives, like getting up to run at 6:00 A.M., or playing golf every day at 9:00 A.M., and tennis at 3:00 P.M., and cocktails, definitely cocktails, at 5:00 P.M. Remember, a hunting dog doesn't lose the instinct to hunt nor does a type A lose the urge to organize the world according to their vision—retirement be damned. You can quickly see that this is not a formula for either a successful retirement or for making friends and having a robust social life because rather than being welcomed as the new "retirement messiah" Type A's are often ridiculed, ignored, or even shunned because of their heavy-handed, misguided, and uncompromising approaches to making friends and influencing people. If you are looking for lonely people to save and bring in from the cold, then look for all those type A's wandering among us—invite them in and let peer pressure and existing social networks work their magic—you just might save a type A's retirement.

Personality Type B's and Retirement

Type B's are the ultimate "good guys or gals," who others seek out to socialize with, to play with, and to ask advice from because they know they will not be criticized or demeaned or made to feel foolish or ignorant. Type B's are there for us; they are more than willing to help out and contribute to whatever needs to be done, even to the point of getting their hands dirty; they do not seek the limelight and are willing to work behind the scenes and to do the tasks that type A's might find "beneath their station." Type B's are not strident or demanding, and they won't take their "marbles" and go home if they don't get their way. They are as gracious in victory as they are in defeat. They are self-effacing without being obsequious and seek neither the favor nor praise of others because they are secure in who they are. They have feelings of self-worth and adequacy and don't feel the need to prove themselves at every turn. Type B's are more than willing volunteers to help those less fortunate, and in fact seek those opportunities in retirement as a way of giving back for all they have been given. They are not sticklers for formality regardless of who they were in their previous lives and prefer to be addressed by their first name over doctor or professor or judge or mayor, as they were known in their working lives. They dress not to impress but rather to be comfortable and eschew displays of wealth or anything that smacks of superiority. They are the consummate friend, confidant, advisor, sympathetic ear, and compassionate truth teller. We can depend on them and call them at any time for any reason—because they will always offer solace and assistance. They are quick to praise and slow to anger regardless of the provocation, but if pushed too far in their defense or in the defense of others they can counter any type A tirade with swiftness and surety. They share the glory and accept blame without recrimination when they feel they have let others down. Type B's are archetypal "everyday heroes and heroines," but they need someone to come to their assistance when they are down or have personal setbacks and concerns, although they will rarely ask for help—so be sensitive to their moods and be prepared to offer type B's comfort and friendship without being asked, because ultimately they will open up and thank you for being there for them. Type B's can be good role models for how type A's should behave in retirement and will patiently and privately try to bring them along. Welcome as many type B's into your retirement life and retirement communities as you can find—you will never regret it.

GOING FROM "A" TO "B," AND NOT THE OTHER WAY ROUND

It's quite obvious from the preceding that those of us with type B Personalities will typically do quite well in retirement. So what about the type A Personalities, what can they do to make retirement a pleasant, satisfying, and ultimately a successful long term experience? I ask the type A's among us to fully consider the suggestions and recommendations being offered in the spirit of comradeship, hope, and the expectation that all of us have a right and an obligation to ourselves and our significant others to live a fulfilling, meaningful, adventurous, and stress-free retirement. Here is my list:

- You are in a different place and a different time, don't fight the same battles—break from old behaviors, ideologies, beliefs, and attitudes that probably did not serve you well in the world of work, and surely will not serve you in the world of retirement. I know, easier said than done.

- Ascribe to the "old saw"—don't sweat the small stuff because it's all small stuff. Let real or apparent misdeeds, missteps, or totally wrong-headed comments slide off, you don't always have to respond to every slight, factual inaccuracy, or perceived insult—*Let it go!*

- Don't live life by the clock—take control of your time and your environment. Retirement gives you an opportunity to disrupt old patterns and release yourself from the "tyranny of time." Don't overschedule your day, let the day evolve. It's okay to take a nap or go for a bike ride or a walk and do that chore you thought you would get to today tomorrow—in fact, "tomorrow" might become your favorite word. It will take some time to adjust to newfound freedoms and to learn new life patterns and not feel guilty—but it will happen, so give freedom a chance, it will never be regretted. You have my personal guarantee.

- Allow your body rhythms to change—don't stick to the same sleep/awake/sleep schedule you had in your working lives. No, I am not suggesting that you sleep until noon and party all night, quite the contrary. In my particular case, I am getting up earlier in retirement than I was in work and typically going to sleep earlier, because my activity levels and interests have expanded. My body is now tuned to the diurnal clock—up at dawn and sleepy and ready for bed at around 10:00 P.M. I never thought that would happen to me either.

- Alter your social persona—yes, you can change your stripes.

- Don't be quick to criticize and value the contributions of others even if they differ from yours.

- Recognize when tension and stress are building and cut 'em off at the pass. Don't let tension build like a pressure cooker that whistles away until you hear and feel that explosion of anger followed by regret for losing control.

- Confide in your significant other about your concerns, fears, and problems arising from retirement. Establish activities you can enjoy together and reserve time for attending events together and just for talking, planning, and dreaming.

- Self-educate—don't self-medicate. Knowledge is more powerful than drugs and alcohol.

- Become a good follower; let others lead and support the team even if you believe you can do a better job of leading.

- Find activities that you enjoy that can also involve others—don't isolate yourself from life or from people.

- Listen first, talk second. Let your brain process before your mouth utters a single word—once the thought is out you cannot get it back.

- Go along to get along.

- Learn to relax by taking up hobbies, not to impress others but rather for their own sake. Find an enjoyable diversion, or noncompetitive sport that will not turn into a fierce competition. Seek fun things to do that are therapeutic and stress reducing and will not become stress *in*ducing. Or how about rekindling that youthful desire to play the drums or the guitar in a rock band? It might just be fun; open yourself to any activity that tickles your fancy.

- Avoid turning everything into a competition—you don't always have to win because sometimes you actually lose.

- Volunteer to help others—be thankful for what you have.

- Join groups, clubs, and organizations with which you have common interests and let others take the lead.

- Talk with others; share your feelings, fears, and thoughts.

- At meetings or social events don't keep looking at the time and never play "Beat the Clock."

- Revive and renew old passions that you pushed aside because of work.

- Refrain from making judgments about others, their ideas, their appearances; we all have different life perspectives and ideas of what is important to us.

- Keep your hostility and anger in check; think before you leap and put yourself in the place of the person you are directing your anger at. Would you want someone to behave toward you in the same manner? And what would onlookers think about you and your loss of self-control?

- Keep moving. Don't let your body down, it needs to be exercised and used—physical activity is probably the healthiest, least-expensive preventative treatment for stress.

- Avoid self-destructive behaviors and habits—you know what they are.

Prepare your own list of behavioral reminders and "mantras" that will take you from bitterness and anger to joy and relaxation; from boredom to action and from solitude to embracing others on equal terms. Give retirement a chance—you will never regret it.[13, 14, 15, 16, 17]

GOING FROM A TO B AND NOT THE OTHER WAY ROUND

CHAPTER 12

■ ■ ■ ■ ■ ■

Why Can't We All Just Get Along
THE IMPORTANCE OF STAYING SOCIALLY CONNECTED

We need people in our lives with whom we can be as open as possible. To have real conversations with people may seem like such a simple, obvious suggestion, but it involves courage and risk.

—THOMAS MOORE

When so many are lonely as seem to be lonely, it would be inexcusably selfish to be lonely alone.

—TENNESSEE WILLIAMS FROM *CAMINO REAL*

LETTING GO, MOVING FORWARD

Most of us didn't live to work, but more fittingly worked to live. Yes, work should have been enjoyable and fulfilling, and yes, it should have been a representation of who we were and where we were at that time in our lives, giving us status and power, a creative outlet for our talents, an opportunity to contribute to society and receive a sense of worth in return from our profession, our business, or the workplace. But ultimately most of us, some with more difficulty than others, separated ourselves from work and committed to retirement, many for the right reasons, some out of necessity, and yet others because they had no real choice in the decision. Regardless, we are all here now; or as Franklin Roosevelt said, "There are many ways of going forward, but only one way of standing still."

Yes, in those first foundering months of retirement we all feel a bit displaced, misplaced, and stuck in constant search mode, or as I call it, a bad case of separation anxiety. And, why is that? Because we have yet to realize or come to understand that, hey, retirement isn't another form of work; rather, *retirement is another way of life*. With that astounding realization, all the bits and pieces start coming together, and struggle is replaced by acceptance. We are all a little slow on the uptake sometimes, but once the light bulb goes off, our tussle with retirement just fades away. No longer is being home treated as a "timeout" for bad behavior, but rather it becomes an opportunity, "now for something completely different," as the Monty Python boys would say as they moved from skit to skit.

WHERE DID ALL THOSE "TOUCHSTONES" GO?

So one day I asked myself, "What is so different about life in retirement from life at work?" And, the answer was, "touchstones," yes touchstones. We no longer have touchstones to guide us through our days, weeks, months, and years as we did at work. Indeed, work touchstones and retirement touchstones are as different as "up" is from "down," they point us in entirely opposite directions. At work we have, or had, a multiplicity of touchstones, perhaps they were goals and objectives against which our "handlers" or managers could measure our performances individually or collectively. We have touchstones that tell us when we must arrive at work and when we can go home, what we can wear, when we can eat, where we will sit, how we will interact with others, how important we are, how we should feel about ourselves, how much money we will be making, and on and on—there is no end of touchstones or rules in the world of work. Indeed, in the military the touchstones are worn on the collar—yup, rank is a touchstone so everyone knows who gives the orders and who has to say "Yes, Sir!" In civilian organizations touchstones are just as prolific and sometimes more confusing than in the military because we don't visibly display our ranks. But, we do know how to distinguish who is more important—by the size of their office, and whether it has windows (and if it does, whether the windows face the parking lot or somewhere more interesting), how many direct reports we supervise, if we have a conference table and a side chair, and by the quality and type of our clothes and whether we wear a tie or not; or as they say, "the cut of our jib," and by the bible we know as the organization chart.

RETIREMENT "UNSTRUCTURES" EVERYTHING

Our lives are controlled, planned, organized, and directed from the day we are born to the day we retire—with the exception of our time at college where we fully believed ourselves to be invulnerable and held tight to the mantra of sex, drugs, and rock 'n' roll that was the hallmark of the '60s. Today, there is, for most of us, comfort in structure and in knowing our place in the social order, with most of us fully accepting those realities. Our social relations were prescribed and proscribed for us by our family, until we figured out how to "politely" chart our own path. Our parents and significant others urged us to follow our hearts, and at the same time, told us what type of professions or jobs we should aspire to, where to go to college, what religion we should adopt, who our friends should be, what type of boy or girl we should marry, and even where we should live. Did we internalize some of those messages?

Probably more than we think. Then the day we retire, all those "work touchstones" that anchored us to reality disappear and we journey unmoored to the other side of work.

BUILDING SOCIAL ASSETS

During the run-up to retirement, most of us (including myself) focused our attention on gathering sufficient financial assets to ease our way into and through the retirement years, while paying scant attention to building what is equally important; that is, our social assets. And then, once the bonds that tied us to the workplace were broken, we had nothing to replace them with and we were set adrift in this huge ocean of humanity to reconstruct the social and support networks that are so critical to shaping successful retirements. Social engagement, hobbies, and interests are all absolutely central to a healthy retirement lifestyle for both your mental and emotional health as well as for your physical well-being. These activities and social networks must either be rebuilt or re-energized in their many different forms, or even be discovered anew. Life requires a healthy amount of passion because a life without passion is a life without meaning. Happiness is transitory. It has to be continually renewed, while passion and the meaning it imparts are everlasting. Retirement is more than flitting from here to there, or mindless trips to absorb time; or just finding things to keep us occupied. Retirement is about meaning and contribution, it's about who we will become and ultimately it is about legacy—never forget that.

NEW TOUCHSTONES TO THE RESCUE

What about those retirement touchstones? When you first retire you may not have many touchstones but don't worry, you will. This time, however, those touchstones will be self-imposed rather than superimposed; they too will regulate your life but in a positive way; they will give you structure, if not meaning, although the meaning will follow in time. It took me about a year to figure all this out, to give myself touchstones, and now I have so many touchstones there is not enough time in my day to get to them all. I am busier, more focused, and more committed to each day—and I mean every day—than I was when working (go figure). Work in the formal organizational sense is in the past—retirement is my future, as it will be yours, so hold on to that dream and don't let it go. And, yes, retirement for some of us can be like having a tiger by the tail, it can give us a thrashing if we don't come to terms with our "inner beasts," but once that tiger is tamed it will be our friend and companion for the rest of our lives—just hold on and enjoy the ride.

MEETING AND GREETING—
FIRST IMPRESSIONS COUNT

When old friends and family meet, the initial greeting is joyful, full of emotional energy, high fives, hugs, and handshakes of all varieties punctuated by "it's great to see you" or "why did we wait so long to get together" and all the other niceties associated with a happy event. When you are introduced to new people or you introduce yourself to an unfamiliar person, the greetings are typically more subdued, polite, and formal. Perhaps a welcome is offered with a handshake or a nod of the head followed by such greetings as, "it's a pleasure to meet you," or "it's nice to make your acquaintance." Salutations have become ritualized, as they have been in the animal kingdom for millennia. While greeting behaviors are hardwired in creatures or animals of every sort, in humans they are learned or nurtured responses with abundant variations, depending on the culture and society in which we live. Sometimes these greetings are warm and sincere, other times perfunctory, and yet at other times there is a hint of unease, if not perhaps distrust or even fear.

Greeting rituals evolved as a more efficient method of determining whether the person approaching was going to kill you or hug you—every animal, including humans, developed rituals to demonstrate, as they say in the cowboy movies, "we come in peace." Greeting rituals, particularly between strangers, insure, at least most of the time, that neither party misinterprets the intention of the other. A socially appropriate greeting shows both parties can be trusted to behave within the boundaries of accepted social norms, and that they will be safe in each other's presence. Communication need not be verbal and in prehistory it was rarely so because spoken language (if there was any) was localized in tribes and rarely understood by others outside that tribal circle, so body language, hand gestures, and facial expressions became the primary way to demonstrate intention.

MATURE MALE/FEMALE SEEKING COMPATIBLE OTHERS

So where do we go from here? You see, when we retire, as discussed previously, we lose our social anchors and the personal contact with our work colleagues, or students, mentors, or customers. We all wished for the day we could put all that stress and all the individual needs and wants of employees, colleagues, students, and customers behind us. When retire, however, we are no longer guided by the work ritual or the discipline it imposed on us and the interactions it required. The novelty of being home soon wears thin and we may begin to wonder if those walls are closing in. We have hobbies, but are they *social* hobbies? And how long do we want to be down in the basement in our woodshop or sitting in our chairs quilting blankets for grandchildren anyway? At some point we start going stir-crazy. So out we go to the malls not only to shop, but to see other humans up close and personal—almost like visiting a human zoo to remind us how many interesting and different varieties of people populate this earth. We join groups and clubs, we attend lectures and plays, but we are still alone or feeling alone. We call old friends, but most of them are still working and their lives are too busy to have more than a monthly lunch or get-together with the "luckiest person" this side of winning the lottery, the one who got out of the dull and boring work routine to find excitement and fulfillment in retirement—so they believe. Meanwhile, we entertain ourselves by reading, watching television, particularly those daytime shows that exploit the failings of humans, and by shopping or playing on our computers and interacting with others electronically, but that is not half as satisfying when we would rather be in places full of walking, talking, breathing people. Perhaps we feel lonely and abandoned because we have forgotten one of life's most important pleasures: the physical presence and company of others.

I WANT TO BE ALONE...DO YOU, REALLY?

In retirement some of us, unfortunately, lose the ability to connect with others. Our social skills have atrophied. Day after day we came home from work exhausted and demoralized and all we wanted to do was separate ourselves from "those people," usually our colleagues, bosses, and customers. Some became addicted not to drugs or drink but to virtual lives, sitting at home behind "electronic walls," and striking up cyber friendships. We wish we could jump through the screen and touch and see those people we have become so familiar with. We don't want to invade their personal space, but yet, we want to be part of their conversation so we settle for electronic intercourse rather than personal intercourse, only in the purest of ways. But do I *really* know that person communicating back to me from behind that electronic wall? *What if he or she is a serial killer?* You wonder sometimes. So, how do we know who is safe and who is not or who is honest and who is not, or who is compatible with our belief systems and who is not, and on and on it goes...until we inevitably ask, *How do I make physical contact with that "image" without embarrassing or endangering myself?* Well, you have come to the right chapter.

As we wander about trying to constructively fill our once fully programmed days, voluntary communication between consenting adults becomes the vehicle for breaking out of our self-imposed social prisons. Communication is the glue that either binds us or separates us. Once retired we no longer have organization charts and supervisors and managers that tell us with whom we can talk and who has the right to say yes or no and to control our lives, our words, and our behaviors. You see, freedom from work does not mean you are free—it means you are left to your own devices, which is an entirely different matter, but wasn't that what you always wanted?

IS ANYBODY LISTENING, DOES ANYBODY CARE?

Retirement, while it should be a time of joy and social richness, can become a "social desert" for many, requiring us to rebuild our social infrastructure, particularly if we did not previously actively pursue outside stimulation because of work, family obligations, or circumstances. Ignore human companionship at your peril because loneliness and boredom are enemies with substance and stealth that creep up on us and steal our energy and joy until it is too late to recover and we become a member of the army of the depressed. Okay, I agree, a bit melodramatic and overstated, but the possibility is real, and we are headed for trouble if collective and corrective actions are not taken, namely to refocus and redouble our efforts to create new and to reaffirm old social networks that provide support, solace, friendship, kinship, and safe harbor from life's stresses, anxieties, traumas, and hassles.

TALK IS CHEAP, BUT I GUESS WE ALREADY KNEW THAT

Talking is not necessarily communication. Yes we can talk, but if we talk in the woods and no one hears us, is that really communicating? (Just ask the tree that fell with no one to hear its crash.) True communication requires a willing sender and a willing receiver, or someone who is willing to listen and then respond. Today, our ability to speak and express ourselves about anything and everything is everywhere and anywhere. We no longer have to be on a corner standing on the proverbial "soap box" to get attention for a cause or an ideology because both feedback and discourse are now instantaneous, thanks to the miracle of technology that spawned social media—particularly Facebook and Twitter—which have become the "virtual corners and soap boxes" for anyone who cares to give voice to their frustrations, anger, dreams, or poetry—whether it be vile or beautiful, helpful or hurtful. Social media allows thoughts to flow without regard to worth and truth—but whose truth are we referring to anyway? Freedom to speak is the bedrock of this nation, but how could our forefathers have ever imagined the interconnected world we live in today? The principle of free speech still holds as true today as it did when enshrined as the First Amendment to our Constitution, part of the Bill of Rights which guarantees, not only free speech; but freedom of religion, press, assembly, and petition. As one insightful and unknown author once said, "Those who have nothing to say chatter endlessly," and that freedom is guaranteed as well.

NEW REALITIES REQUIRE NEW RESPONSES

When we leave work we lose our "currency" very quickly, but that is both expected and desired. Retirement is our time to move on, to renew and refresh ourselves, or perhaps even reinvent ourselves, but at the least, to do something different. This new reality compels us to build new social networks and this is best done around common interests, whether they be sports, hobbies, volunteer work, cultural activities, or a myriad of things we might have interest in but never pursued, or a secret passion like music or poetry we never revealed to others. Building new personal relationships is neither easy nor comfortable at times. We are out of our element and are no longer being sought out, but rather we become the seekers. Yes, we meet people at community meetings on our blocks and at events. But think about this, how many of us have close associations with our neighbors other than polite greetings and perhaps borrowing an item or two? So consider that in retirement, when we seek comfort and social contact from other people, how do we go about identifying and finding compatible others? Some of us seek out our former colleagues who have also retired, but the conversation always harkens back to what once was rather than what is. Others join clubs and volunteer or join in group activities and attend free concerts in the hopes of meeting like-minded individuals. As we wander around the world, our neighborhoods, adult communities, our apartments and condos, we see others who look like us, dress like us, and perhaps behave like us, and who are as lonely as we are. Do we approach them, and if so how do we introduce ourselves? I don't know who they are and they don't know me, you think. So, you walk silently on with your head down as if eye contact would demonstrate commitment, and you are alone once again. At work, we are thrust together by the requirements of our jobs, we have to talk, cooperate, and plan together with our colleagues what we do at the office or factory, and we get to know each other and then, perhaps, we invite each other out to lunch and eventually to our homes. In retirement we lose that "centering," that social gathering place work provided for us.

DON'T LET INSECURITY SEPARATE YOU FROM THE WORLD

Believe it or not, I am still on task here. Stick with me. At work, we have the opportunity to interact with others repeatedly over time and this can aid us in determining status, financial condition, common interests, and even in roughly determining an individual's or colleague's personality profile, or how they interact with the world, and their communication styles. This allows all interested parties to make an educated guess about compatibility for friendship or romance—sounds like a dating site. But in the retiree world, where the incentive to leave our well-appointed, self-imposed prisons is much diminished, the opportunities to socialize and to meet others is both less frequent and less structured, more angst inducing and quite frankly, embarrassing to some who are decades out of practice with how to get involved in the social scene which can be scary. So, we do nothing, regardless of how lonely we are. And, when we do go to a local event, or to the park, or join clubs, we have precious little time to make judgments about compatibility or worthiness and whether they would be a good match or have common interests, beliefs, or shared political views; or perhaps what skeletons are hiding in their closets.

DID YOU EVER NOTICE?

We all interact with others either in structured or informal settings and environments. When you participate in meetings, community events, lectures, or even friendly discussions, notice how difficult it sometimes is to achieve consensus on what seems to you to be a blatantly obvious solution. Consider why something so apparently simple and straightforward can spark such heated debates and even anger. If that is in fact the case, then, my friends, you have scratched below the surface of comity right down to the bedrock of what is called "deeply held beliefs" and the accompanying unwavering perceptions of the world. And, once these beliefs have been fully verbalized, there is little anyone can do, or probably should do, to change such foundational life assumptions, at least not in the heat of the moment. The only way out of this standoff, short of raising interpersonal tensions to the boiling point, is to simply agree to disagree and then move on to a less contentious subject.

Did you ever notice that at work or in social gatherings, when a group is standing around chatting someone is always the spoiler or the naysayer or the contrarian, no matter how trivial the matter or how polite the conversation starts out? And, when attending these formal or informal meetings or social events did you also notice that you could predict how certain individuals would respond to a suggestion or to a discussion before they even opened their mouths? Did you ever notice that some of us are more thoughtful than others in how we treat people and how we interact with others? Some of us don't use our brains to filter what we say and to whom we say it before we speak. Did you ever notice that certain of us play well with others, allowing them to get a word in edgewise, while others of us are always judgmental and critical of everyone and everything?

What you have noticed, my fellow travelers, is that we all tend to respond in certain patterned and predictable ways to life events, situations, challenges, threats, verbal cues, and what I call "trigger words" and the personal quirks of others. All of us—well at least *most* of us— have, more or less, developed "a human persona," specific to us that is learned, conditioned, or baked-in. Our persona is more commonly and appropriately called our "observable" or "manifested personality," or our "visible behaviors" as perceived by others, or put more simply, our "personality." Some of us learn to turn our behaviors and subsequent personalities off and on to realize a personal end; satisfy or gratify a personal need; or achieve a personal advantage over others, and these types of individuals I call "manipulators." Some of us respond to the world and to people in our life spaces by constantly adapting to the needs and wants of others, avoiding unpleasantness regardless of the personal costs, always agreeing regardless of our own personal beliefs, saying yes to every request and demand placed upon us and being fearful of displeasing anyone over anything. These types of individuals I call "pleasers." These are but two of the five "behavioral dimensions" that will be introduced and discussed in depth, providing insight into why people say what they say and do what they do. Personality is very much like an iceberg, with most of it being under water and not readily visible; we don't wear signs indicating whether we are warm and fuzzy, prickly or unapproachable, friend or master, mentor or soul-sucking demon—wish it were so.

PEOPLE READING PEOPLE

But, indeed, we do send signals and symbols to others continuously through our behaviors, our words, and the way we interact. And that is what allows us to categorize and analyze, and predict somewhat accurately, how an individual will behave in certain types of situations or communicative acts. And if we are honest with ourselves, by using the information and tools provided, we could even understand why we behave and react in certain patterned ways. It is much more difficult to see ourselves as others see us, but we must try or we will be living false lives. Once familiar with these personality classifications, we will not only gain a richer understanding of who we are, and perhaps who we want to be, but will assuredly possess new perspectives as to why we get along with certain individuals and not with others.

Retirement is about choices and options, the decision to either engage with others or isolate ourselves, to seek acceptance or to court rejection, to build lasting friendships, or to forever remain on the sidelines of life; stark choices no doubt, but real nonetheless. The following concepts and their accompanying techniques afford broader understandings of human behavior and offer choices and options for approaching and engaging others, for interacting and communicating with and responding to others in ways that could either increase tensions and conflict or maximize acceptance and cooperation. It isn't magic, it is the art and science of social interaction, or how we behave and communicate with and among others.

From our early years, we developed an ability to "read" people even as young children. We knew who we should stay away from, or which children it was fun to play with—we did not know why or what made them act that way, but we were sensitive to those behaviors. Think back to when you were in elementary school, now try to recall the types of kids that shared classrooms with you. There were the shy ones, the bold ones, the naughty ones, the bossy ones, the clowns, the whiners, the bullies, the teacher's pets, the doers, the strivers, the forever smiling ones, the forever sad ones, the eager beavers, the angry ones, and the fearful ones. As you moved into junior high and high school, did your fellow students change their "stripes"? Perhaps they matured physically and some even emotionally, shedding some behaviors and adding others, some fueled by free-flowing hormones, but in bigger bodies, whether good or bad. And then, by the time we have become adults, courtesy of government edict, our personalities and their consequent behaviors have for all intents and purposes become frozen in place making us who we are, as perceived by others, and who we believe we are, as seen from within—with the two not always being in alignment.

LOOKING FOR FRIENDS IN ALL THE WRONG PLACES

As a general rule we want to be liked, accepted, valued, and treated with respect by others. Some of us, however, have difficulty establishing relationships and friendships. Some of us believe there is something about us that chases potential suitors, acquaintances, or friends away; that we are somehow deficient or not worth knowing. Perhaps those spurned might believe it is the other's loss if someone chooses not to engage them; and that they just threw away an opportunity to get to know someone who could have become very important in their lives, if they had only given the relationship a chance to develop. Well, get ready to be informed and perhaps even enlightened. There are reasons why some of us can connect or engage others, easily building diverse and wide-ranging social networks. Just as there are reasons why some people struggle with or even fear or evade active social engagement; and as there are reasons why we prefer or seek out or even target certain "types" of people to befriend.

We oftentimes see ourselves through the eyes of others and adopt their perceptions of who we are as our own. And conversely, we ignore the behaviors, foibles, and misdeeds in ourselves that we would neither tolerate nor condone in someone else. Or as Carl Gustav Jung, the founding father of analytic psychology, reminds us, "Everything that irritates us about others can lead us to a deeper understanding of ourselves." So while it is important that we define and understand ourselves, we must also be aware and sensitive to how we are perceived by potential friends and foes alike. Invariably, we will occupy the same physical space, purposely or by chance, with a heterogeneous fusion of others and the outcome is never certain, regardless of our expectations and desires. These doubts and fears leave us forever wondering why we so easily connect with some but not with others. The answer is not in the cards—it is within us. Mystical, isn't it?

ARE YOU TALKING TO ME?

Let's get back to the original question of this chapter or, Why can't we all just get along? I'm going to tell you why. We are all different people with different perspectives, different beliefs, different values, different cultural heritages, different lifestyles, different social classes, different religions, different educational backgrounds, different prejudices, different races, different food preferences, different work ethics, or just all around different anythings. The question then becomes, with all these differences, what actually brings us together; and that is the real nub of the question, why indeed. What brings us together are common interests, overarching values, and beliefs, like our common flag, our common ages, our common fundamental beliefs in freedom, and the right to practice those freedoms, or shared religious preferences. I will show how to decode what I call the behavioral mechanics of human interaction, or why some of us can easily navigate their social environments to form bonds and relationships while others continually flee or fail. Prepare to be informed.

THE BUILDING BLOCKS TO BETTER CONVERSATION CHECKLIST

SOME COMMUNICATION PRINCIPLES— THAT ACTUALLY WORK!

☐ Connect with an individual, a group, an audience, or even a nation by first establishing *trust*, *credibility*, and *common interest*—the "Big Three of Communication." In other words, who you are, or appear to be, is oftentimes more important than what you say—just ask any successful politician. Listeners evaluate who you are first and what you say second.

☐ People are predisposed to like and spend time with those who have similar belief patterns and values. Social walls can be quickly overcome by first establishing mutual understanding.

☐ Try to speak like the people around you, using their idioms and a common vocabulary. Avoid loaded or "trigger words" like "you people" or "all old people should"—those are "fighting words," literally as well as figuratively.

☐ If your values, cultural touchstones and religious beliefs are different from those around you, that's fine, as long as you recognize their right to have and hold differing belief systems. If you want the conversation to continue, avoid attacking their beliefs.

☐ Be both an empathetic and a good listener. No matter how anxious you are to get into the conversation, don't interrupt others while they are talking.

☐ When attempting to move an individual or an audience off a deeply held belief or behavior, first attempt to find common ground. For example, trying to convince someone to stop smoking; a smoker might not care what happens to them, but they *do* care what happens to their children or grandchildren. With common ground to stand on, build on that logic chain by offering alternative options to smoking. Above all, don't make them feel like a bad person; rather than attacking their right to smoke, rationally discuss the impact of smoking to keep the conversation going.

☐ If a discussion appears to be getting emotionally charged and tempers are flaring up, bring down the rhetoric and agree to never talk about it again, or better yet agree to revisit the topic when cooler heads prevail. It's always best to move quickly away from "emotionally" loaded arguments or discussions to knowledge and factually driven arguments and discussions.

THE BUILDING BLOCKS TO BETTER CONVERSATION CHECKLIST

CHAPTER 13

■ ■ ■ ■ ■

We Are Who We
Are Until We Aren't

*The true triumph of reason is that it enables us to
get along with those who do not possess it.*
—Voltaire

*The most important single ingredient in success is
knowing how to get along with people.*
—Theodore Roosevelt

THE GAMES PEOPLE PLAY

I have been pondering relational dynamics for decades and have developed a model for observing, understanding, interpreting, predicting, and ultimately, decoding the behavioral mechanics of human interaction; or why certain of us connect while others do not; or why some people can easily form social bonds while others struggle for even a modicum of attention; or why some of us are listened to and others ignored; or why some of us get to be in the center of the circle while others patrol the fringes. I call my model "The Behavioral Compatibility Matrix" (BCM), an intuitive method for performing interpersonal "quick reads" into our personal interactions and behavioral styles, or why we and others say what we say and do what we do. These quick reads allow us to make predictive judgments about the potential for interpersonal compatibility. How many times have we asked ourselves why we ever got involved with this person or why we joined this group or why this person makes us happy and that one always gets our blood boiling? Would you like a tool that will help you avoid potentially embarrassing situations, or prevent nonproductive relationships from even happening? Well, now you have one.

The model posits five behavioral/communication modalities, allowing each of us to self-categorize and place ourselves into the behavioral profile that most closely fits our self-observed communication and interaction styles. We all have different social preferences and approaches. Some always want to be the center of attention, while others always hang back, yet others are constantly swiveling their heads, flitting from person to person or from group to group, shopping for the opinion leaders as if their reputations would rub off on them. Likewise, did you ever wonder why we actively invite some people into our personal space, and passively accept the presence of others, while outright shutting the door on some who can't easily take a hint? Or, why some communications and interactions foster productive and sustained relationships while others either never get started, or quickly end in discord?

It's better to know why, how, and where we fit into the relational world and why we get along with some and not with others. I urge all to take the time, energy, effort, and perhaps even muster the courage to go through this process with me because so many of us live under false assumptions, about both ourselves and how others truly view us. Indeed, we might be surprised by the outcomes, but at the very least we will be able to identify our own predominate communication and behavioral profiles and the profiles of those we come across in our daily lives, and hopefully understand why some of our relationships prosper while others quickly wither on the vine. Our behavioral profiles have profound implications for how we lead and operationalize our lives, above all, whom we socialize with and who will engage with us.

Self-analysis, as psychically painful as it might be, is the highest form of self-awareness and ultimately leads to self-improvement—and after all, that's what retirement should be about. Let's begin!

PREPARE TO BE TROUBLED AND ENLIGHTENED

The Behavioral Compatibility Model is a theoretical representation of how we communicate, interact, and engage with others, one that will fit most people most of the time. The five Behavioral/Communication Profiles are: (1) the Dominator; (2) the Critic; (3) the Pleaser; (4) the Achiever; and (5) the dreaded Manipulator.

BEHAVIORAL PROFILE #1:
THE DOMINATOR

Includes these variants: The Boss, The Big Dog, The Rule-maker, The Dictator, The Dispenser of Favors and of Pain, The Mover and Shaker, The All Powerful One, and The Big Guy/Gal.

Dominators are readily identifiable because of their overt pushiness, their overbearing and sometimes boorish behaviors, their egocentric physical and emotional posturing, and their constant efforts to control every conversation, social situation, meeting, and even informal encounters with friends—if they have any—or with new acquaintances. They are at times intolerant and disinterested in hearing the viewpoints of others, and oftentimes have an inflated sense of entitlement. They are never mistaken for a "warm-fuzzy," and are more likely described by others as a "junkyard dog," although they can even give these poor beasts a bad name. They are the school yard bully everyone loved to hate but always wanted around just in case some other bully showed up. So why are some people attracted to Dominators? Because Dominators project an image of importance and power and have forceful personalities; and people want to be around others who appear important, those from whom they can get a figurative pat on the head or recognition that they exist.

Dominators rarely see themselves as others see them—as overbearing bores, that is. They tend to be at best indifferent to the needs and sensitivities of others and can be arrogant, dictatorial, and authoritarian in both manner and style, believing they are superior to everyone else on planet earth until another Dominator happens along—and then you might get the *Clash of the Titans*. Dominators tend to have a pessimistic worldview and can be rude, insensitive, and dismissive of others and demonstrate those behaviors through word and deed—no one is safe from the Dominator's wrath and displeasure. They see disaster around every corner and they are the only ones capable of steering the Ship of Fools, as they might characterize their friends and colleagues. They firmly believe the world would collapse and the sky would fall if not for their presence. They can be welcoming and manipulative to get their way, but if that doesn't work, they revert back to the Bully persona. But behind that curtain, much like the Wizard of Oz, you will probably find a man or woman who is in reality emotionally weak, insecure, and constantly needing the praises and admiration of others to validate their self-worth.

Dealing with the Dominator: Getting to Know You

Everyone stands in awe of the powerful and the wealthy, and Dominators, in particular, see themselves as powerful in their life spheres, perhaps wealthy, and, even sometimes famous. So how do mere mortals approach and communicate with individuals that either believe they are somehow different from the rest of us or, actually are because of their status, position, and wealth? Typically, Dominators set themselves apart by where they live—usually behind guardhouses and fences. I previously stated that in retirement we are all equal; and yes, we are equal in that we can no longer rely on what we did and who we were to give us our self-worth, but rather must find new purpose and meaning in life. That includes both the powerful and wealthy, and the ordinary Joes and Janes, because we all are searching to find our places in this new social order, but each in our own way.

So how do we connect with others, including Dominators, should we have that desire? Relationships are typically formed around common bonds and interests and sometimes, just sometimes, those we believed to be "above our station" are there with us—traveling with us, biking with us, golfing with us, sailing with us, supporting charities with us, joining clubs with us, going to plays with us—in fact, they are us. Dominators are no different from us—the term merely reflects their approach to dealing with life—it is neither right nor wrong, it's just who they are. Yes, you can spot them because their demeanor, posture, and even dress signal that power, forthrightness, and competence reside in "this" body. But don't shy away nor be intrusive or fawning, rather be open and welcoming as they should be to you. In other words, find common ground around which to build a friendship as you would with any other new acquaintance; and while not ignoring their status, do not play up to it, rather let relationships develop organically—you do not want to be a "go-fer," you want to be a friend.

BEHAVIORAL PROFILE #2: THE CRITIC

Includes these variants: The Know-It-All, The Judge, "Chicken-Little," The Pessimist in Our Midst, The Constant Complainer, The Fault Finder, or "The Glass Is Always Half Empty."

The Critic and the Critical Personality have some of the characteristics of the Dominator but from a different perspective. They didn't typically have corporate playgrounds upon which to practice their special type of bile, and it was probably their lack of success at work, in life, or in social situations that made them into the embittered souls they are. Critics developed their hard outer shell as a defense mechanism to mask their failures, low sense of self, and their panoply of insecurities, and to convince themselves they are superior to others, if not in wealth or status, then in intelligence and moral rectitude. They see themselves as superior to us mere mortals and as arbiters of what is right and wrong in society, large or small; they are not tolerant or accepting of the opinions and positions of others if they conflict with their belief systems. Critics make pronouncements rather than invite discussion and debate. Critics are verbal bullies. As a result, they can be dismissive of others. You see, they have the right to criticize you, but you have no right to criticize them. They always want to be the center of attention in any social situation because they are the voice of authority. Interestingly, the Critic sees no need to justify their opinions, viewpoints, or conclusions because they are the experts, and one only has to watch *Judge Judy* to fully understand this particular personality type.

Taming the Critic

So how do we deal with the critics among us? When a critic or critics attempt to monopolize and/or redirect a meeting or a lecture or anything else for their own personal entertainment, how should an individual or a group deal with them? First of all, don't debate and confront or throw out your own inaccurate facts and numbers to counter their inaccurate facts and numbers. That's what they want—they love the debate because they truly believe they know more about everything and will prevail in any battle of wits. Rather, thank them for their input, then indicate we must move along to the next question or comment and quickly proceed to another topic or speaker. Do not sink to their level of negativity by censuring the Critic for bad manners, or for offensive behaviors, or the worst offense of all, correcting their "facts." That can only add fuel to the fire. Above all, do not ignore them; instead, recognize their right to ask questions and request clarifications, at the appropriate time at least. At the same time, keep them from dominating the discussion by pointing out that others have yet to speak or contribute their ideas. No person has the right to demean another person, and if the Critic engages in this disreputable form of comment, take them aside and let them know that this is not tolerated, and if it happens again, they will be shown the door. Now if you happen to sit next to and become the unwitting sidekick of what I call the "muttering critic"—you know, the ones who provide a running commentary of whatever event you are attending, chattering incessantly directly into your ear canal—be politely pro-active and inform the miscreant that you are trying to listen and would appreciate it if they could save any comments until after the event, and then turn away and do not even appear to be interested in their private mutterings. Or if that doesn't work, simply move your seat at an appropriate time, if you can.

BEHAVIORAL PROFILE #3:
THE PLEASER

Includes these variants: The Shapeshifter, Everybody's Friend, "Go-Along to Get-Along," Mommy's Little Helper Grown Up, The Follower, The Kiss-Up, The Puppy—I just need to be wanted, or The Everyday Sycophant.

The Pleaser is the ideal friend, colleague, relative, new acquaintance, or someone you would be fortunate to sit next to on a long overseas flight. Pleasant almost to a fault, they are easy to like, to be around, to work with, to tell your troubles, to accompany you to the doctor's office when bad news is expected, or to ask for advice and assistance when you are at wit's end. They are your typical active PTA member, coach, hyperactive volunteer, community advocate, and the first to send condolences or congratulations, and to offer to babysit for a friend or go shopping for an elderly neighbor. Because they are so involved in the lives of others they often give short shrift to their own needs or their family's by sacrificing themselves on the altar of being liked, needed, and wanted. Such dramatic time commitments require the Pleaser to be very organized which they are to a point, but they often get over-whelmed because they are just like the girl who "can't say no" in the musical *Oklahoma*. Pleasers abhor and avoid conflict or disagreement at almost any cost, personal or otherwise; they are not only Pleasers but "appeasers." Indeed, they will tell people what they want to hear to avoid any hint of rancor, even if it violates every principle they hold. They are consummate "shape-shifters," trying to conform to the image and expectations of the person standing in front of them, agreeing—always agreeing.

And, why do they do this? Some psychologists attribute these driven helping behaviors to the compulsive need for constant approval as validation of self-worth, the need to be wanted and valued by others, and the need to assuage their constant fear of rejection, or perhaps even the need to avoid dealing with their own personal life challenges and problems. The Pleaser's personal motto, whether they know it or not, is "never rock the boat," or "why can't we all just get along?" They avoid conflict at any cost and are the archetypal "yes person."

Dealing with the People Pleaser

Engaging and communicating with the People Pleaser presents a totally different type of challenge. In this case, it's not about what we say to them, but how they communicate with us. Pleasers are the consummate "parrots," they first ascertain the answer you want by listening to your communication and then rejoin with a compatible non-contradictory or non-threatening response. So, if it's pouring outside and the speaker says, "What a nice day this is," the Pleaser will respond, "Yes, the sun will come out soon." People Pleasers are all about making others happy; or at the least, never adding to their woes or distress. They live for the approval and praise of others. They hope to attain this approval by presenting a mirror image to anyone sharing their space, never challenging, never being unpleasant, never displeasing, and always being helpful. As a result, our task is to make it possible for the Pleasers to express themselves without self-censoring, to say what they really feel and not what they expect others want to hear. The only way to accomplish this complete turnaround is to *empower* the Pleaser, to let them know it's okay to express their own feelings and opinions and to be critical of others when needed and appropriate. First, when engaging a People Pleaser in a conversation encourage them to express their thoughts freely, because you are asking for advice and value their opinion. Second, ask the People Pleaser if they truly want to be helpful to others. If they respond yes, then posit when someone asks for your opinion or advice, is it because they believe you to be a knowledgeable and wise person, or because they believe you to be someone of limited breadth and depth? The answer is obvious: they are seeking your guidance on a matter important to them because they respect your opinion. Therefore, would withholding your "wise counsel" help them or hurt them? So, when communicating with a People Pleaser, strip away the clutter and reduce the conversation to choices that leave the People Pleaser little room to prevaricate, moving them toward actually making a "statement." Don't become a crutch but rather a mentor, much like Henry Higgins to Eliza Doolittle in the movie *My Fair Lady*.

BEHAVIORAL PROFILE #4:
THE ACHIEVER

Includes these variants: The Get-It-Done Person, Action Hero, Dudley Do-Right, The Champion, The Optimist in Our Midst, The Guru, The Glass Is Half-Full Person, The Mentor, The Statesman or "The Mensch," The Hero, or how about "Mighty Mouse," Always There to Save the Day.

The Achiever, ah, the Achiever, everyone is in awe of the Achiever. This is the person we can always count on to get things done; the quintessential go-to, can-do person, always there to save the day. Achievers are not gender specific, they might not be the flashiest guy or gal around, but if something needs doing, they get it done. While Achievers can be ambitious, they typically work in the background, sharing the credit with others. Dynamic and effective leaders, they use strength of personality and competence rather than position or title to earn respect and cooperation from others. Achievers have optimistic worldviews, are straightforward in their dealings, motivated by the thrill of the hunt, always looking for new challenges and obstacles to hurdle. Like scientists, Achievers are analytical, methodical, and tough-minded in their approach to solving problems. They are data driven, persistent, self-motivated, and they do not need reminders as to what they need to do or are supposed to be doing because they are always two steps ahead and focused on the problem at hand, refusing to be distracted by extraneous events. They are thoughtful, contemplative, innovative, and entrepreneurial, willing to do things differently rather than stay with old worn-out methodologies and approaches to solving problems. They do not tolerate impolite and destructive behavior from any quarter; they are inclusive rather than exclusive, and more than willing to mentor others. They are everyone's vision of the perfect companion, friend, colleague, and team member. And, oftentimes they are silent heroes, letting others take the credit for the successes while willing to accept the blame for failures—for that is their way.

Dealing with the Achiever: The Facts, Just the Facts, Ma'am

The Achiever is the archetypal "Get It Done" or "Go To" person that is essential to every effective high-functioning social system or organization. While Achievers can be effective communicators, they can eschew small talk, wanting to get down to the nub of the opportunity, problem, or issue that is being confronted at the moment. As a result, they prefer, or even demand, that discussions and communications be focused, stripped of embellishment, factually supported, preferably with numbers, and to the point. Achievers particularly both distrust and dislike emotionality in verbal and written communications. They view emotion as both a weakness and a distraction that can cloud the thought process—it's about the facts not about conjecture. Indeed, they expect the facts and logic to carry the arguments. Communications, in any form, must be precise and concise—no wasted words or alliterations. Meetings likewise are highly focused, open, and direct, no wasted time for socializing and small talk, always on task. The Achiever's communications, likewise, tend to be non-emotional and to the point, very directive and precise as to expected outcome. While they are not great socializers, preferring to have a couple of close acquaintances rather than an address book full of names, they are comfortable in both formal and informal settings, as participants and as presenters or speakers.

They are dynamic and highly energetic, but prefer solving problems to talking about them. Those who want to be part of an Achiever's retinue must be prepared for quick action, expect to be challenged (and sometimes strongly so), not easily discouraged, willing to turn on a dime, non-complaining, and willing to get to the point, both in meetings and in personal communications.

BEHAVIORAL PROFILE #5: THE MANIPULATOR

Includes these variants: The User and Abuser, The Bad Actor, The Exploiter, The Phony, The Troublemaker, The Opportunist, The Intriguer, or how about The Politician and The Salesperson—when the shoe fits.

The Manipulator is the Prince or Princess of Darkness, the "people user" par excellence with few or any redeeming qualities as a person, partner, friend, family member, or acquaintance. Manipulators can be truly toxic people and if you ever encounter one—and I will provide some cues as to how to spot them—always be polite, professional, and perfunctory, and then don't walk, but *run* away as if the hounds of hell are chasing you. Without going into the psychology of how we manage to produce so many Manipulators in our society, or the why's and wherefores, it is sufficient to say that our darling children, or "little manipulators," sometimes grow up to be big adult Manipulators.

Beware the Manipulators, They Speak with Forked Tongues

Manipulators love drama because it forwards their interests, so they create it whenever they can. They thrive on playing the victim—so they can be saved by their "mark," or target. They are experts at building guilt, and never ease their grip on their target until they get what they want. They mask their social and personal aggression, lest it betray their "victim" status; and, as we know, every victim requires a savior or a hero. Life is all about them; and they attack, attack, attack until they achieve their goal, which is getting their target under their control to do their bidding; and, if they resist, there are many other tools at their disposal to regain obedience, power, and domain. Psychological blackmail including deception, deceit, and outright lying are commonly deployed weapons of personal conquest. Manipulators typically have underdeveloped (to say it kindly) moral or ethical centers with little compassion for others; and a pessimistic view of the world with a stunted sense of humor. Manipulators enjoy wielding their particular forms of twisted thinking over groups. The Manipulator "gets off" on the angst and drama they have created—the more angst, the better, and they are highly skilled at exploiting the weaknesses of others, only caring about their personal needs and interests. Their tactics for obtaining compliance are only constrained by their distorted imaginations. Some Manipulators fall within the pathological spectrum.

Handling the Hard-Core Manipulator

I use the terms "handling" and "hard-core" advisedly because we can "handle" the Manipulator but not change them or redirect them into more positive behaviors, particularly the "hard-core" Manipulator, who could quite possibly be pathological. Now the Rules of Engagement:

Rule # 1: Avoid, flee from, get out of Dodge, or run like the wind if you have even an inclination that the person standing in front of you is a Hard-Core Manipulator.

Rule # 2: Always follow Rule #1. If you can't run and there is a Manipulator in your midst, consider taking the following actions to protect yourself and to minimize the impact and consequences of their manipulative behaviors and actions.

- Manipulators will distort everything you say, and then use what you didn't say against you—how neat is that? So beware. Don't engage the discussion and don't worry about hurting their feelings, they have none for you, it's all about them.

- Manipulators are superb at identifying and exploiting weakness and emotional distress in others by drawing out their concerns and problems. So, never, never confide in a Manipulator, whatever you say will be used against you, for their amusement and benefit.

- Manipulators seek and enjoy engagement, it gives them an opportunity to spin their webs, and display their entire arsenal of bad behaviors, lies, and deceptions. Don't get into an argument with a Manipulator. No matter how hard they try, just walk away.

- Manipulators are guilt mongers and are only serving their personal interests and needs and will play the guilt card to bring their mark back under their control by making them feel remorseful or sorry for their unhappiness or despair. Don't get suckered, hold your ground, and stay away from their webs of despair.

- Manipulators are never wrong—never. They can make your head spin with all the convoluted thinking, rationalizations, and blaming, but these verbal "farts" have no purpose other than to deflect blame from them to others. "It wasn't my fault," they say over and over again. When that happens, clearly and calmly inform the Manipulator that you do not buy their explanation and that not only was their behavior unacceptable but if those behaviors are repeated, there will be consequences.

- Manipulators always play the "mine is bigger or worse than yours" game or one-upmanship on steroids. Don't call them out, just walk away and they will know you didn't buy any of it.

- Don't even attempt to "save" the Manipulators from themselves, particularly if they are of the "hard-core" or pathological variety. Leave that to the professionals. Deal with their behaviors and actions, not how they think or why they think that way.

SO WHO GETS ALONG WITH WHOM AND WHY?

It's time to reveal, after much personal insight and self-reflection on your part, why some people connect easily and others do not; or why some of us endlessly wander outside the circle of social engagement looking for a way in, while others are always in its center. Let's begin.

- The **Dominator** doesn't do well with other **Dominators**; all are pack leaders, and when a pack has more than one leader, there is only way to settle that discrepancy in the wild, a fight to the death or until one or the other flees the area and is banished for life. This is neither practical nor sanctioned in polite society where the battle for dominance happens in more subtle ways, or not, but typically ends with one conceding control to the other and either accepting a minor role in the drama or leaving the field of conflict for greener pastures. The **Dominator** does not get along with the **Critic** because **Dominators** are never wrong and don't accept criticism very graciously, regardless of how accurate it may be. **Dominators** often seek out **Pleaser** types as assistants, sidekicks, or "go-fers" and **Pleasers** willingly comply because they can hide behind the **Dominator's** authority and when forced to answer "why," they say because "the boss says so" and "don't shoot the messenger." **Dominators** very much need **Achievers** to get the work done so they can take the credit for a job well done—but above all **Dominators** need and seek constant reinforcement of their importance and personal attractiveness and that they are "always" right. The **Manipulator** fills that bill because they are flatterers par excellence, and as long as the **Manipulator** is the **Dominator's** manipulator they will be used to good effect, oftentimes as hunter-killers.

- **Critics** don't ever like other **Critics** because there can be only one "smartest" kid in the class. When one **Critic** surfaces to sing their own praises, another **Critic** lies in wait for an opportune time to discredit the competition. **Critics** are the consummate contrarians. If you say red, they say green. Even the **Pleaser** has to make an effort to hang with the critic, but they do. **Critics** avoid **Achievers** because they know their hijinks won't be accepted, or if they don't, they will soon learn. **Critics** are so naive they see **Manipulators** as potential comrades, as the spider said to the fly. **Dominators** eat **Critics** for breakfast. So, **Critics** are very lonely people unless they choose to mask those negative behaviors even for a short while, but most can't.

- **Pleasers** want to please everyone, **Dominator, Critic, Achiever, Manipulator** alike; they don't want to disappoint anyone and they agree with everybody. **Pleasers,** unfortunately for them, accept everyone at face value, but they eventually will learn—one hopes.

- **Achievers** are willing to work with **Dominators**, even if the **Dominator** takes the credit because the rest of the observers or participants fully understand how that success *really* happened. **Achievers** can quickly assess "players" and have no time for dogmatic naysayers—can you say goodbye, **Critic**? **Achievers** oftentimes seek other **Achievers** because they have small egos and thrill in the chance and the chase of tackling complex problems and enjoy the company of like-minded individuals. **Achievers** have particular sensitivity to potential troublemakers, particularly **Manipulators**, because of their propensity to sew confusion and unhappiness in well-functioning team environments or in social situations. **Pleasers** are welcomed, but they have to independently contribute to solutions rather than be cheerleaders and parrots.

- **Manipulators** believe they can twist anyone and everyone who crosses their paths to their will and are master "puppeteers." They thrill in making other **Manipulators** jump to their tune, hence they seek the challenge of confronting (subtly or otherwise) their fellow **Manipulators**, but look to each other when there is mutual interest or common enemies. **Manipulators** join together and separate just as quickly. They can also get into the heads of **Dominators** and twist them to their desires by using praise or sexual innuendo to exploit their prey. Even **Dominators** can be turned by a pretty face and lots and lots of: *you're so smart, you work so hard, and you saved the world—I just like being around such a great person like you*; this is manipulation cloaked as praise—case closed. **Manipulators** typically know enough to stay away from **Achievers**, but can easily turn **Critics** to their own devices; and **Pleasers** are easily subdued. **Manipulators** are the unredeemable "users" of others.

LOCKED IN CAN GET YOU LOCKED OUT

If we are locked in to one behavioral profile, never varying from its script whether it is helpful or hurtful to us or to others, we have been effectively "captured"; or, as I like to say, "locked in" to that specific behavioral profile. We have effectively become the proverbial "one trick pony" which limits our ability to move between profiles, allowing us to select the response or the behavior most appropriate for particular social or business situations. In other words, we unfortunately become a stereotype of ourselves if we rarely vary what we say, what we do, and how we respond to both predictable and unpredictable events. So, we become identified as Clara "Critic" or David "Dominator" or Phoebe the "People Pleaser"—you get the point. We, all of us, must find ways to adapt to specific environments, people, and situations. We all need to retain the freedom and ability to slide between profiles as situations and etiquette requires; even if we typically communicate and relate from a core profile. However, if you are so unpredictable that no one knows who they are talking to or dealing with at any particular moment, or whether your switch is on "flip" or "flop," this can be as disturbing and communication killing as being locked in. Find the happy medium.

THE BEHAVIORAL COMPATIBILITY MATRIX (BCM)

	Dominator	Critic	Pleaser	Achiever	Manipulator
Dominator	D	C	C	C	MI
Critic	D	D	C	D	MI
Pleaser	C	C	C	C	C
Achiever	C	D	C	C	D
Manipulator	MI	MI	C	D	MI

LEGEND:

C = COMPLEMENTARY: Communications are reciprocal and relationships are typically enduring, self-generating, and mutually supportive.

MI = MUTUAL INTEREST: Communications and relationships built around contemporaneous shared interests and common concerns, typically of the "I need you when I need you" type, usually ending when those mutual interests have been either satisfied or are no longer relevant.

D = DISCORDANT: Communications and relationships that rarely go beyond perfunctory greetings and social niceties because of deeply held contradictory beliefs, incompatible behavioral profiles, and prior antagonistic histories.

THE MATRIX IS TALKING TO YOU, SO LISTEN UP

Perhaps the Matrix will be a wake-up call for some of us who, possibly, now understand why they were having difficulty connecting with some individuals but not with others, and who now understand what behavioral/communication profile they personally "own." No, we do not have to be locked in to any particular profile. Remember, we have free will, and we can change and modify our behaviors and communication styles over time, allowing us to slide into a more compatible or more personally acceptable behavioral profile, if that is our preference. But I am relatively certain that we all learned something new about ourselves; and if that is the case, this exercise was worthwhile. Remember what I have incessantly repeated: retirement is not about who we were, rather it is about who we will become.

With these new understandings as to why some people find it easy to connect, while others fail or find it difficult to create enduring relationships, perhaps it is time to use this newfound knowledge to our advantage; that is, to up our engagement profiles; to get out of the house and greet the world. This could well become a turning point, your chance to reshape who you are into who you want to be. We are not talking about a personality makeover; we are talking about changing behaviors that were perceived as being somewhat off-putting to others, the others you wanted to get to know and tried to engage with; but you were not successful and didn't understand why. Well, maybe now you know. It's hard to see our personal flaws, but easy to see flaws in others. We can change our behaviors, we can apologize for past transgressions, and we can start anew—amazing ourselves and our new friends.

REACH OUT AND REALLY TOUCH SOMEONE

Without engagement, no communicative act is even possible. Engagement requires two willing participants. But we live in a different, technologically connected world, and the forms, if not the substance, of our engagements have substantially changed. Today, because of technology, we no longer have to be face to face to be engaged with a partner, whether it is an individual, group, or a universe full of people. Events happen in an instant and communication and knowledge of those events, whether good or bad, follows with startling rapidity. However, with speed comes thoughtlessness, mindless responses, and inane drivel intended more to fill space rather than contribute to the debate, wherever out there it actually is. We incite rather than quell—we want and crave to be noticed and recognized by others, fulfilling our personal needs to be heard, regardless of the worth of our purported contribution. Whether emailing, texting, tweeting, Facebooking, or Skyping, we all must recognize that what we say leaves an electronic crumb trail right back to us—so don't say anything you will regret, or that you want to keep private— you've been warned. Many of our communications are what I call "fact or content free," that is, solely created to satisfy our need to be part of the engagement process to be recognized as being alive, even electronically, to fill empty space with useless information thereby reducing the impact and importance of all communications. People have an insatiable desire to be heard and listened to—to be recognized and valued by others as someone special in some way or another, whether for good deeds or bad. The price we pay for freedom is the freedom to be bombarded by countless appeals for money, inane drivel, drunken tirades, endless advertisements for male enhancement pills, and otherworldly offers of millions of dollars if you just send some Nigerian official your bank account information—and you know, some people actually do, so what were they thinking?

Because many, if not most, of our communications and interactions occur electronically, we are losing the ability and the willingness to communicate and interact face to face, to see and read critical and elucidating facial expressions and the body language so important to the communicative act. Yes, you are correct, we can view each other on our computer screens, as finally the promise of the 1950s has come true for us all, and it's free thanks to Skype. But we are hiding behind our HD screens, oftentimes building false impressions of who we are, giving up the opportunity to see and touch, to empathize and to comfort that only human to human contact allows. Anyone, regardless of message, whether life affirming or life destroying, can reach vast, anonymous audiences, and the more absurd the video or the message, the more likely it will spread, reinforcing the constant regurgitation of more and more useless garbage masquerading as communication and information.

CAN YOU SING "KUMBAYA"?

So there you have it, a quick trip through the world of "us," our behaviors and how those behaviors are played out in the many and diverse environments we co-inhabit. Can you spot yourself in this ménage, or are you fearful of looking underneath your own blankets? Actually few of us interact with or confront the world from a single behavioral profile. Indeed, the true measure of a socially adept person is their ability to find multiple ways for communicating with diverse audiences and individuals. Don't label yourself or anyone else, no one is beyond salvation, even the dreaded Manipulator. Accept people for who they are and how they can enrich our lives, and we theirs, because we all have value and we all share this earth. Now, let's all sing the Peter, Paul and Mary classic that filled our young heads with love for mankind, when we were naive and telling our parents how wrong they were about everything: a one and a two and a three—sorry that was a Lawrence Welk moment—*Kumbaya my Lord, Kumbaya; Kumbaya my Lord, Kumbaya; Kumbaya my Lord, Kumbaya.* Now hold hands and give each other a giant drug-free hug, just like the old days. Right-on!

CHAPTER 14

■ ■ ■ ■ ■ ■

The Power of Wonderment
KEEPING OUR BRAINS
CREATIVELY OCCUPIED

*Anyone who keeps the ability to
see beauty never grows old.*
—Franz Kafka

*We are perishing for want of wonder,
not for want of wonders.*
—G.K. Chesterton

OUR AGING BRAINS

As we age it becomes ever more important to keep our brains operating at peak capacity. Perhaps this is my way of introducing a topic that is literally on all our minds, and perhaps the number one fear for many of us—*will my brain fail me?* There is no polite or easy way of saying this. Yes, our brains do change as we age and not necessarily for the better. According to the National Institute of Aging, we can expect these changes in our brain as we age: certain parts of the brain actually shrink, particularly the areas controlling learning, memory, and the ability to perform complex mental activities; brain neurons lose some of their ability to communicate with each other slowing response times; blood vessels get smaller and harder, compromising blood flow within our brain; plaques gum up the works; free radicals run wild and aggressively go after healthy brain molecules; and as our body attempts to fight off disease, inflammation throughout our body increases. The net result is as we age some of us will notice becoming more forgetful; and that it's sometimes harder to learn new things and perform complex tasks. This is certainly a scary list of possible "horribles," but do not lose hope because we can fight back, physically, mentally and emotionally, and keep the scourge of dementia and other neurodegenerative diseases at bay.

LISTEN TO YOUR BRAIN, NOT YOUR STOMACH

As usual there are the same-old-same-old suggestions and nostrums that we hear at every doctor's visit and read in every article on healthy aging; but as much as we understand their implications, many of us fail to heed the advice. So, one more time, what can we do to help our brains remain healthy and fully functioning? The answers remain the same, we have to do it on our own; no one can do it for us. Basically, it involves controlling the risk factors that lead to heart disease and diabetes, which can ultimately compromise our brains. So here it goes one more time: (a) eat a healthy diet; (b) maintain a healthy weight; (c) get regular exercise and be physically vigorous; (d) remain intellectually active and curious; and, (e) stay socially engaged.[18]

But how many of us actually take these recommendations seriously? We have to commit to doing these things; and that's what this book is all about—getting the most out of the rest of our lives—and we can't do this if we are attached to tubes and machines, or can't remember our own names. But there is a way forward and dementia does not have to be us. It's time to address, perhaps, what we least understand—how to keep our brains active, fully engaged, and healthy.

TAKING OUR BRAIN OUT TO PLAY

There are many ways to stimulate our minds and imaginations, some are healthy and others not. My recommendation is to take the healthy road to brain stimulation, and many of us who experienced the '60s know what I am talking about. It might appear, at first blush, counter-intuitive, but my approach is to release the child within us, you know the curious little being that is always exploring, asking questions, and constantly seeking and experiencing that sense of wonderment we all knew as children. The thrill of discoveries big and small, like figuring out where your brother actually came from, or seeing your first movie on a big screen is the wonderment that drives society and civilization forward, and keeps us constantly curious and life engaged.

INDEPENDENT THINKERS WANTED

In the technologically driven world we now inhabit we never have to leave our homes to be informed, educated, entertained or shop because the world comes to us. Our home technological inventory has grown in size, ubiquity, and as some would say, iniquity. Our 60-inch high-definition 3D television screens and our computers, iPads and smartphones are the new portals to the world, or what I call "reality-light." Everything we see and hear is filtered and siphoned, translated, transmuted, and tortured before it ever reaches our eyes and ears; so we only see and hear what others want us to see and hear—this is sadly our new reality. We no longer seek independent or personal verification, we just accept what we get from our media devices and computers as gospel. No need to inconvenience ourselves; or to go outside and get wet or cold to attend a concert or a play; or cheer on our grandchildren in their first sporting event or school performance; or to just observe the world in all its beauty and ugliness; or to shape our own views and opinions based on observation and personal experience. Rather, we are being told what is right or wrong; or what we should believe in or not believe in. Mass media is for the masses and those who control the media control us. We have, to a great extent, lost our individuality and reclaimed the herd mentality where some must die so others can live. Rugged individuality is scorned and derided. We are a one-for-all and an all-for-one society, where conformity is rewarded, and heretics, or those who do not accept the prevailing dogma, are literally and figuratively hounded out of town or burned at the stake.

Or we could simply avoid the "inconvenience" and stress of either running with the herd or declaring ourselves nonconformists and swimming upstream by just agreeing with "Big Brother" and simply adopting the politically correct flavor of the day. If we don't find that alternative to our liking we can feed our brains alcohol or other stimulants to the point that we just don't care about anyone or anything, but only about where our next high is coming from, legal or otherwise. While there are many ways to keep our brains entertained and active, isolating ourselves in our homes, and viewing the world through an HD screen is in actuality a false idol separating us from humanity, the touch of others and the joys and sadness of life on planet earth. Sticking our heads in the sand, metaphorically speaking of course, is not the path to enlightenment; rather, an escape from our personal realities that each of us must confront and come to terms with. As I see it we have two choices, we can either remain fully engaged with life with all its shortcomings and flaws; or seek isolation mentally and/or physically from what is admittedly an imperfect world.

THE WORLD WILL ALWAYS BE A MYSTERIOUS PLACE

We are so over-stimulated that we have become desensitized to the ugliness and the beauty surrounding us. If it isn't loud, in our faces, scaring us, or amusing us we don't pay attention. And don't you think those in the business of selling us the things we "need" whether it is ideology or products haven't learned that lesson. We are bombarded by appeals and deals everywhere we turn, but retirement should be our time to get back to basics, to slow down and at least smell some of the roses; and to once again view our world with constant wonderment. My world, our world remains a mysterious place where sometimes, just sometimes small can be big and big can be small. Do you remember, as a young child, looking up at the heavens and seeing those twinkling tiny spots of light blanketing the sky from horizon to horizon? I distinctly remember doing just that while walking home alone on a dark country road, gazing in wonderment at the magnificent light display over my head. Did I know that each of those gleaming tiny pinpoints of light could swallow planet earth whole; or even that our sun was a star? Heck no, all that knowledge came later on, but I remember that evening like it was yesterday. So, something actually very big, like a star in the sky, can look very small to a child. How about the first time you came across a spider, and rather than squashing it you let it live and observed how it built its web, so delicate looking but so intricate and strong that it could ensnare all sorts of creepy flying and crawling things. That spider was one of life's tableaus that once frightened me, but later held me transfixed as the spider wrapped its victim in a cocoon of silky threads. I did not know why the victim was mummified until I sought out a book at the public library. Here something a little like a spider spinning its web takes on a new, much larger dimension in a child's fertile mind, as I wondered what would happen if I got caught in a spider's web; this is the stuff that dreams and nightmares are made of. How many of us changed our life course based on these scenes of wonderment and became the scientists, the explorers, the doctors, the builders and even the astronauts who so boldly went into space not knowing if they would ever return or what they would find. We are shaped by what we see for ourselves and what we learn from others; and by how that knowledge is digested by our brains and then translated into behaviors and actions.

We should always be living in this constant state of wonderment—always looking, always questioning, always thinking; and above all, always learning. It's never too late to learn about ourselves, about our histories, and even more importantly, about our futures and the futures of our progeny. We are all different, but in some ways very much the same. Some of us are givers, others takers; some are trustworthy others are not; some are everyday heroes some scoundrels; some are dreamers, and others hardcore realists; some see the cup half full, others half empty; but in the end we all must share this planet and learn to live or die together. I want to view and feel the world with all my senses never becoming complacent or bored, because the world is my schoolyard, as it should be yours; and we should never, never become inured to the trials and tribulations of others who share this planet with us—man, woman, beast or bug—because sometimes small can be big; and big can be small.

VIEWING LIFE IN FIRST PERSON

Staying engaged with life and with others and keeping our brains stimulated, occupied, and fully entertained is something we need to work at—it doesn't just happen on its own. Here are some suggestions and some approaches that worked for me. First of all, don't view the world through intermediaries, whether it is the media, technologies of any shape or form, friends, or significant others. Whenever possible do it in first person. Be a marcher in, not a viewer of life's passing parade. Resist the temptation to hide away regardless of the reasons, legitimate or otherwise, that reverberate in our heads. Hobbies are great, as long as they are not singular. Join affinity clubs of all types civic or otherwise. Volunteer because it is a double win both for you and for those you associate with as a volunteer. I find the opportunity to interact with children of all ages most rewarding, because aren't they the future us? There are literally hundreds, if not thousands, of local opportunities to volunteer. There are websites devoted to matching organizations seeking volunteers with perspective—volunteers, especially seniors, who have the time, the experience and the desire to help their communities.

While television is no longer the waste-land it once was, it now contains hundreds of channels of drivel, but amongst them are some gems. Even with those few saving graces television can actually distort reality as do the mega million-dollar movies and computer games packed with violence. The images that flicker before our eyes actually create a false reality turning us into voyeurs; a reason to stay home to watch a favorite program and an excuse for not getting out and about. But we must force ourselves to see the world through different lenses and not shut out viewpoints and lifestyles that differ from ours; after all, we don't have to adopt them, we just have to understand them. Every type of personal taste or entertainment preference can be satisfied on those ever-expanding television and computer screens from the prurient to the artistic, from the pugilistic to the patriotic—it's all there in living color. And sports, ah all those sports—indeed, we never have to leave the house except to replenish our stores. But if watching others get hurt, sweaty, and rich is not your cup of tea, then stop being passive participants or "cheerleaders"; rather, get outside where you can became sweaty, tired and dirty, if not rich.

LIFELONG LEARNING REQUIRES A LIFELONG COMMITMENT

We are always learning, perhaps not in the formal sense, but learning nonetheless. Sometimes those learnings are helpful to us and other times not so much, because we learn bad habits as well as good ones. We learn by being around others and modeling those behaviors and thoughts; or through the various media; or, through trial and error; or through observation; whether we know it or not. Sometimes we set out to learn new things because they interest us and add new dimensionality to our lives; because, if we are not actively learning and adding to our stores of brain cells, knowledge, and experience, then the only possible outcome is a sometimes slow and other times rapid loss of our cognitive abilities.

So how do we prevent our brains from getting soft on us? The answer is actually quite simple: use it or lose it, as they say. That's right, put stress on your brain, take it out of its rut, see and do new things, surprise the brain, break from routine, and you will surprise yourself. Like any body part, what is not used will atrophy whether it is our hearts, our muscles, or our brains. What better way to keep our brain occupied than to take it back to school, that's right I said "school." Going back to school is becoming popular amongst the senior set as we seek new opportunities to exercise our bodies and brains. Typically going under the rubric of "Lifelong Learning," many, if not most, colleges and universities around the nation offer educational opportunities to us seniors, typically the over-60 set, at no cost to the student, except perhaps for some course fees and books. At these and similarly named institutes, seniors can re-experience the joy of learning by enrolling in noncredit courses designed to appeal to the "gray heads," or by allowing us to audit; that is, enroll in almost any course in the college catalogue, on a space-available basis, again at nominal cost. And while you will not get course credit, you should be prepared to complete all assignments and meet all course requirements, if you want to get the most out of the experience. Once enrolled, either as an audit or in specifically designed courses geared to seniors, you are considered a member of the college community and can use most college facilities including libraries, computers, and athletic facilities, and even attend college-sponsored athletic events, performances, special lectures; but no, you still can't bring alcohol to the stadium.

Even if you didn't go to college, or it was more "animal house" than "school house," these experiences will take you back to those most memorable years; but this time you will actually learn something, because you now possess something very important called "maturity." These formal and informal learning opportunities will enrich your life by keeping you mentally engaged; break you out of your less-than-positive life routines, and out of your house and onto college campuses, rubbing shoulders with the next generation responsible for keeping our social security coming. It will also create new social opportunities; teach you how to confidently form and articulate thoughts and ideas; and perhaps most importantly, sharpen your thinking and build cognitive skills that fortify your brain against all those nasty neurodegenerative diseases. So what do you have to lose—try it, you might like it, just ask Mikey.

LIBRARIES REACH OUT TO SENIORS

Colleges and universities are not the only places where we can exercise our brains. Libraries have become safe havens for the older set who still enjoy the written word and who like to hold books and turn actual, not virtual pages. In addition to providing reading materials many libraries offer seniors access to computers and printers. Many provide digital literacy programs as well, a fancy way of saying teaching us older folks how to use that stuff. We live in a digital world and we don't want to be left behind, now do we? There are many benefits to becoming digitally literate. It not only connects us to our families, our children and grandchildren in living breathing color on Skype; it also connects us to the world; and perhaps, most of all to Amazon and eBay, and almost every big box store where we can let our fingers do the shopping without having to drive in bad weather, or brave the heat or the cold. Even more importantly, it puts knowledge at our fingertips, provided you can separate the junk science and the scammers from the legitimate purveyors of truth, knowledge, and informed discourse on almost any subject. It provides portals to governments at all levels and to information, services, and assistance that we didn't even know were available to us.

Libraries also support social engagement by sponsoring lectures, book clubs, and hosting small concerts and theater groups geared to the older set; and by providing free books to seniors oftentimes donated to the library by patrons for just that purpose. Many libraries also take their services directly to the senior community through bookmobiles and into senior centers, nursing homes, congregate care facilities, and adult homes and hospitals.

THE LOCAL CONNECTION—SENIOR CENTERS

Many cities, towns, and counties sponsor senior centers that promote active and healthy living, while also serving as a safe haven and gathering place for our community's seniors, particularly those who do not have other opportunities for positive socialization and engagement. The senior centers are often supported by local or regional transportation systems that get seniors to their doctor appointments, or to the supermarket; and to special events, whether they are walking under their own power or in wheelchairs. Volunteers and staff provide intellectual stimulation, tips on healthy living, entertainment, and a friendly place to gather and to meet and greet and share a communal meal with others.

TRAVEL WITH A PURPOSE

I have discovered that travel is one of the most fulfilling learning experiences we will ever encounter. Visiting new places, meeting new people and experiencing different cultures can be life-changing events and can give you an entirely new life perspective. For those with the wanderlust, and the cash to support it, seeing the world and joining the army of senior travelers just might be your cup of tea. You can do this solo, with significant others or friends; or in the company of like-minded seniors who actively navigate our world by seeking pre-planned group travel opportunities. Travel is truly a first-person experience and you can make it as exotic, as physical, and as comfortable as you please—it's your choice. While making travel plans, particularly to far-away places, can be exciting, they can also be complex and oftentimes scary because we don't know what we are walking in to. So many of us leave our travel plans to the experts and nonprofit organizations such as Road Scholar, formerly known as Elderhostel. Road Scholar provides, as they call it, "educational adventures for adults 55 and over." These adventures typically combine travel and educational opportunities to seniors in the United States and in 150 countries around the globe in which students can "experience in-depth learning and behind-the scenes learning opportunities, from cultural tours and study cruises to walking, biking, and more"—these are their words, not mine. If you have the financial wherewithal this is a good way to go because all those "nitty gritty" details are taken care of by knowledgeable travel professionals. Depending on where you are traveling, there are staff and experts familiar with those regions accompanying you throughout the journey. Fellow travelers are quickly embraced by a similar demographic with similar interests, experiences, and expectations; it's the type of environment that makes single travelers feel welcomed. You will learn from each other, from experts; and more importantly, by interacting with fellow travelers and residents of the communities in which you are temporarily living. But most importantly, travelers come away with a better understanding of how different cultures and people live, whether at home in the United States or around the world. New, perhaps lifelong, friendships will be formed; new discoveries about yourself and others will be made that will educate and elucidate to make you a more knowledgeable world citizen. Ultimately, you can come away with a better understanding of how different and really similar we are regardless of where we live, our ethnicity, our politics, our cultures, or religions. New pictures will be added to photo albums and new memories added to our memory banks that will last a lifetime.

While my wife and I have traveled extensively around the U.S. and Europe on our own, we have yet to visit those more exotic places or seek out group travel opportunities. We recently broke the mold and did our first river cruises with an outfit called Grand Circle Travel, which proved to be an excellent and safe way to see new and interesting places in the company of compatible others. The river cruises are done on purpose-built vessels with a guest capacity of about 150, so they can get through the canals, which are actually quite narrow in Europe because they were built so many years ago. You quickly get to know your fellow travelers, to socialize, share your meals, and tour with, who come from all over the U.S., each with a different story to tell, and lasting friendships can result. The neat part of river cruising is once you get on the boat you never have to move your luggage again, because unlike bus tours you are fed, housed, and entertained on the same vessel throughout the entire trip, docking, most of the time within walking distance of all the main attractions of the villages, towns, and cities along the route.

And like Road Scholars, knowledgeable program leaders accompany you on the trip identifying sites along the way and educating guests about the cultures, the people and the histories of each country, village, town, and city we pass through, as well as leading land-based group tours at all the stops. It's a fun, convenient, educational, and socially enriching way to travel.

DOING GOOD, HELPING OTHERS

Volunteer organizations offer opportunities to travel, appreciate new cultures, and to help at the same time. Volunteer vacations, sometimes known as "voluntours" provide the opportunity to give back while traveling, regardless of ages, skills, or interests. While many nonprofits offer these opportunities, I will identify the three that I am personally familiar with (although I do not endorse these or any other organization of this type nor do I suggest you run out and blindly sign up—this is solely for edification and consideration).

- **Appalachian Trail Conference:** Want to stay local? Then what about helping to maintain the 2,000 mile long Appalachian Trail in return for food and very basic accommodations.

- **Peace Corps, Worldwide:** This is the same Peace Corps that attracted the idealistic young but is now looking for the idealistic and skilled among the senior class who were young when it all started—what comes around goes around. A commitment of 27 months is required.

- **Habitat for Humanity:** They are dedicated to providing affordable housing for low income families and do great work in this country and all over the world.

A FINAL PLEA

Staying mentally engaged is the key to, if not longevity, then to pre-serving our most important asset—our brains. When we do this life is interesting; because without dreams and something to look forward to, there is no reason to get up every morning, to get dressed just to stare at the television or our computer screens. We must fight the urge to fade into the background to become the unseen; rather, we must break with routine and seek new experiences because we are never too old to learn, or too old to make new friends and travel to new places whether it is around the world or around our block. We have seen it all and done it all, and now is our time to do it again, and again and again—never, never go silently into that dark night. We must first find and define ourselves, and there is no better time to do it than now. Enjoying the rest of our lives with others surrounding us should be our new mantra because one is the loneliest number we'll ever know; or so they say.

CHAPTER 15

■ ■ ■ ■ ■ ■

The Adventurous Retiree
AROUND THE WORLD OR
AROUND THE CORNER

*You cannot discover new oceans unless you
have the courage to lose sight of the shore.*
—Andre Gide

I haven't been everywhere, but it's on my list.
—Susan Sontag

VIRTUAL WORLDS, NONVIRTUOUS BODIES

We live in a virtual world, but we don't have virtual bodies—at least not yet. Thus, every so often our "bodies" should be taken out for air and exercise, although I recommend more than a casual outing with your body every so often—way more. It's sad but true, as noted in previous chapters, that many of our contemporaries are enjoying the "good life," eating too much and moving too little, and the net result of such behaviors is expanding waistlines and greater exposure to a host of debilitating conditions and diseases. Work has become less physical, travel has become less physical, interacting with others has become less physical, recreation has become less physical, shopping has become less physical—because we play, travel, shop, and interact on our computers.

And, what makes all this slothfulness possible? Yup, you got it, the wonderful world of technology and the ever growing selection of "apps" (which I guess is geek-speak for "applications," or in my view, for never having to get off our butts.) Not only do all these apps afford us the prospect of never having to leave our homes or apartments by providing us with the limitless ability to find anything; and then have others do all those pesky daily chores and activities that we apparently have no time or desire to do any longer. But, it also isolates us from our neighborhoods and impedes contact with other human beings who we just might casually encounter when out and about. What's missing from our lives is chaos, serendipity, and happenstance that we once counted on to save us from boredom and routine—or any excuse to do some-thing different than whatever we were doing at the time, like homework or housework or even no work. We over-plan, overthink, over-spend, and overindulge in the wrong things. Let go of your iPads, iPhones, and iPods. Go outside your door and walk around, you just might be surprised by what you find; and then travel to a country that has yet to even see the technological shackles that bind you—and by the way, leave them home because if you are where you can "get a signal" you're in the wrong place.

WHAT DO YOU MEAN BY "ADVENTURE"?

Jules the Kiwi (a New Zealander with a YouTube presence) defines adventure as "extreme circumstances recalled in tranquility." Adventure is probably harder to describe or define than it is to find, but let's try. Adventure is something we do, not something that is done to us. It is something we seek—adventure does not come looking for us. Adven-ture can be a sport, hobby, travel, or any activity that challenges your physical self, takes you out of your comfort zone, or makes you sweaty and tired. Adventure can be right outside your door or across the globe;

it can be 30,000 feet in the sky or hundreds of feet below the oceans or the earth. It is something we want to get better at or have never done before. Adventure requires us to accept risk but at the same time to do everything possible to avoid getting injured. Adventure is something we can master, but is still worthwhile if you fail—the adventure is in the attempt, not the result, because failure becomes the bridge to success. Adventure is something we talk about and remember for a lifetime. Adventure releases us from our Zombie-like existence; it wakes us up and welcomes us back to the "land of the living" like a cold splash of water on the face in the morning. Adventure is the opposite of boring, of comfortable or of mundane. Adventure takes us to new places; some are beautiful to behold, some exotic, some just plain depressing as we become observers of how most of the rest of our planet lives. Adventure is never giving up and always moving forward. Adventure is overcoming fear and becoming the stronger for it. Adventure is when fear turns into an ally; and when fear becomes our strength. Adventure is sometimes getting injured, but wounds heal and we go forward again, and then again until both our fears and our challenges are conquered. Giving up is not in our vocabulary. Adventure is exploration of who we are as people—what we are made of and what we want to become. Adventure is our muse and partner throughout life—don't abandon her—embrace the spirit if not the result, or as Samuel Beckett, an Irish playwright, poet, and novelist, so wisely told us, "Ever tried. Ever failed. No matter. Try again. Fail again, Fail better."

RETIREMENT WILL ONLY BE AS GOOD AS OUR LAST ADVENTURE

If nothing else, adventure will break you out of your stupor and get you moving, dreaming, and thinking once again about all of life's possibilities. It will give purpose and meaning to your life—this is your quest to be better at something, to conquer something, to plan something you previously could not have even imagined doing, to do something with your partner and to become an "adventure team." Life is not without risk—sometimes we just have to want to "walk on the wild side" to confront fear, to challenge both our physical and mental selves and to come out the other side bruised, perhaps, but not defeated, and with renewed courage and commitment to a life of action, exploration, and renewal; or of doing things we have never done before.

Age should never be a barrier to leading an adventurous life because life itself should be an adventure at every age. Rekindle that childlike wonderment, fearlessness, and urge to explore. As a child, were you worried about every bump and bruise? Probably not. Rather, you were excited by the "hunt" and not concerned with the consequences. Remember when Mom or Dad found out you left your proscribed boundaries to explore the neighborhood or to visit a friend? Sure, you paid the price, but you also came away with new knowledge and confidence about yourself and the world; it wasn't so scary, now was it? Children today are rarely allowed to experience independence or failure in their overprotective worlds. This generally leaves our children, at whatever age we finally release those bonds, exceptionally unprepared for the vagaries of life and the real world they will encounter when set free to roam the planet on their own. Some of us go to the extreme and abuse our newfound freedoms, learning life's lessons perhaps the hard way, while yet others eventually discover life's balance point, some more quickly than others, between freedom and responsibility, called self-discipline, a necessary prerequisite for adulthood, a time when all parents can breathe a bit easier.

AGE SHOULD NEVER BECOME A BARRIER TO ADVENTURE

As we age, we become fearful not only of new experiences but also of damaging our fragile bodies. But that's the point—our bodies become fragile because we are afraid to move them, to exercise them, to challenge our physical selves; and, like any biological or physical system, if not used, our bodies will atrophy. Everybody has a "season" and a purpose and we need to prepare our bodies for each season and the specific purpose that our bodies will be used for—so my bicycle body is different than my skiing body and my hiking body is different from my sailing body, and I look forward to those transitions as I look forward to the change of seasons, full knowing that new and old adventures will greet me with a "where have you been—let's get going" élan, and I will say, "I missed you." Life is a smorgasbord, so sample all it has to offer—the ordinary and the risky, the beauty and the ugliness, the sadness and the joy—and never regret what you did or did not taste because there is still time to feast at the table of life.

Adventure can be tame or wild and woolly—it's entirely up to you. A gentle hike of two miles through woods and streams is just as adventurous to most of us as a climb up Mount Everest would be to a seasoned expert. Remember the words of Lao Tzu, "a journey of 1,000 miles begins with a single step," then, at the very least, take that single step.

LITTLE SEPARATES THE BRAVE FROM THE FOOL OR FROM THE JUST LUCKY TO BE ALIVE

I believe you get the point. This is not a contest to see who is the bravest or most foolish among us, because little separates the brave from the fool or from those who are just lucky to be alive. Indeed, adventures can have danger attached to them—after all, that is what makes them adventures. But there are all manner of adventurous activities we can engage in, from literally, a walk in the park to climbing the tallest mountains in the world—it's our choice. But most importantly, we must not let others make the decisions for us or goad us into activities we are not yet mentally and physically prepared for. It's better to walk away than expose ourselves to injury or harm because both bravado and fear can surely get us hurt.

TAKE LIFE FROM DULL TO DARING

The goal of this book, and particularly of this chapter, is to bring some controlled chaos and serendipity back into your life and to provide the incentive as well as the ability to break the bonds of comfortable routine in which many of us probably find ourselves today, and to take your life from dull to daring. We are going on a journey of discovery and adventure, hoping to find and then reconnect with our inner child, who has lain dormant in our bodies, yearning to get out and play yet again. I urge you to choose the adventure road as Ralph Waldo Emerson so eloquently encourages us to take, "do not go where the path may lead, go instead where there is no path and leave a trail."

And why is adventure so important? First, a life of boredom can literally and figuratively kill us. Boredom will suck out our souls, damage our psyches, and push us to replace constructive behaviors and activities with self-harming behaviors, like alcohol and drugs, to fill the time. The feelings of hopelessness and helplessness common to those having too much time and too little to do, can drive even the healthy into depression. Second, those among us who challenge their minds and bodies live longer and have a better quality of life. Physically active seniors remain stronger, healthier, more flexible, and agile, and more mentally alert than those planting themselves in front of computers or televisions or driving around in golf carts rather than walking. That's my approach, and I'm sticking to it, whether you believe it or not. You see—my way is more fun, or as Truman Capote tells us, "failure is the condiment that gives success its flavor." Retirement shouldn't be a race to see how many bucket list items you can cross off—it isn't about impressing your friends and neighbors; rather, it is about recapturing the joy and thrill of life; allowing yourself to test your limits and abilities; challenging yourself in the environment in which you live; and the will to seek adventure in all its forms and to experience the world in the first person and not virtually. Are you there yet? Well, maybe yes and maybe no.

PREPARE TO GET LOST IN ADVENTURE— THE WORLD AWAITS

Active, adventurous retirees are always searching for new experiences—particularly if they have the means, the desire, the health, and the time. One of our favorite pastimes is travel; particularly tempting are those tantalizing offers that cross our computer screens screaming at us to take this trip or that one for an amazingly low price—the cognoscenti among us call, "*last minute travel deals!*" and who doesn't like a deal? Some of us, however, have gotten a bit jaded about what I call "ancient mariner" type travel opportunities, those trips catering to the less adventurous among us, like cruises to nowhere in particular; or eight-hour "stops and goes" on ships bigger than most towns with kitschy entertainment and bland but well-presented foods. If your travel tastes have gone beyond these pre-programmed types of travel, then a new world awaits you—it's called "adventure travel." Just remember, it's called adventure travel for a reason; it is an inherently active experience where the traveler is not an onlooker or bystander but rather a participant. The range of adventure travel experiences runs the gamut from leisurely (where almost anyone can enjoy the adventure without fear of injury or exhaustion) to "extreme adventure" where you have to be fit, skilled, and willing to undergo hardship and discomfort, but the payoff to your psyche is well worth the effort, and the stories and pictures you will bring home will reverberate in your memory until your last days on earth—remember when . . .

Henry Miller, a playwright and novelist of distinction but sometimes better known as the husband of Marilyn Monroe, once said, "One's destination is never a place, but a new way of seeing things." Travel indeed opens our eyes to sights never seen, to cultures never experienced, and to wonders never imagined. Clearly, the new, the different, the sometimes vile smells emanating from fetid living conditions are as important as the "lilies of the field"—because travel is not about entertainment, it is about finding the truth within ourselves and the truth about the world we live in. Indeed, we will come away from every adventure with a new way of "seeing things."

THERE'S SOMETHING OUT THERE FOR EVERY ONE OF US

An entire industry has been created to satisfy the ever-escalating cravings for another adrenaline rush of those "adventurous travelers." These experiences can range across the entire adventure spectrum from posh, where our every need is catered to, whether in the deepest jungle or the teeming cities, and where the worst that can happen is to twist an ankle or encounter an insect on our person, to extreme adventures, where there is no safety net, and nothing between us and potential injury or death other than our own abilities. Where you are positioned on this spectrum is up to you individually—and to the adventure outfitter, who also makes judgments about your capabilities to withstand the rigors of the experience you are seeking to participate in.

The first question we must ask ourselves is, *Am I ready for adventure travel?* Be careful what you wish for. We must determine where we are on the adventure scale, including our fitness for physical activity and our tolerance for a certain degree of discomfort. Once we have established our personal limits then it is time to dive into the world of adventure travel and select the experience that best fits our interests and our pocketbooks, because some can be quite expensive.

START WITH THE FAMILIAR AND THE COMFORTABLE

Before gallivanting to the four corners of the world, we might want to start our adventure travels in more familiar territory. How about the United States and Canada, where there are unlimited opportunities for adventure travel? In fact, our own states and regions are sources for almost untold adventure opportunities. But if that is too close to home then Western Europe beckons—where walking, hiking, climbing, and all sorts of adventure experiences await. Indeed, moderate climbing expeditions are quite common and done by all, old and young. Europeans tend to be enthusiastic walkers/hikers, even in the winter. Just to provide some additional perspective on what we seniors can do when adventure becomes part of our lives, former President George Bush went tandem skydiving to celebrate his 85th birthday on June 12, 2009, just as he did on his 75th and 80th birthdays. When asked why, he responded to the question by saying he was in good hands, and "just because you're an old guy, you don't have to sit around drooling in the corner."[19] Get out and do something. Get out and enjoy life.

Just like former President George Bush, become a nonconventional thinker—you have earned that right. Don't let others convince you that you can't or that it is "foolhardy" or even worse, "to act your age." Get that Harley-Davidson', yes, there is a possibility you might come to an untimely end, but if that is the thrill you seek then go for it, you can break a hip reaching for your iPad too. Conventional thinkers and doers don't challenge themselves or others, but that's how we grow as individuals and become better people, by constantly challenging who we are, what we believe, what we know, and who we want to become.

ADVENTURE IS RIGHT OUTSIDE OUR DOORS

If traveling to exotic or faraway places with cultures, environments, and dodgy political regimes is not high up on your bucket list; or, if engaging in sometimes dangerous pursuits does not fit within your comfort zone or financial abilities, then how about finding adventure right outside your door? For those of us willing to go farther afield, how about visiting countries with common languages and histories, or where our forbearers came from—because we are, after all, a land of immigrants. There are literally hundreds of "adventure activities" available to seniors that we can learn, do, and become good at, if not ultimately master—yup, we *can* learn new tricks. Some of these activities have a nominal cost of entry, while others can be equipment intensive and extremely physical, requiring great skill and fitness with perhaps a hint of danger, which might appeal to some but not to others.

I have selected a sample of these adventures/activities; the ones that I believe are most relevant and amenable to people of our age and ones that will demonstrate the breadth and reality of what is available to us right around the corner. The standards used to narrow the field for inclusion in my list of reachable sports/activities are the ones that best support and contribute to senior health, fitness, and physical capabilities, and their inclusion on this list was based on the following criteria: (1) get us moving and keep us moving; (2) keep us fit and don't tend to overstress any particular parts of our body; (3) stay close to home—we don't need to venture far from home to enjoy these newfound interests; (4) take us outdoors, where we can appreciate the wonder of nature, the change of seasons, and smell the fresh air—warm, cold, or otherwise; (5) are accessible: don't have to be a finely honed, well-practiced athlete to enjoy them; (6) are activities we can enjoy as a novice, and even more so after achieving greater and greater levels of proficiency without getting bored; (7) are adventures that can be shared with others—that's half the fun; (8) are adventure activities supported by clubs, organizations, and retailers, at whatever level we are, providing instruction, advice, mentoring, practice, and lessons in the "field" and brother- sisterhood opportunities for its members. Do we need any more reasons to get off our collective butts? I don't think so. So get out of that chair and let's get started!

WALKING FOR HEALTH, CULTURE, AND FUN

I find it interesting that what separates us from other animals, namely walking upright and true bipedalism, is something so many of us strive to avoid. Walking is typically our last option when setting out to get someplace. Many of us see walking as medicine or something health professionals tell us to do. I see walking as a way to enjoy life in slow motion—to get from one place to another while fully considering the beauty of life and of God's creations. I particularly enjoy walking with my wife in the downtown areas of both small and large cities, appreciating their rhythms and their diversity; or on paths designed for walkers that meander through hill and dale, and particularly so with our grandchildren. Without the grandkids knowing about it, I use these walks as learning opportunities both for them and for us. It was with this same spirit that my wife and I (more her than me) first planned and then realized a long dreamed-of walking tour of Merry Old England. The only equipment needed was good daypacks, water bottles, maps, a GPS, comfortable walking/hiking shoes or boots, walking sticks, and the proper togs typically made of polyester (not cotton because cotton absorbs sweat and polyester moves sweat away from our bodies, allowing it to evaporate and keeping us nice and dry in the winter and comfortable in the summer). It was a magnificent way to see the "other" England—or the "not London." We spent three weeks crossing town, hill, and dale, visiting the Lake District, York, Cambridge, Bath, Cornwall, Dartmoor, Royal Tunbridge Wells…the list goes on. Yes, we had a vehicle to take us to our destinations and haul the gear, but after arriving we parked the little beast with its steering on the wrong side and set out on foot, visiting pubs and local establishments and meeting other walkers and locals, seeing more and learning more than we possibly could have if we viewed England from the passing window of a bus, car, or train. We walked the moors, climbed over dozens of stiles, hopped over ancient rock walls, and climbed sturdy fences, wandering through churches and forts, through castles both restored and ruined, through estates and gardens, around Stonehenge and Castlerigg (a monument even older than Stonehenge, populated mainly by sheep), through museums and WWII airfields, through Winston Churchill's ancestral home, Wordsworth's cottage, and Beatrix Potter's farm, past the house where Karl Marx wrote his "Manifesto," and the birthplace of Oliver Cromwell.

We enjoyed that experience so much that we followed the England trip with a walk through the American West, exploring the numerous national and state parks in Utah, Colorado, Wyoming, and Montana. Once again our only gear was good walking or hiking boots, a couple of daypacks, some water bottles, and our walking sticks. Interestingly we were more familiar with Europe than with our own country, having never traveled to the western states of our magnificent nation, which is figuratively right outside our door when compared to traveling "across the pond," as they say.

DAY HIKING

Day hiking is a pleasant way to spend a day—something to look forward to and an opportunity to commune with nature. It gets our bodies moving and refocuses our thoughts, from mundane issues to what is really important, enjoying the outdoors, enjoying each other, and staying healthy. Even day hikes require preparation and planning. There are numerous guidebooks that identify local or regional hiking trails, and specify where the trailhead is located, the difficulty of terrain, the altitude rise, and the mileage you will be covering. It is absolutely critical, regardless of how easy you believe the hike will be or how well marked it is supposed to be, that you carry a detailed map of the area and of the trail you will be hiking. Check the weather forecast and current conditions and dress accordingly. You can always shed clothes, but you cannot add layers unless you have them with you. Wear comfortable, sturdy hiking boots and don't try to break in new boots on the trail. Let a friend or family member know where you are going and when you anticipate returning home. Don't go on a longer hike than you can comfortably handle. Gradually build up to the longer treks by starting with shorter adventures on familiar and comfortable trails. Make sure your daypacks contain all the necessities, including first aid supplies, bug repellent, flashlight, maps, compass, GPS (if you have one), snacks, lunch, and plenty of liquids (primarily sport drinks). Also beware of wildlife in the woods, especially those bigger than you—remember, they were there first. If there is a box at the trailhead containing trail maps and a sign-in ledger, record your name, address, and a contact name or cell number, noting the time you entered the trail and the time you anticipate exiting, and make sure that when you return you remove your name from the ledger or note that you have returned. Start early in the day to allow plenty of time to complete the hiking route well before dark. Pace yourself, bring a camera and preserve the beauty for others, and do not separate from your companions. Always stay on the marked trails and be aware of trail mergers, which can be confusing. Be familiar with the types of snakes and potentially harmful insects that you might encounter. Once you have mastered day hiking skills in familiar territory then you can expand out to longer and more challenging hikes. Eventually, you might even consider backpacking and camping in the wild—but that's for a different day.

GEOCACHING

A relatively new and growing activity, geocaching is like an adult treasure hunt using a combination of technology in the form of a GPS and our finely honed orienteering skills. Geocaching requires the collaboration of two separate parties—those who hide the caches and those who seek the caches, and usually each does both. When a cache (which typically contains non-valuable trinkets or toys and a logbook) is hidden, the party that did so records and publishes the longitudinal coordinates using a GPS. These coordinates are then published on known geocaching websites, such as geocaching.com, and then other geocachers search for these hidden "treasures," using their own GPS devices. When a cache is discovered the finder typically takes a few items and leaves a few new ones in return for future geocache hunters. The finder then signs the logbook, usually contained within the geocache, and records the date it was found and their pre-established geocaching code name. It is estimated that there are more than 1 million hidden caches around the globe. It is a great way to get out of the house and to do something fun and worthwhile that requires both skill and knowledge. And for many converts it turns into their "quest" or even a compulsion. After all, who doesn't like a treasure hunt? It's something enjoyed by old and young alike, especially a treasure hunt covering thousands of acres and requiring every bit of skill you can muster. A good quality backwoods or hiking specific GPS will set you back from $300 to $600.

BICYCLING FOR LIFE

Bicycling is one of the healthiest activities we can choose to become proficient at. It builds aerobic capacity and, unlike running, it doesn't stress our knees or feet, which may lead to a host of problems later on. And remember—it's just like riding a bike, meaning we never really forget how to ride a bicycle or the joy we felt when mastering the balance trick of staying up on two wheels without Mom or Dad holding the seat as off we went. As children, biking spelled f-r-e-e-d-o-m. We could go three times as far with less effort and still be home before our parents figured out where we were—what great memories we had of trips on our bikes. Today freedom is not our goal—because finally we have that—but rather we wish to enjoy our freedom, and there is no better way than on a bicycle. In a car the world rushes past you, when walking you see the world in slow motion, but on a bicycle the world comes into focus—not too fast and not too slow.

The bikes we rode as children are clearly not the bikes we ride today. Now there are essentially three general categories of bicycles to match our anticipated riding profiles. What differentiates bikes from one general category to another, with many variations within each category, is function, or what we intend to do with our shiny new two-wheeled beauty. Also, within each category there is wide variation in costs, based on the quality of components, the level of technology, and the material and sophistication of the bike. The three "simplified bicycle categories" are: (1) Road Bikes; (2) Mountain Bikes; and (3) Hybrid Bikes. And a helmet is mandatory equipment with each.

Road Bikes

I call this category "skinny tire" bikes. If you believe road biking is appealing and you are interested in purchasing this type of riding machine, my first and most important recommendation is that you purchase the best road bike you can afford, which also means the lightest road bike you can afford, because buying a cheaper bike is self-defeating and ultimately more expensive in the long run. When buying a road bike, especially, work with a bike specific retailer, but check them out first. Don't buy until you find a retailer that will allow you to test several models and a store that can properly fit you to the bike—this is critically important. The bike brand you ultimately purchase is less important than the quality of components and its weight. A good road bike should weigh in at around 20 pounds—anything less and you will pay a premium. The lightest road bikes are "full carbon" but that adds significant cost and some very good road bikes are made from aluminum. Remember, it's the quality of the components—the wheel sets, the crank, and the gear/derailleur—that make up much of the cost. You can expect to pay around $2,000 or more for a full carbon bike, and you could buy a very good aluminum-framed road bicycle, with perhaps some carbon bits, for around $1,000—think of it as an investment in yourself. If you have a friend who is an avid road biker, take him or her with you, an experienced eye always helps.

Mountain Bikes

If you want to ride off trail in the woods or hurtle down large or small mountains (sometimes under control and sometimes not), or jump off cliffs with your bike (hopefully still attached to your body), then this is your ideal bike. This bike is not, however, for the weak of heart, if you are using it for its intended purposes. I am not saying that some older folks don't ride mountain bikes, but if you are starting or renewing your acquaintance with bicycling after many years, put mountain biking off until you know what you are getting into. Mountain bikes typically have big knobby tires and a seriously strong frame, some with suspension systems and others without (for the hardcore who want lighter bikes so they can go faster, jump farther, and possibly hurt themselves more). Mountain bikes with all their accoutrements are not very efficient on roads, or even on dirt-packed trails because of their weight and fat tires. Real mountain bikes have a specific purpose, and that is to go up a hill and then back down it as fast as possible on a trail designed for maximum thrill and difficulty. Think twice, cut once if you are considering a mountain bike. Prices for mountain bikes range from around $500 for a plausible one to well over $4,000 for a professional-grade competitive bike.

Hybrid Bikes

Get a hybrid bike when you want to mate either the best or worst parts of a road bike with the worst and/or best parts of a mountain bike. The hybrid bike is a compromise, but a compromise with a purpose. It makes a very capable commuter bike or a bike to put panniers and baskets on so you can go shopping or traveling and camping with your new two-wheeled friend. It typically has a more comfortable seat than a road bike, and it sometimes has suspension components. You ride in the upright position and it's strictly for leisure riding, not long distance. Hybrids are typically made of aluminum and come as "fixies," single speed bikes, or with full multispeed derailleur setups. You can buy hybrid bikes for around $200 all the way up into the thousands for handmade models. Buy as much bike as you can afford, you will not regret it.

SNOW SPORTS

If you are fortunate enough to live in the colder climes, or willing and able to reverse the seasons by traveling, then snow sports are for you. They come in many forms, but I am addressing downhill or alpine skiing and cross country skiing. Cross country skiing has a low cost of entry and typically is a safer form of playing in the snow. You can cross country ski in almost any local park, in some golf clubs, in many state parks, or at commercial cross country facilities; downhill or alpine skiing, however, requires a visit to a ski resort.

Cross Country Skiing

Cross country skiing is quite invigorating and burns lots of calories, to say the least, for the active aficionado. It requires some skill to navigate both prepared and virgin trails, but with a little effort you will get the hang of it. Cross country skis are totally different from alpine skis. They are narrower, often without metal edges, and your heels are not locked into the skis because you are propelling yourself through the snow without benefit of gravity, at least most of the time—you have to get yourself up the hill and then you have to navigate these long narrow skis, which don't turn very easily, back down the hill. There are two types of cross country skis: (1) touring skis, or those designed for groomed trails with tracks, and (2) metal edged touring skis which are shorter for better maneuverability, grip on ice, and flotation in deeper snow and un-groomed trails. Cross country skiing is a great workout; it gets you outside in winter, and provides the opportunity to see nature in winter's dress, with animal tracks galore. You will need ski specific boots and proper clothing for winter sports of this type, and always remember to stay hydrated. You can rent cross country skis, boots, and poles and take lessons, which I strongly suggest you do prior to making any purchases—see if cross country skiing is right for you before you buy. A cross country ski package for a novice or an entry level skier with mounted bindings, poles, and boots can be purchased for around $300 and that does not include winter specific clothing or other gear you will want to wear on your adventure, including helmets. Oh, and if you see Sasquatch say hello for me.

Downhill or Alpine Skiing

This can be one of the most exhilarating sports on earth. We click into our bindings with our rented boots on our rented skis and proceed to the ski lift for a breathtaking ride up to the top of the mountain. Then we find the trail marked with a black diamond that friends told us was a piece of cake, point the skis down the hill, and, as Jackie Gleason used to say "away you go." Not so fast, buckaroo, you are not only putting yourself at risk but also all those who are within your cone of devastation. So who needs skiing lessons? The answer is simple: every-one and anyone who believes they can ski on difficult trails without knowing how to stop or slow their forward motion, as well as anyone who doesn't understand how gravity works. It's one thing to knock yourself out, but another to wipe out a squad of boarders and skiers by becoming a human bowling ball. The moral of this story is that downhill skiing can be, and is, exhilarating and exciting for those prepared for its challenges, but downhill skiing has never been kind to "fools" because the mountain will win every time. Skiing safely, enjoying all the sport has to offer, and skiing on increasingly difficult terrain is not about the equipment, it's about the *skier*. Skiing is a technical sport that needs to be learned and then practiced and then practiced some more, but that doesn't mean that novices cannot enjoy the sport. Then, after some more lessons, and practicing on incrementally more difficult trails, novice skiers will soon enough get to appreciate both the thrills and the eventual spills that make downhill skiing or boarding—and the attendant adrenaline rush—so exciting and almost addictive. Age is no barrier to this sport, some of my instructor colleagues are in their 80s and some of my guests are likewise. I learned to ski in my early 50s. The best way to approach downhill skiing is with enthusiasm and caution, starting slowly and taking lessons and then more lessons, and renting your skis and your equipment until you are confident that this is a sport for you. Properly equipping yourself for downhill skiing, including skis, boots, poles, helmet, goggles, ski gloves, and ski pants, will cost around $1,000 if purchased wisely.

CANOEING/KAYAKING

Purists would be aghast at even mentioning canoeing and kayaking in the same sentence. But, we're not purists—at least not yet. Both canoes and kayaks, although each have different purposes, shapes, and paddling techniques, offer us more mature folks an opportunity to get outside, to be on the water, and to get our bodies working in a beautiful setting at a relatively low price point—hey, it's cheaper than a yacht. Novices can enjoy their first outings as long as they stay within very defined and safe boundaries. And, since both types of vessels are fairly portable with the proper cartop carrier, you can take them wherever you go. I strongly suggest that you do some pre-buying research, then visit a canoe and/or kayak dealer; yes, most do carry both "species." Many of these retailers offer test floats in the spring and in the fall at very reasonable prices to help shed inventory and make way for the new models. Find a canoe or kayak to fit all your needs or purposes; for example, if there are two of you, then get a two-person canoe or kayak. Both canoes and kayaks tend to be tippy and both take practice and skill to use properly and safely, and that is why safety equipment is so important anytime you are on the water, no matter how deep or how big it is—"Safety First" is rule #1.

There are many variations on theme in both canoes and kayaks, so please consult someone who is quite familiar with these crafts or a dealer who has your interests in mind and not necessarily their own pocketbooks. Either of these vessels can take you into new worlds— worlds of flowing streams or overhanging foliage or tranquil lakes. Our ancestors' highways were the streams and rivers, as the native populations will attest, so go back to a simpler time and you just might find floating and paddling under your own power to be a delightful and meaningful experience—as long as you stay away from those pesky motorboats, that is. I know that when my sailing days have come to an end, I will seek the "skinny waters," the tranquility and the sounds of running streams, to keep me close to nature and on the water. The cost of entry into either canoeing or kayaking is dependent on the type or function you want the canoe or kayak to perform and the build quality, including the materials used, and the weight, strength, and durability of the vessel— lighter is better and more expensive. At the low end, you can get into two-person kayaks or canoes with paddles and basic safety equipment plus a cartop carrier for around $2,000. But, remember this warning—try before you buy, and take lessons and a safety course before setting out on your own.

WHAT'S STOPPING YOU?

Well, we have just concluded our trip through the world of adventure. Many, if not most, of these adventures are right outside your door; some have nominal or almost no cost of entry, like walking and day hiking, while others require a commitment of money and of the time to learn how to safely engage in the activity of choice, whatever it is. It doesn't cost more to take your travel from boring to exciting, so why not seek travel opportunities that offer a hint of adventure to start and then ramp up your experiences and their difficulty from there, as you become acclimated or better yet, addicted to the thrill, the energy, the feeling of well-earned fatigue, and finally the joy and excitement of adventure sports and of looking around the next corner, wondering what mysteries will present themselves. This is your time to "fly and be free" so take advantage of it while you are healthy enough, willing enough, and financially secure enough to do something different tomorrow than you did today. The formula for a healthy, satisfying life in retirement is, repeat after me, "Eat! Sleep! Move! Think! Pray!" And, keep smiling—it confuses people!

THE ADVENTUROUS RETIREE'S CHECKLIST

These are some of the qualities inherent in adventurers of any stripe or age. You don't have to possess all of them (or even most of them) so long as you are willing to tailor your adventure quest to your comfort and ability levels. Adventure can be tame or wild and wooly—it's entirely up to you.

As the oft-quoted Lao Tzu once said, "A journey of 1,000 miles begins with a single step." *So take that single step!*

WHAT DOES IT TAKE TO BECOME AN ADVENTUROUS RETIREE?

☐ Be willing to unleash your "inner child."

☐ Be eager to do something different tomorrow than you did today.

☐ Seek out challenge and adventure, rather than waiting for it to come to you.

☐ Be ready to accept "controlled risk" as being part of adventure.

☐ Prepare to "fail" in order to ultimately "succeed."

☐ Be motivated to take the path of "most resistance."

☐ Let adventure becomes a "way of life" rather than a one-time occurrence.

☐ Be prepared to "switch-on" your "adventure brain" at a moment's notice.

☐ Be confident and strong of mind and body.

☐ Be eager to travel to unfamiliar places and experience unfamiliar cultures.

THE ADVENTUROUS RETIREE'S CHECKLIST

- [ ] Hold comfort as an afterthought, challenge and discovery take precedence.

- [ ] Always be thinking about and planning your next adventure.

- [ ] Advocate for the "adventurous life," and try to enlist friends and others to join the adventurer tribe.

- [ ] Enjoy reading about the adventures of others, always looking to expand your knowledge and reach.

- [ ] Belong to adventure-specific clubs, groups and organizations.

- [ ] Make every effort to stay fit and healthy.

- [ ] Understand that adventure and social engagement go hand-in-hand—it's a no-lose situation.

CHAPTER 16

■ ■ ■ ■ ■ ■

Is That All There Is?

Life is without meaning. You bring the life to it.
—Joseph Campbell

*We don't find the meaning of life by ourselves
alone—we find it with another.*
—Thomas Merton

SOMETHING'S STILL MISSING, BUT WHAT?

We chased our bucket list and explored new places and challenged our bodies, if not our sanity. Some were fulfilling and exciting; some downright frightening, in a good way; others were informative, relaxing, and even culturally enriching; and still others were dull and perhaps a waste of time. But, we did it. Yet, it feels like something is still missing, but what? We ask ourselves, "What remains to be done or what do we need to do, before we are no longer able, and time just runs out?" Perhaps the bucket list got too big or too controlling, the list appeared to be telling us what we should do, not the other way around. Our retirements should be more, much more, than a "treasure hunt," buying cheap trinkets and souvenirs from around the world to give our grandchildren or display in our homes, so we can say, "Been there, done that."

TOUCH THE WORLD

When we travel or seek adventure we are often separated from the cultures we visit by tour guides; itineraries that skirt the unkempt and the untidy parts of town where most people actually live, work, and play; and by our own discomfort and fear of the unknown or of the "common folk." We look but do not see, we hear, but do not listen. We, just as Dorothy, do not gaze behind the curtain, so we come away with a filtered or sanitized version of reality that the tour guides or, as I call them, "handlers" want us to witness. My wife and I, whenever possible, avoid the guided tours, stepping out on our own to talk with the "real" people of all social and economic classes who populate a city, town, or village. We visit their churches, their markets, and sometimes even their homes to experience and touch and smell—pleasant or not—the rhythms and realities of the communities we set out to discover, and those we just by happenstance find after taking a wrong turn, which sometimes proves even more enlightening. Eventually we all get travel fatigue, and that is most obvious when we can no longer distinguish, or even remember, where we have been, what we have seen, and what tourist sites were in what country. When that happens, it's time to stop the travel chase and find something more fulfilling and meaningful, and a bit less frenetic.

MINE IS BIGGER THAN YOURS

Life for many of us, before retirement, was a competition; a race to see who had the biggest and fastest, the newest and the most desired; or who was the richest or the most important or the most powerful; or whose name appeared in the news the most times; or who had the most people reporting to them; or who could raise the flags of vanity and victory the most often, and all those things that confirmed and nourished our self-image but not our souls. You see, we were not in the business of soul building. We were family building, or business building, or power building, or money getting, or reputation building, or whatever we believed was important to us at that time.

But all that conceit will flow away when we are tethered to machines, as many of us will eventually find ourselves, contemplating our last trip, you know, the one with a ticket stamped, "No return—one way only." Yes, medicine can extend our lives but it cannot extend our souls, because that is up to us as we ask ourselves, "Will I be remembered?" And now, everything else just becomes background noise; all those previous wants and needs, those cars and expensive clothes and trinkets we thought so important recede from consciousness, and the only images flooding our minds are those life memories that perhaps we did not believe important, at least until now.

WE CAN SEE MORE CLEARLY NOW

"There has to be more," we say to ourselves; and with that simple insight, we finally get it—that fulfillment, meaning, joy, and our life force comes from within, not from without. We achieve that ultimate understanding when we fully recognize that no amount of "things" are worth a tinker's damn when we come face to face with our humanity, our destiny, with who we have become, and with the realization that our time on this planet is finite. With this awareness comes a renewed willingness to separate the important from the trivial. We can see more clearly now that life is not about how much money we have amassed, or about the trinkets that clutter our houses and that we plan to give to our children—full knowing they don't want them. But rather, life is about the good we have done, the people we have touched, and those who touched us along life's many roads. Those are the memories we should hold most dear, not the trappings of life we desperately wanted as displays of wealth and status and believed so important to our very existence—or is this new epiphany just a "conversion of convenience"?

THE "MEANING" OF MEANING

When that happens; that is, when we've had all the excitement and adventure our bodies and our psyches can stand, then it is time to move on to retirement's sixth and final building block—contemplation, introspection, retrospection, reflection, fulfillment, giving back, and spirituality, which for the purpose of this discussion is placed within the orbit of a very powerful (if mostly misunderstood) word: "meaning." And why is it misunderstood? Because the word meaning has different meanings for everyone. It is one of those words that can evoke different feelings, different actions, and different beliefs in each of us, depending on how we view our personal worlds; and no, I am not talking about Monty Python's The Meaning of Life. Please allow me to put my spin on what "meaning" means to me to establish a common reference point for the next two sections. If something, anything—an act, a behavior, a memory, a place, an object, a value or belief, a person, a song, an event, whether happy or sad—has a special place in our hearts or evokes memories, it clearly has importance or "meaning" to us. If we constantly flash back to that event or that "something," it has become imbedded into our very being to be played and replayed, whether it was the birth of a child or the death of a loved one, or anything in between.

WE CAN GIVE AND ACCEPT THE GIFT OF MEANING

Some seek meaning by donating money or time to a worthy cause, whatever that might be; and some give with the expectation that their name will appear (depending of course on how much they donate) on a plaque, in a brochure, mentioned on radio, scrolled on television, and even the holiest of holies, for those so inclined, on a monument or a building; yet others choose to be anonymous. We all want to feel needed and important and worthy of the attention of others—and I call these individuals "meaning-seekers." One person's selfless gift of time to an elderly person in need, or $100 anonymously donated to a food bank gives more personal satisfaction to an individual of limited resources than a gift of a million dollars donated to a worthy cause by an individual of immense wealth, who is then adulated and acclaimed for their great "sacrifice" and for their public spirit and kindness to needy others. While we can buy the *appearance* of meaning, we cannot buy *true* meaning. We all have the power to provide the gift of meaningful moments to others and to accept the gift of meaningful moments from others and grant meaningful moments to ourselves, and our willingness to do so is not dependent on the size of our bank accounts, but rather on the size of our hearts, metaphorically, of course.

MEANING IS NOURISHMENT FOR THE SOUL

"Meaning" is an internal state of being; indeed, it is nourishment for the soul. It is not granted or purchased. Major corporations have caught on to the "meaning craze." How many commercials have you seen lately that scream at you that for every purchase of this or that useless product a company will donate so many pennies to this cause or that one, tying their commercial interest to a cause and thereby cheapening both. You see, meaning sells.

We all have to decide what has meaning for us because we all march to the beat of different drummers. It could be devotion to family or helping raise our grandchildren that has meaning beyond our generation, particularly if all goes well. I know numerous grandparents who have given up their dreams and stepped into the breach to save their grandchildren from less than happy circumstances. But please, don't confuse "meaning" with "sacrifice"; while they may be coterminous, one does not necessarily lead to the other. Then, there are those who find meaning in spirituality or in their religions, or in the everyday wonders of nature. What about the tens of millions of volunteers who serve thousands of worthy causes—do they do it for meaning, or do they do it because it is worth doing, or do they do it because it is the right thing to do? Motivation and meaning, while important, don't make the effort any more or less worthwhile. I will hazard a guess that each of us can recall the most "meaningful" moment or moments in our lives. Oh yes, we will all identify our weddings and some might also include divorces, the births of our children, and those meaningful family events that brought great joy to our lives. But meaning also comes in different forms and packages. I am going to ask you to recall the most personally meaningful event in your life; and I will tell you about mine.

GO, JOHNNY, GO—MY MOST MEMORABLE LIFE EXPERIENCE

First, some background. Paul Newman, one of my favorite actors, had two passions that I knew about, racing his fleet of high-powered cars and giving children with serious medical conditions a chance to live life, even for a short time, outside the envelope of their illnesses and disabilities. I know about his racing exploits through the press, but I personally know about his dedication to sick children as a volunteer in one of the camps he founded, and which has since grown into the world's largest family of camps for children with serious medical conditions, known as the "Hole in the Wall Camps." The movie Butch Cassidy and the Sundance Kid, the one that propelled both Paul Newman and Robert Redford into stardom, was the source for the name. Self-effacing as usual, when Mr. Newman was asked, of all the good things he could have done, why did he choose to put his money, his personal energies, and prestige into this particular project, he responded, "I wish I could recall with clarity the impulse that compelled me to help bring these camps into being. I'd be pleased if I could announce a motive of lofty purpose. I've been accused of compassion, of altruism, of devotion to Christian, Hebrew, and Muslim ethic, but, however desperate I am to claim ownership of high ideal, I cannot. I wanted to acknowledge Luck; the chance of it, the benevolence of it in my life, and the brutality of it in the lives of others, made especially savage for children because they may not be allowed the good fortune of a lifetime to correct it."[20] These camps look, for all intents and purposes, like ordinary camps replete with cabins, horseback riding, lakes, and all the typical sports and camping activities, including ghost stories and treasure hunts, but with one major difference. Housed within its walls are medical facilities and medical professionals of all types to make sure the children can be sustained and cared for outside of the hospitals they so frequently visit, insuring they can fully enjoy their time at camp, regardless of the severity of their conditions, and at no cost to the campers or their families. This worked so well it was decided to open one of these camps, the Double H Hole in the Woods Camp in Lake Luzerne, NY. It was different from the others: this camp offered snow sport opportunities to both children and their families (primarily skiing). And they came from all over the East Coast, again at no cost to the campers or their parents. Remember, these were particularly fragile children, many with complex physical, emotional, and severely life-threatening disabilities, many unfortunately doomed to a life of pain and an untimely demise. My wife and I volunteered, along with dozens of others, to be ski instructors and to bring some light and joy into their lives allowing them to experience winter in all its beauty and glory; to get them out of their houses regardless of their medical conditions, and to see winter in a different way, not looking at it through a window flat on their backs, but rather to become part of winter and to touch and play in the snow, as their more fortunate brothers and sisters could.

One lesson, one family, one child on one weekend changed my life. I was assigned, along with another instructor, to a young man of around 12 years of age, let's call him Johnny, who was completely paralyzed. His mother wheeled him into the lodge and then onto the snow, hauled him up from his wheelchair, and gently placed him in what we call a "sit ski." Think of a sled with a high back and lots of straps, buckles, and safety points to keep the disabled skier in the device even if it overturns, but unlike a sled it has two skis on the bottom instead of runners. Johnny's mother informed me that he had complete awareness of his surround-ings, was able to read, and had the intelligence of any other child his age, and although he was not able to speak or verbally communicate, still he could communicate with his eyes. I was trained to work with and teach skiing to the disabled, but I was not prepared emotionally to confront such a profound disability in such a young child, and sadness overwhelmed me. The mother could tell by the caution I was taking when buckling Johnny into the sit ski, when placing him on the lift, and then slowly skiing him down this modest hill in total fear of dumping the sit ski, and Johnny along with it. After one of those slow meandering runs, Johnny's mom came up to me and in a very loving way said, "You know, Rick, you are taking wonderful care of Johnny, but I want you to understand that there is nothing you can do that would 'damage' Johnny any more than he already is. Enjoy the time with him because he has never moved on his own in anything but a wheelchair or car, and this is the first time, and perhaps the last, that he will enjoy the thrill of speed, the cold and wind in his face; you cannot 'break' him more than he is already broken." Well, with renewed confidence I put Johnny back on the lift and we went for run after run; and yes, I managed to dump Johnny, although he remained in the sit ski, and for the first time, I saw Johnny "smile with his eyes." That was and remains to this day, as it will for the rest of my life, the most meaningful moment in my life; not because I did something for Johnny, but because Johnny did something for me. He changed my life in a very profound way by telling me with his eyes that this was the happiest and most exciting day of his life, and mine as well. With tears in my eyes and a smile on my face I said goodbye to Johnny and his wonderful mother. Go, Johnny, go, wherever you are.

MOVING BEYOND SELF

So how do we achieve this state of "meaningful grace"? It won't be easy; but is anything worthwhile ever easy? Meaning from which joy and happiness flow comes from within, not without. Introspection is feared by some and sought by others; we all need and crave constant external approval and reassurance that we are smarter, handsomer, and prettier than whomever, and so on and so on. The need for external validation was never matched by our inner voices, because our insecurities were hidden from public view and even from our own inner gaze. We needed, no we *demanded*, constant praise or reassurance from without rather than the quiet and very personal reassurance from within that we've done good. We do good things for others, not for selfish aggrandizement but solely for the inner joy of seeing someone other than ourselves grow, succeed, and thrive. It is when we have achieved the realization that life is not about us, but rather how we can be in the lives of others that we have that special moment or epiphany about the "meaning of life," and perhaps for the first time, move beyond self.

In order to truly become a certified adherent of retirement's sixth building block, we have to give "ourselves" up to "ourselves." And you thought I was going to say something like a "higher power," but in a way you are right, because perhaps it was a "higher power" that created us and in a way we are giving ourselves up to that "higher power" when we are in control of ourselves, when we take responsibility for ourselves and for our actions. No more excuses, no more "I'm sorry," no more following the herd, no more leading from behind. From earliest childhood we have been shaped and reshaped by our religions, our cultural antecedents, the rules of others, the beliefs of others, the traditions, the laws, the morays, and folkways of others—with little say in those matters. As children, it was our responsibility to heed our parents, our elders, our teachers, and religious leaders, but as adults things changed. We had access to life's best teacher, experience. We know that life isn't always fair, that some people are bad actors to be avoided, and that some are needy and require assistance, as will we one day. As we age, we start thinking less about "things" and more about life's ironies and abstractions. We are more contemplative and thoughtful, less quick to anger, and more forgiving of others as we seek our rightful places in this world beyond work. In other words, we have become "inner directed," listening to our own voices rather than mindlessly accepting the views and beliefs of others simply because it was expected, or was always done that way, or because it is so written.

WE ARE NOT ALONE

The most important gift we can give our children and their children is the gift of knowledge, of what is right and wrong; and with that gift comes the gift of self-determination, the freedom to do what is right for ourselves, our families, and our communities. Some might praise us for this, and some might damn us, but we always must be true to ourselves, without, of course, being hurtful to others and always respecting both their rights and obligations to hold their own personal beliefs. Tolerance and acceptance of the rights of others is what makes civil society possible. But our right to hold differing beliefs and opinions and to move forward and act on those opinions does not mean we can live outside the rule of law. I am not suggesting that our personal beliefs override the rights of others—or our obligation to be good citizens—rather, we accept the premise that we are in control of us and that we have the power to make choices for ourselves that likewise impact our significant others, and those choices should be life-enhancing not life-destroying because we are not alone. Others depend on us and care for and about us; and if we hurt ourselves, we damage them as well. That is the end of this sermon.

NO REGRETS

By the time we have reached retirement's Last Stage and Age, and we are contemplating retirement's sixth building block, there is way more life behind us than left in front. We have moved through most of life's benchmarks, both formal and informal. We are indeed the fortunate ones because we are still one with the world and we must honor the memories of those who have left before us. Likewise, we should accept the reality that our time on this earth is in its final phase; just as the moon goes through its phases and is yet reborn, we too move through phases, but are not reborn in body, at least not on this earth.

Nostalgia and familiarity can be very comforting to us at this time in our lives because memories can be very powerful stimulants. Fall back to those earlier times when life was perhaps simpler—tell stories and pass on memories of when you were a child to your children and grandchildren—apocryphal or not, they always want to know what it was like when you were their age. Retirement is about collecting and experiencing unique moments which make for better memories. It is both a privilege and an obligation to pass those memories on to others, to linger and incubate in the minds of our loved ones, to be called forth at a later time as they endeavor to navigate life, so they not only learn from us but can dream forward for us, recalling our stories and how we confronted life, our fears, and demons, and how we came out the other side safe and stronger for the effort.

Our health is perhaps declining, our minds are not as sharp and agile as we would like, our bodies no longer respond to our every demand, but we still endure and in most cases even thrive. The walls of our lives are closing in with the realization that life is not infinite and we probably attend more funerals than weddings. It's time to make amends and apologize for our transgressions, both to ourselves and to our loved ones and friends, for none of us is without fault or stain. It's our time for redemption and reconciliation, and to allow peace and tranquility to surround our hearts and souls. It's time to realize the inevitable will actually show up at our doorsteps, maybe not today or next month or next year or even next decade, but we all feel its presence. Our spirit is perhaps still strong, but our desires and our bodies are weakening—yet the spark of life still burns bright within us.

DO NOT LEAVE WITH A HEAVY HEART

We must all plan for the inevitable, whatever you want to name it. We have lived a good life, now it is time to bring our affairs into order. Never leave with a heavy heart—don't let anger and revenge take us, resist the urge to get even or settle real or imagined grievances. Some of us will become empty vessels, our minds taken over by the demon Dementia. Some of us will lose all awareness of who we are, who we were, and thankfully of what we are yet to become. Some of us seek invisibility, hiding our fragilities and our aging bodies. Some of us move into clouds so dark we no longer have a sense of self or of how hurtful we become to ourselves and to others. Some of us will leave our homes for institutions where others will care for us, feed us, diaper us, and sometimes they will even be kind to us, like the helpless infants we have once again become. Some of us will be predeceased by our loved ones, and in that case, I wonder who is the more fortunate of the two. Fight the urge to let our humanity steal away in the night, fight the urge to disappear within ourselves, fight the urge to strike out at others, and prepare for the inevitable—pray for release from the body and mind that is no longer you.

OUR LEGACY IS OUR GIFT TO THE WORLD

Death and dying have become an industry of immense proportions and we are its products and purpose. We linger, almost in a state of suspended animation, hovering between life and death, but death is our only salvation. For even in our dying bodies, our minds are still working and back in its recesses we hear a reassuring voice telling us that we have done well for ourselves, our families, for others, and for our country, and that we will leave this earth a better place because of our presence on this planet, and that our good deeds and loving hearts will make a difference to those we knew and touched and our progeny, and those others that crossed into our circle of life will carry us and our memories forward, and we will live once again through them. Our legacy is our gift to the world.

YOUR PERSONAL RETIREMENT NARRATIVE—YOUR LIFE, YOUR WAY!

Wouldn't it be mind-bending if we could see into the future? Well, in a way, we can.

We all have our life stories or narratives to tell. Some are programmed in by others; some are self-ordained; some are embedded in our DNA; yet others are assiduously planned, while many seemingly unfold in living color, right before our eyes. These life stories become our futures. Retirement is one of those rare opportunities to rewrite our life's script that may not have served us well. We need to take control of our retirement destinies—retirements don't just happen—and we have to make them happen our way. And we can do this by writing or rewriting our "personal retirement life narratives," rather than letting others do it for us. Retirement is not about who we were, or thought we were; it is about who we *want* to *become*. Its life's only "do-over," and your last best chance to reshape your life.

Following along with the prompts below, write down your personal retirement narrative. In retirement, life will be different; hopefully a "good different," but that remains up to each us.

This will require some introspection and retrospection—but it won't hurt (at least not very much).

INSTRUCTIONS

Treat each of these questions as a paragraph in your "Retirement Narrative." This narrative enables us to move from the present, and what we know, into the future and what we don't know. If you have a spouse or partner, each of you should complete this exercise separately. No peeking! If you don't have a spouse/partner, enlist a friend or family member as a co-author to challenge you to explore new avenues of possibility.

Plan to set aside at least two hours to complete your narratives. Once the agreed-to time has elapsed, share with your partner/spouse, swapping narratives with each going to separate rooms to read, contemplate and take notes. When you have done your homework, find a calm, safe place where you can write—the kitchen table works best, as it is where most of our conversations begin and evolve. Go down the list of responses, first by summarizing, and then by adding context, with your significant other or friend doing likewise.

Now let the dialogue begin. First, identify common interests and understandings about how life after work should evolve. Now comes the hard part—address differing views and life perspectives, because it is these differing visions of the future that must be reconciled. Our life stories are often intertwined with others; we learn to shift from "I" to "we" by weaving these two disparate stories into one coherent narrative or life script.

RETIREMENT NARRATIVE OUTLINE

- What are your core retirement values? What is most important to you in retirement? For example: staying healthy, seeking adventure; sharing more time with family and friends, spending quality time with your partner/spouse, pursuing cultural enrichment, going back to school, learning to play an instrument, volunteering to help others, traveling to every continent, starting a new business, running a marathon—it's up to you!

- What are your greatest fears as you enter your retirement years? How do you plan to counteract them? Identify the challenges you are currently facing, and those you believe you might be facing when retired. How can these challenges be mediated?

- In general terms, describe the type of life you would ideally like to lead in retirement. How much freedom will you allow your spouse/partner (if one is present in your life) to pursue their personal dreams and bucket lists?

- What activities, hobbies, interests, and experiences are you currently pursuing? Which of these will be carried over into retirement? Which of these can be shared? What activities will be expanded or diminished? What new or different activities would you like to add to the "retirement menu?"

- How will you and/or your spouse/partner organize your average day—do you always have to be together, or will you have your own separate interests and friends, as well as mutual interests and friends?

- Do you recognize that change, compromise, and collaboration are sometimes necessary to achieve your future vision? Are you willing to make those positive personal decisions and compromises?

- Where do you want to live during your retirement years? If moving is in your future, how will you make it happen?

- What provisions will you make for your care as you age (long-term care insurance)? Do you plan to remain in the home as long as possible, or live with your children? Are they aware of your plans?

- Do you have a bucket list? If yes, what is on that list? Has the list been jointly agreed to and prioritized?

- Are you financially ready for retirement? Is there a gap between what you anticipate spending (based on your desired retirement lifestyle) and what you will be receiving from all income sources? If yes, how will you bring them back into equilibrium—incur debt, reduce expectations, get a part-time job?

- Are there health issues or health constraints, physical or psychological, which can impact your retirements? How do you plan to deal with these health constraints? Do you have health insurance? If not, what are you going to do about getting it?

- When you retire from something, you have to retire *to* something— what are you retiring to? How will you positively fill your newfound time (which work and colleagues previously monopolized)?

CHAPTER 17

■ ■ ■ ■ ■ ■

What a Wonderful World

*I bid you fair winds and following seas
and long may your big jib draw.*

—ANONYMOUS

*Being the richest man in the cemetery doesn't
matter to me. Going to bed at night saying we've
done something wonderful is what matters to me.*

—STEVE JOBS

ALL ROADS LEAD TO RETIREMENT

What originally separated us—what we did, who we were, where we worked, how much money we earned or had, what part of the country we lived in, our languages and accents—ultimately brings us together in retirement. Our many roads to retirement eventually converge into only one, the day we decide it's our time to retire and announce our intentions to our family, our employer, Social Security, and the rest of our extended network of friends. Some of us, in our previous lives, achieved great wealth, recognition, and perhaps a modicum of fame or even notoriety, while others found happiness and psychic wealth living everyday lives, raising families, going to jobs, helping others, celebrating life's joyous occasions, and joining together in common bond to provide solace and support to those facing personal loss. Rich or poor; black, white, yellow, or red we ultimately make peace with ourselves and move on to the next life stage, carrying both our baggage and our dreams, hoping for the best but prepared for the worst.

Retirement gives us the opportunity to shape the rest of our lives and brings life's realities, or what is or is not important, into true perspective. Former anyones and anythings are more approachable, small problems are less concerning, and our children finally realize that parents will not be with them forever and might in fact one day need their support, love, care, and guidance.

Yes, some of us have more assets than others; some of us have finer homes, cars, and other "toys"; yet others might have stronger family and friendship networks, or passions and talents that are both fulfilling and emotionally satisfying; while still others might have very little in the way of "things" but the will and the devotion to help others less fortunate than they. The ultimate determinant of how well we will live in retirement is actually defined by us and made real by seeking what is truly important to us and valued by us and our loved ones without the drama, the pressure, and the overhang of our previous lives at work. Retirement is about how we choose to live the rest of our lives and whether our new lives are meaningful and satisfying to us without worrying about what others believe or think. It's about the quality of our retirement years, not the quantity; that is truly the defining factor and that is how we and others should measure our worth and place on this planet and in retirement.

Indeed, to retire or not is a very personal decision that each of us, at some time in our lives, must come to terms with; but personal doesn't mean "alone." Our decision to retire has implications for all who surround us, our life partners, our children, our employers, our friends and family, and even our neighbors who wonder where we will be going and who will move into the neighborhood when and if we leave. The choice of whether or when to retire is as much emotional as it is intellectual, as much financial as it is our perspective on life, for we must consult our hearts as well as our minds before we undertake such a life-altering action, one that is difficult to reverse. Retirement in many ways is our personal "final frontier."

WE BID YOU WELCOME

There are many reasons as to why, when, or whether we will retire—some more profound than others. Sometimes the "when" is entirely taken out of our hands, because of health, family issues, personal issues, or employment dislocations, while other times the "when" is totally within our control. The "why," however is totally another matter, and those reasons and rationales can be legion. For some the "whether" to retire is a simple calculation of how much money we will need to sustain ourselves in our retirement years; and the "when" is how long it will take to reach that magic number, and as soon as the "cash register of life" lights up like a Las Vegas slot machine, you're out of there. Or, perhaps you just had enough of the everyday grind, or the commutes were becoming intolerable, or your work, the pressures, and the new young boss they brought in to shape the place up were emotionally sucking you dry; or maybe your colleagues had retired, leaving you the last man or woman standing, and you had had enough and knew it was your turn, your time to retire.

We all have been working to design our retirements for many years, whether we knew it or not, and we now find ourselves closing in on our final destination, believing ourselves ready, willing, and able to retire, as it should be. By some force of nature, it appears to us and our children that we are somehow getting smarter and, in fact, we are. We can't have lived on this planet for sixty or more years without learning some life lessons and indeed we all have; one of those is the knowledge of what's waiting for us on the "other side of work" and what we need to do to get there with as little wear and tear as possible. And, just perhaps, the insights, strategies, and tools this book has provided will help make your retirement years the best and most fulfilling of your life.

Retiring, or even the thought of never having to go to work again, might seem like a dream come true on the surface, but you and I both know it not only signals the end of one of life's most hectic, rewarding, and challenging times, but also presages moving into another life stage, the third act of a three-act play. It is in the third act of life and in theater that all the plots come together after much "misdirection," sometimes to a happy and other times to a tragic conclusion, depending, of course, both on who is writing and who is directing our "personal life scripts." So, I will close with words of caution and words of welcome. You and your loved ones must be the authors of your personal retirement life script, don't allow others to decide your future or your fate. You can do this by refocusing your collective energies on the "good" that life in retirement has to offer, while sidestepping the bad and the ugly. Please take to heart what I have been saying throughout these pages, that retirement isn't about the money or about who you were, or thought you were; it is about who you are yet to become. Please accept retirement as the new beginning and as the gift and the privilege it really is, and above all, don't squander this last, best chance for meaning, joy, purpose, and happiness because there won't be another.

UNTIL WE MEET AGAIN

I write these last words, full knowing we are the next generation to visit God's waiting room, and that I was perhaps more wrapped up in my temporal life than I should have been and didn't do all the things I could have done for my wife, family, and my parents when I had the time, but not the motivation or the inclination, because I was too "busy" at work or too engaged with my own problems or just too mystified by life that seemingly ebbed more times than it flowed. Those days are gone now. I am more centered, more thankful for what I have, more focused on doing right rather than being right, and less concerned with what other people think or do, and how others view me through their distorted lenses, because finally I am at peace with myself, in my happy place, where making memories is more important than making money. In hindsight life has been good to me, and probably to most of us, and it isn't over yet, not by a long shot. The best is yet to come, and I mean to squeeze every last experience out of life before I let go and say my final goodbyes—should I be so fortunate as to have that opportunity—full knowing that I live in a wonderful world, in a wonderful time, and I wish us all a wonderful rest of our lives. Because, my brothers and sisters of the Boomer Generation, we left our marks on this world, we made it a better place in some cases and a different place in all cases. We took, we gave, we laughed, we cried, we married, and we died; but through it all, I remain thankful for being here in this time and place and continually marvel at the mystery and beauty of the world, our world.

My mind, as I write the last words of this chapter and this book, continually falls back to the lyrics of "What a Wonderful World," sung in Louis Armstrong's soulful, gravelly voice, with his signature trumpet solo; it brings tears to my eyes every time I hear it: *"I see trees of green...red roses too...I see 'em bloom for me and you...And I think to myself...what a wonderful world ..."*

Oh, and by the way, it's still rock 'n' roll to me!

Endnotes

1. Sir Arthur Conan Doyle, *The Sign of Four* (London: Penguin Classics, 2001), 37.

2. www.live.com/news/detroit/index.ssf/2012/09/Michigan-lottery-winner-amandah; accessed online November 11, 2013.

3. www.anial.hubpages.com/hub/winning-the-lottery-a-dream-come-true-or-a-curse; accessed online October 18, 2013.

4. Beth Howard, "What to Expect in Your 60's," *AARP The Magazine*, October/November 2012, pp. 51–61.

5. Andrew R. Sommers, "Obesity among Older Americans," Congressional Research Service, 7–5000 (www.crs.gov.RL34358), February 20, 2009.

6. Curtis L. Triplitt, Pharma D, "Examining the Mechanisms of Glucose Regulation," *The American Journal of Managed Care*, 18, November 1, 2012, Supplement; published online January 28, 2012.

7. Holy St. Lifer, "5 Ways to Prevent Diabetes," AARP Health Report, *AARP The Magazine*, October/November 2012, pp. 16–17.

8. www.nimh.nih.gov/health/publications/the-numbers-count-mental-disorders-in-america; accessed online November 20, 2013.

9. www.minddisorders.com/Kau-Nu/major-depressive-disorder.html; accessed online November 20, 2013.

10. Home Page Topics A to Z, "Prescription and Illicit Drug Abuse"; http://nihseniorhealth.gov/drugabuse/improperuse/01.html; accessed online November 20, 2013.

11. Ana Veciana-Suarez, "Baby Boomers: The Hooked Generation?" www.miamiherald.com, Health, November 13, 2012.

12. Haya El Nasser, "Life's Good for Older Americans," *USA Today*, August 8, 2012, usatoday.com/news/nation/story/2012-08-07/aging-americans-attitudes; accessed online November 20, 2013.

13. Kathleen Lynn, "Many Retirees Still Carry a Mortgage," *Sunday Times Union*, October 28, 2012, pE3.

14. Meyer Friedman and Diane Ulmay, *Treating Type A Behavior and Your Heart*, (New York: Knopf, 1984).

15. Ray H. Rosenman, "Type A Behavior Pattern: A Personal Overview," *Journal of Social and Behavioral Personality*, 5, pp. 1–24.

16. Wikipedia, "Type A and Type B Personality Theory," http://en.wikipedia.org/wiki/Type_A_and_Type_B_personality_theory; accessed online November 26, 2012.

17. The American Institute of Stress, "Hans Selye: Birth of Stress," www.stress.org/about/hans-seyle-birth-of-stress; accessed July 29, 2013.

18. www.nia.nih.gov/alzheimers/publications/part-1-basics-healthy-brain/changing-brain; accessed May 22, 2014.

19. www.latimesblog.latimes.com/outposts/2009/06/former-president-george-hw-bush-skydives; accessed online November 20, 2013

20. www.holeinthewallgang.org; accessed November 19, 2013.